Planning the Urban Forest

James C. Schwab, General Editor

TABLE OF CONTENTS

Acknowledgments

The work upon which this publication is based was funded in part through a grant awarded by the Northeastern Area State and Private Forestry, USDA Forest Service. That grant was matched collectively by the three partner organizations involved in the project: American Planning Association, American Forests, and the International Society of Arboriculture (ISA).

APA would like to thank the following people for their participation in the March 22-23, 2006, symposium that helped launch the project: Buck Abbey, Louisiana State University; Melinda Adams, City of Fort Worth, Texas; Rachel Buice, City of Columbus, Georgia; Lynn Desautels, U.S. Environmental Protection Agency; Peter Gutowsky, AICP, Deschutes County, Oregon; Peggy Harwood, USDA Forest Service; Eric Kasarjian, ESRI; Cheryl Kollin, American Forests; R.J. Laverne, Davey Tree Expert Company; Donald Outen, Baltimore County; Phillip Rodbell, USDA Forest Service; James Skiera, ISA; and James Urban, Urban and Associates. For their assistance in reviewing the manuscript, APA would like to thank Robert Benjamin, ISA; Kendra Briechle, The Conservation Fund; Keith Cline, USDA Forest Service; William Elmendorf, Pennsylvania State University; Susan Mockenhaupt, USDA Forest Service; as well as Peter Gutowsky, Cheryl Kollin, and Jim Skiera. Clearly, we are grateful to all those listed on the title page who contributed case studies or other material to the report itself. Finally, for other helpful advice and direction, we wish to acknowledge the assistance of Tracy Boaz, Missouri Department of Conservation; Mark Buscaino, originally with USDA Forest Service and subsequently Casey Trees; Terrance W. Clark, Associate Director, Science and Education, Society of American Foresters; Barbara Deutsch, Casey Trees; Maureen Hart; Michelle Harvey, Sustainable Urban Forests Coalition; James Hecimovich, former editor of APA's Planning Advisory Service Reports; JohnPaul Kusz, Illinois Institute of Technology; David Nowak, USDA Forest Service; and Kathleen Wolf, USDA Forest Service.

CHAPTER 1

Bringing Nature into the City

By Cheryl Kollin and James Schwab, AICP

Consider the following: The U.S. Environmental Protection Agency (EPA) was created in 1970, only 39 years ago, under the administration of President Richard M. Nixon, and most major U.S. environmental legislation has been enacted since then. That fact would be shocking to many. Indeed, the growing public awareness about the environment and concern for its protection over the past 39 years has been nothing short of amazing.

Urban forestry is one of the numerous environmental issues that have risen to the forefront of public awareness during that same period. Particularly in the last two decades, scholars, practitioners, and community leaders have documented many more ways in which trees, especially as part of a regional or urban green ecosystem, help create a better quality of life. By quality of life, we mean the sum of all things that make life enjoyable and meaningful, including physical, mental, economic, psychological, aesthetic, and recreational benefits. But first things first: let's define what we mean by urban forestry.

DEFINING URBAN FORESTRY

In discussing urban forestry fully, we need to examine the ecological, climatic, urban, political, and cultural conditions that foster or inhibit the growth and survival of trees. For planners, then, any working definition of urban forestry must specifically relate to all these conditions.

The Dictionary of Forestry definition echoes this holistic understanding. It defines urban forestry as "the art, science, and technology of managing trees and forest resources in and around urban community ecosystems for the physiological, sociological, economic, and aesthetic benefits trees provide society" (Helms 1998). In a similar vein, the National Urban and Community Forestry Advisory Council, which advises the U.S Forest Service, defines it as "The art, science, and technology of managing trees, forests, and natural systems in and around cities, suburbs, and towns for the health and well-being of all people." This emphasis on benefits helps get us to the heart of the entire purpose of discussing planning for urban forestry. Without a focus on anticipated benefits, a community simply has open space awaiting development or vacant lots that have gone fallow because of blight. Trees may well sprout in such places if they have not been paved over, but no planning is involved and the benefits are strictly serendipitous (and perhaps unrecognized).

The green infrastructure illustrated in this photo evokes the interconnectedness of nature and people in urban areas.

Gary Moll

The Sustainable Urban Forests Coalition, which supported the publication of this Planning Advisory Service Report and to which the American Planning Association belongs, also echoes this large role for urban forestry: "The Coalition views urban forests as the aggregate of all community vegetation and green spaces that provide benefits vital to enriching the quality of life."

APA also spoke to three urban forestry experts to see if these definitions were accurate reflections of the state of the art. All agreed that these holistic definitions were indeed reflective of current practice and understanding.

But we needed to expand our definition because this PAS Report is not just about urban forestry. Other books and reports addressing urban forestry generally appear in our references and resources. This report is specifically about the intersection of urban and community forestry with the process of community planning, and about where and how planning can advance the goals and benefits of urban forestry. In that context, we drafted a definition of urban forestry that addresses it as a planned outcome of community visioning and goal setting. This report, then, defines urban and community forestry as "a planned and programmatic approach to the development and maintenance of the urban forest, including all elements of green infrastructure within the community, in an effort to optimize the resulting benefits in social, environmental, public health, economic, and aesthetic terms, especially when resulting from a community visioning and goal-setting process."

The foremost logical question that flows from this definition is how a community can quantify and document the benefits it claims for urban forestry.

The economic benefits of a healthy urban and community forest are often discounted or ignored in development decisions. These "ecosystem services" are extremely valuable and need to be considered in any evaluation of benefits.

THE BENEFITS OF AN URBAN FORESTRY PROGRAM

In the 1960s and 1970s, Dutch elm disease decimated urban forests in the eastern and midwestern U.S., changing the look of urban and suburban communities forever. From this crisis, the profession of urban forestry was born. Over the last three decades, the profession has evolved, as researchers and practitioners learn more about the structure and function of trees and their unique role in providing environmental, economic, and social benefits to urban areas. The following sections show how urban forestry provides each of these benefits in differing circumstances: as infrastructure, as part of design and development, and as efficient and productive providers of economic development.

The Environmental Benefits of Urban Forests

Providing "green infrastructure." Infrastructure, a city's physical "capital assets" (e.g., sewer, utility, and transportation systems), can be divided into gray and green elements. Gray elements are composed of buildings, roads, and utilities, all of which are vital to a community. Gray elements are also impervious, forcing stormwater to run off roofs, parking lots, and streets into stormwater sewer systems. Wastewater picks up surface pollutants that must be removed before the water enters rivers and lakes. In contrast, green elements are composed of trees, wetlands, shrubs, grass, and other vegetation. They interact with other natural systems of air, water, and soil. Green elements are porous, allowing stormwater to soak into soil, which naturally filters pollutants before entering rivers.

Benedict and McMahon (2006) offer this definition of green infrastructure: "An interconnected network of natural areas and other open spaces that conserves natural ecosystem values and functions, sustains clean air and water, and provides a wide array of benefits to people and wildlife." An urban forest can certainly be part of such a system.

The economic benefits of a healthy urban and community forest are often discounted or ignored in development decisions. These "ecosystem services" are extremely valuable and need to be considered in any evaluation of benefits. (See the sidebar on the following page for a definition of ecosystem services and a useful reference.)

ECOSYSTEM SERVICES

Ecosystem services are an emerging area of economic and scientific inquiry related to healthy forests. Forest ecosystems provide numerous benefits to society that have traditionally been regarded as free social goods—benefits like wildlife habitat, biodiversity, carbon storage, and scenic values, among others. Undervaluing these services in economic decisions makes the forests supporting them more vulnerable to development and conversion to other uses, often significantly increasing real economic costs for environmental protection after the damage has been done. Valuing the benefits of the urban forest thus contributes to an understanding of ecosystem services. The USDA Forest Service provides valuable background information on this topic on its website at www.fs.fed.us/ecosystemservices/.

Treating stormwater runoff. Trees and soils function together to reduce stormwater runoff. Trees reduce stormwater flow by intercepting rainwater on leaves, branches, and trunks. Some of the intercepted water evaporates back into the atmosphere, and some soaks into the ground reducing the total amount of runoff that must be managed in urban areas. Trees also reduce the volume of water that a containment facility must store. For example, in the metropolitan Washington, D.C., region, the existing 46 percent tree canopy reduces the need for stormwater retention structures by 949 million cubic feet, valued at $4.7 billion per 20-year construction cycle, based on a $5/cubic foot construction cost (American Forests 2002). Many other cities have turned to green infrastructure as a tool for managing stormwater. For example, the Milwaukee Metropolitan Sewerage District, which serves 28 communities, is pursuing a conservation plan to identify and acquire easements on properties at risk for development that can provide flood prevention benefits. Bellevue, Washington, combines the use of parks with stormwater management (Erickson 2006) and for two decades has worked actively to protect riparian open space (Sherrard 1996).

American Forests' studies estimate that impervious surfaces have increased by 20 percent over the past two decades in urban areas at a cost to taxpayers of more than $100 billion (American Forests 2000).

Trees and other vegetation act as a nonengineered stormwater management system by slowing stormwater runoff and filtering pollutants out of water before it enters waterways.

When stormwater hits impervious surfaces in urban areas, it increases the water temperature and also picks up various pollutants, such as excess lawn fertilizers, salts, bio-toxins, and oils on roadways. This nonpoint pollution translates into water quality problems when large volumes of heated stormwater flow into receiving waters, posing threats to temperature-sensitive species, such as anadromous fish (i.e., fish that migrate from salt water to spawn in fresh water—salmon, for instance), trout, and small invertebrates, as well as providing conditions for algal blooms (i.e., increases of algae in a water body that cause increases in bacteria, which, in turn, use up oxygen and result in the death of plants and animals) and nutrient imbalances.

Exactly what role trees can play locally in improving stormwater management is an issue that requires local study because of wide variations in topography, hydrology, development patterns, and other factors. The principles, however, are consistent everywhere. Pervious surfaces containing trees, with their extensive root matter, along with shrubs, grass, and other vegetative land cover, act as a sponge for precipitation, holding a great deal more of it than bare soil and far more than impervious surfaces. Moreover, trees hold some rainwater in their leaves and branches, resulting in some evaporation of water that never reaches the soil. The percentage varies from 12 to 48 percent in the U.S., depending on local climate and the species involved, but the impact where tree canopy exists is clearly significant (Kohrnak 2000). One needs to look at all the green infrastructure, including wetlands, for the total effect, but the end result is that some stormwater that would end up in creeks and streams instead percolates through the soil to regenerate groundwater. This slow percolation process cleans the water and helps cities meet their total management daily load standards. The total reduction in runoff varies with the density of forest canopy, but Duryea, Binelli, and Gholz (2000) note one study from Dayton, Ohio, that found a 7 percent reduction in runoff with the existing forest there and a potential 12 percent reduction with a slight increase in canopy cover.

The EPA regulates water quality, including nonpoint-source pollutants, such as those from stormwater runoff. As cities recognize the high costs of controlling stormwater with gray infrastructure, such as stormwater sewer systems, they are looking for innovative ways to implement effective controls inexpensively. In 2003, new federal Clean Water Act regulations issued under Municipal Stormwater-Phase II permits required communities with populations of 50,000 to 100,000 to create stormwater management plans to improve water quality. Phase I (cities with populations greater than 100,000) and Phase II permits provide cities with opportunities to incorporate urban forestry and green infrastructure into specific best management practices.

Shading and cooling the urban heat island. Between 1979 and 2003, excessive heat exposure—temperatures that hover 10 degrees or more above the average high temperature for the region and last for several weeks—caused 8,015 deaths in the United States (Centers for Disease Control and Prevention 2006). Trees provide enormous cooling benefits, principally through direct and indirect cooling. First, because they absorb sunlight and provide shade, trees prevent sunlight from reaching surfaces such as concrete, asphalt, and brick, which radiate heat. Buildings require less energy to be cooled, so air conditioning costs are reduced. Also, trees release water vapor through tiny openings in their leaves called stomata. This process, known as evapotranspiration, uses the released water vapor to absorb heat directly from the air and cool it. Trees are also stressed by the urban heat island that radiates heat from buildings 24 hours a day, reducing an urban tree's ability to recover from the heat.

The urban forest provides indirect benefits by reducing the urban heat island effect, a phenomenon of warmer air occurring in city centers, compared to lower ambient temperatures in the surrounding countryside. This occurs in cities where the predominance of gray infrastructure and its impervious surfaces absorb sunlight and convert it to heat. Temperatures in the city centers have been measured at five to nine degrees Fahrenheit (F) warmer than in the surrounding countryside. Groupings of trees have a greater cooling effect than single trees, as evidenced by cooler temperatures measured in urban parks. On a citywide scale, the National Lawrence Berkeley Laboratory measured the additional urban energy use caused by the urban heat island effect. In summer, the costs in Washington, D.C., were $40,000 per hour; in Los Angeles, the energy costs soared to $150,000 per hour (Petit, Bassert, and Kollin 1995, 9).

The urban forest provides indirect benefits by reducing the urban heat island effect, a phenomenon of warmer air occurring in city centers, compared to lower ambient temperatures in the surrounding countryside.

Trees are efficient air-cleaning machines. Trees remove many pollutants from the atmosphere, including nitrogen dioxide (NO₂), sulfur dioxide (SO₂), ozone (O₃), carbon monoxide (CO), and particulate matter of 10 microns or less (PM₁₀).

McPherson et al. (1994) quantified the energy conservation benefits of trees from direct shading on one- and two-story residential buildings. Using its formulas for measuring cooling benefits, American Forests found that Frederick, Maryland, residents receive almost $1 million per year on average in cooling effects from existing trees (Kollin 1994). If those trees were placed around houses to strategically maximize shade, the savings would be an additional $2 million per year.

Others have found that urban forests can simultaneously improve both cooling and air quality if they are planted in ways that consider air flow and air quality patterns. The technique to do such mapping is not even new, although the analytical tools have improved greatly over time. Spirn (1984) describes how Stuttgart, Germany, which, like some Rust Belt cities in the U.S., faced frequent air inversions that exacerbated air pollution problems from industry and traffic, discovered that clean, cool air flowed nightly down from ravines from hillsides above the city. By restricting development and preserving tree cover on those hillsides, as well as implementing pollution control measures for industry, Stuttgart was able to engineer what might be called citywide air conditioning to improve both air quality and the quality of life for urban residents. The Stuttgart experiment has been replicated elsewhere in Europe and has become a global model in this regard.

Reducing air pollution. "Air temperature is directly related to air pollution. Polluted days may increase by 10 percent for each five degree F increase. In Los Angeles, for example, ozone levels are not likely to exceed the current National Ambient Air Quality Standard (NAAQS) when temperatures are below 74 degrees F. Above that threshold, however, peak ozone levels increase. At 94 degrees F and above they reach unacceptable levels" (Akbari et al. 1992, 21).

Air pollution in cities and suburbs is a serious concern as described in the section on health benefits below. Burning fossil fuels has introduced a steady flow of deadly pollutants into our atmosphere, yet very few urban areas can meet national clean air standards. Trees are efficient air-cleaning machines. Trees remove many pollutants from the atmosphere, including nitrogen dioxide (NO_2), sulfur dioxide (SO_2), ozone (O_3), carbon monoxide (CO), and particulate matter of 10 microns or less (PM_{10}).

David Nowak of the U.S. Forest Service conducted research in 55 U.S. cities and developed a methodology to assess the air pollution removal capacity of urban forests with respect to the five named pollutants (American Forests 2004). Economists multiply the number of tons of pollutants by an "externality" cost; that is, a cost that society would have to pay in areas such as health care if trees did not remove these pollutants. (See Table 1-1.) Dollar values for pollutants are based on the externality costs set by the Public Service Commission in each state.

TABLE 1-1. TREES AND AIR QUALITY AROUND THE COUNTRY

City	Pounds of pollutants removed annually by trees	Annual value of trees with respect to air pollution
Washington, D.C.	878,000	$2.1 million
Atlanta, Georgia, Metro Area	19,000,000	$47 million
Portland, Oregon, Metro Area	2,000,000	$4.8 million
Denver, Colorado, Metro Area	1,100,000	$2.6 million

Storing and sequestering carbon. In addition to combating the urban heat island effect and improving air quality, trees are able to absorb atmospheric carbon, which reduces greenhouse gases thought to contribute to global warming. The carbon-related function of trees is measured in two ways: storage (the total amount currently stored in tree biomass) and sequestration (the rate of absorption per year). Tree age greatly affects the ability to store and sequester carbon. Older trees store more total carbon in their wood, and younger trees sequester more carbon as measured annually.

Carbon trading has begun to attract attention in the U.S. as it has in markets overseas. While carbon reporting is currently voluntary in the U.S., the increasing concern over global warming may change this to a mandatory requirement. The ability of trees to store and sequester carbon may play a role in that market, providing cities with a greater economic incentive to do better urban forestry planning.

Providing wildlife habitat. Trees located within urban forested parcels, along meadow edges and stream banks, and within corridors contribute to the diverse cover, food, and nesting needs for a wide variety of wildlife. A U.S. Fish and Wildlife Service survey reported that more than half of all adult Americans participate in urban wildlife-related activities, such as feeding, observing, and photographing wild animals. Most of these activities occurred close to home (Ebenreck 1989). Wildlife and their habitat bring nature into our cities and provide a welcome respite for people who live in urban areas. Butterflies, songbirds, and other flying species are well adapted to urban areas. Citizens enhance their backyards to attract wildlife through programs such as the National Wildlife Federation's Backyard Wildlife Habitat Program.

At a larger scale, municipalities also recognize the multiple values of urban open space, many of which create wildlife habitat in parks and on other public land. In addition to urban parks, cities have enhanced wildlife habitat and promoted wildlife-watching in cemeteries, golf courses, floodplain zones, and riparian corridors, such as within Rock Creek Park in downtown Washington, D.C.

Linear urban infrastructure, such as highways, railroads, and utility corridors, also serves as an important source of wildlife habitat. These linear travel routes, especially ones left unmowed and planted with wildflowers and other native vegetation, provide feeding, nesting, and dispersion routes for wild animals.

State conservation agencies conduct urban wildlife inventories to identify critical habitats and then take steps to preserve them. The Missouri Department of Conservation, for instance, purchases small wilderness tracts in urban areas and then leases them to local municipalities to manage. In Tucson, Arizona, critical roadrunner and javelina habitats are identified and conserved to safeguard their movements within and outside of the city.

The Social Benefits of Urban Forests

Health benefits. According to a survey by the U.S. Center for Disease Control (CDC: www.cdc.gov/nccdphp/dnpa/obesity/), "Since the mid-seventies, the prevalence of overweight and obesity has increased sharply for both adults and children. Data from two National Health and Nutrition Examination surveys show that among adults aged 20–74 years, the prevalence of obesity increased from 15 percent (in the 1976–1980 survey) to 32.9 percent (in the 2003–2004 survey)."

Louv (2005) examines generational views of recreation and open space. He believes the escalating obesity epidemic in the U.S., especially child obesity, is tied to the declining interest in outdoor recreation and the lack of access to open space. He testified before the U.S. House Interior Appropriations Subcommittee in May 2007 that public land managers and Congress must

Trees located within urban forested parcels, along meadow edges and stream banks, and within corridors contribute to the diverse cover, food, and nesting needs for a wide variety of wildlife.

recognize the direct link between the two and address this problem as a public health issue. State programs such as Connecticut's "No Child Left Inside" and Texas's "Life Is Better Outside" have already made the connection between obesity and lack of recreation by boosting family attendance at underused state parks.

A sedentary lifestyle increases the risk of overall early mortality (two- to three-fold), cardiovascular disease (three- to five-fold), and some types of cancer, including colon and breast cancer (Dannenberg 2005). Furthermore, obesity-related health care costs exceed $100 billion per year, which is more than smoking-related costs.

Another health-environmental connection is sun exposure and skin cancer. According to the American Cancer Society, melanoma has doubled in the U.S. since 1973 with more than 1 million cases each year (www.melanoma-center.org/basics/statistics.html). Trees help protect against harmful sun exposure in playgrounds and other outdoor urban settings with reflective surfaces. Trees reduce exposure by about half, so that it takes twice as long to burn in the shade as in the sun (Heisler, Grant, and Gao 2002). Recognizing this problem, the Arkansas Forestry Commission's Urban and Community Forestry Program created "Shade Trees on Playgrounds" (STOP; see www.forestry.state.ar.us/community/stop.html) and is planting trees to prevent skin cancer in children.

Asthma rates have also increased, especially among children. In 2003, the American Lung Association reported that 8.6 million U.S. children have asthma, a 37 percent increase over the rate of occurrence in 2001 (Dannenberg 2005). Asthma has been linked to air pollution as observed from the 1996 Summer Olympic Games in Atlanta. During the games, peak morning traffic decreased 23 percent and peak ozone levels also decreased 28 percent. During the same time period, asthma-related emergency room visits by children decreased 42 percent, even though children's emergency visits for non-asthma causes did not change during that period. As discussed previously, trees act as air filters, absorbing air pollutants. An acre of trees absorbs 2.6 tons of carbon dioxide, which is equivalent to the emissions spewed by a car driven 26,000 miles annually.

Preserving and enhancing urban forest and open space serves dual purposes: providing recreation opportunities for health and well-being, and increasing nature's ability to filter urban air pollutants.

Mercer Slough Nature Park, City of Bellevue, Washington

In addition to the communitywide health benefits of trees, a person's immediate landscape or even just a view of it can greatly influence patient recovery time after surgery. Roger Ulrich documented the reduction in pain medication and reduced recovery time of gall bladder patients when looking at a landscaped view from their hospital room compared to looking at a blank wall (Ebenreck 1989).

Environmental justice. Environmental justice seeks to protect ethnically and economically disadvantaged people from unfair environmental impacts (Arnold 2007). Often this segment of the population lives in the bleakest parts of a city, where green space is lacking and areas are dominated by tall concrete buildings. Even though urban forest activists have attempted to engage these communities in greening their neighborhoods, Madeline Williams, Executive Director of the National Association of Black Environmentalists, believes that residents have been apathetic about such efforts. She attributes this attitude to their struggle with day-to-day economic and social problems, which then contribute to social and psychological barriers, which then preclude interest in improving their environment.

A study conducted by Kuo and Sullivan (2001), however, demonstrated that minority populations do indeed respond favorably to urban forests. They compared the social behavior of inner-city low-income residents living in the same high-rise building complex. One part of the high-rise complex was planted with trees and other vegetation, while another part remained barren of landscaping. Residents living in the attractive outdoor setting met and socialized with their neighbors. Residents who formed social ties felt safer and less stressed, and experienced less violence. They were also less likely to abuse their children. In contrast, residents without a treed environment knew few neighbors, had few visitors, and relied on social services more often than on their neighbors or friends. As this study shows, efforts to cut costs for subsidized housing by eliminating trees and landscaping may exacerbate the social ills of disadvantaged urban communities, resulting in greater overall costs.

Perhaps the most successful efforts to improve one's environment come from within the community itself. Elena Conte grew up in the South Bronx in the shadow of heavy industry. With asthma rates in this African-American and Latino community ranked the second highest in the nation, local residents got together and created Greening for Breathing, a local nonprofit organization. Their mission: to plant trees strategically for air pollution mitigation and to create a green buffer zone to protect the community from nearby heavy industry. Through a partnership with the New York City Parks Department, the residents turned their vision into a plan. They are transforming their neighborhood through planting, community stewardship, and technology.

Because environmental justice issues are often closely correlated with community development, it is worth noting that other studies have shown that tree planting and related participatory environmental projects (even including voluntary cleanup) can help to increase community capacity and build social structure (Westphal 2003).

The Economic Benefits of Urban Forestry

Even though many residential neighborhoods are well canopied with trees, many people don't realize the economic value that urban forests contribute to real estate—both commercial and residential.

Wolf (1999), for instance, documents that shoppers are willing to pay more for parking and often stay longer in shops in downtown business districts that have many large, well-maintained trees. She also found that customers who shop at venues with tree-lined landscapes believe the quality of the

Efforts to cut costs for subsidized housing by eliminating trees and landscaping may exacerbate the social ills of disadvantaged urban communities, resulting in greater overall costs.

merchandise sold there to be higher and are willing to pay, on average, 12 percent more for goods and services.

In addition, the quality of landscaping along approach routes to business districts has been found to positively influence consumer perceptions, according to Wolf. She found that in tree-lined areas, property values may be up to 6 percent greater than in similar areas without trees.

An ARBOR National Mortgage survey (1994) found that, of 1,350 real estate agents responding, 85 percent believed that a home with trees would be as much as 20 percent more salable than a home without trees. C.P. Morgan, a developer in Indiana, found that his wooded lots sell for an average of 20 percent more than similarly sized nonwooded lots (Petit, Bassert, and Kollin 1995). A few nice trees can add $10,000 to $15,000 to a base lot price of $60,000.

The Trust for Public Land (TPL) has calculated the various values that urban parks bring to a community. The organization's methodology and calculator are discussed on its website: www.tpl.org/tier3_cd.cfm?content_item_id=20878&folder_id=3208. The first published case study of the methodology is of the Philadelphia's parks and recreation system (Harnik 2008). Economic factors that help determine a park's value include clean air and water, property values adjacent to a park, user happiness and healthfulness, total community value, and neighborhood social capital (i.e., the time and money people contributed to an urban park). TPL is currently developing a calculator so that municipal managers can determine the value of their urban parks and thus prove their budget worthiness.

Homes surrounded by trees are more desirable—increasing sales values and strengthening community character.

Measuring Green Infrastructure

Traditionally, cities have conducted urban forest inventories to determine the number of publicly owned trees and to track their maintenance needs. While these data can be very useful to the tree management department, they do not alone provide city leaders with the information they need to build budgets or manage municipal environmental needs using green infrastructure. Using a geographic information system (GIS), however, a community can calculate the benefits of all the trees in the city, not just those growing in public spaces. The trees can be viewed as citywide assets when they are given a spatial location rather than a street address.

Urban planners can develop a digital GIS representation of green infrastructure—a green data layer. GIS technology not only allows planners to determine existing tree cover, but, using specific GIS applications, also al-

This high-resolution, satellite imagery is more than just a pretty picture. Its multispectral qualities provide the basis for classifying imagery into land cover and calculating the land cover's ecosystem services.

lows them to calculate its ecosystem benefits and economic value. This, in turn, gives them the means to establish levels of priority and importance for both preservation and acquisition of various elements of tree cover within an open space plan or comprehensive plan element.

Collecting, storing, and using object-oriented gray infrastructure data are the standard business practices in most municipal planning, engineering, and GIS departments today. Adding a tree cover data layer to this information makes good sense. With this data, the location of a tree, light pole, or sidewalk can all be stored in the database and displayed on a map by any department at any time. By storing green and gray infrastructure data in one database using a GIS, all department heads and citywide decision makers can view the same data and identify opportunities and conflicts before making decisions on specific actions.

The first step in creating a green data layer for use in GIS is to acquire land cover data from satellites or specially equipped airplanes. The data are acquired during the growing season, when the leaves are on the trees.

Two types of satellite imagery are useful for determining tree cover in cities. The Landsat satellite has been circling the earth since 1972 and therefore can provide a good view of the historic changes that have occurred. Landsat data are used to evaluate change over time in tree cover. As of 2000, more recent satellites carry high-resolution sensors that capture detail on individual trees. At this scale, a digital green data layer is useful for ongoing land-use planning and project-specific decision making.

Aerial imagery also offers a community an excellent opportunity to map tree cover and separate the landscape into gray and green objects. Landsat data are best used to understand trends and to support general public policies. In contrast, high-resolution satellite data are used to create a digital representation of a city's green infrastructure. This green data layer integrates well with other GIS data layers and is most useful for daily land-use planning and management.

A person hired or appointed to manage a city's urban forestry program may be a forester, but is just as likely to have a four-year degree in arboriculture, horticulture, landscape architecture, or another natural resource specialty.

Specialists classify the images into different land cover types—trees, grass, open space, or impervious surfaces, such as parking lots, buildings, and roads. This analysis produces a digital green data layer and is used with gray infrastructure and other data sets commonly used in GIS for local planning. The data are now ready for analysis.

American Forests created a GIS software application called CITYgreen (see sidebar) to automate the complex calculations needed to quantify the effects urban forests have on stormwater, air and water quality, and carbon sequestration. This peer-reviewed software calculates the dollar value of green infrastructure by applying scientific and engineering models to the digital GIS green data layer. In addition, the software allows planners to create different development scenarios and compare the environmental and economic impacts of each. Planners can use the tools and data to incorporate green infrastructure into land-use planning. In doing so, policy makers build their capacity to better plan and manage their cities.

WHO IS INVOLVED IN URBAN FORESTRY?

The success of an urban forestry program does not hinge only on the talents and work ethic of a small group of professionals trained in this field. It also rides on the commitment of allied professionals, appointed and elected public officials, and the citizens and local businesses who represent the community. In a successful program, all of these people are involved at different levels, and all bring something vital and necessary to the process.

The First Tier: Forestry and Parks Professionals

Arboriculture deals primarily with the management of individual trees and tree species. Commercial arborists provide tree care and management services on private and public property, utility arborists deal with tree management issues along utility rights-of-way, including line clearances within municipalities, and municipal arborists are those employed or contracted by municipalities to manage tree programs. Arborists, as the International Society of Arboriculture (ISA) definition in the sidebar on page 14 indicates, are basically trained in the art and science of tree management, which includes pruning, planting, and other functions aimed at maintaining tree health. ISA manages the certification program for professional arborists.

Foresters, on the other hand, have typically earned at least a four-year baccalaureate degree in forestry and are trained to analyze and understand whole ecosystems (Helms 1998). Often licensed by states or otherwise credentialed by professional organizations such as the Society of American Foresters, their skills lie in managing forests at a systemic level. Foresters with advanced degrees are also likely to be engaged with urban forestry as researchers and scientists.

A person hired or appointed to manage a city's urban forestry program may be a forester, but is just as likely to have a four-year degree in arboriculture, horticulture, landscape architecture, or another natural resource specialty. Titles of those managing urban forestry programs have included urban forester, city forester, municipal arborist, and city arborist, among others, reflecting an overlap in the experience, training, and skills of individual professionals who lead municipal urban forestry programs. Overall, says Jim Skiera (2007), the executive director of ISA, the differences between foresters and arborists are "a matter of macro and micro."

In addition to arborists and urban foresters, another group of professionals working largely in local government has evolved to manage public parks and open spaces. Parks and recreation has thus become recognized as another profession in its own right, with its own university academic programs and certification standards. APA's City Parks Forum (www.planning.

CITYgreen AND i-TREE: TWO VALUABLE SOFTWARE PROGRAMS TO HELP PROTECT AND MAINTAIN THE URBAN FOREST

Throughout this PAS Report, authors will refer to software programs that can be of immense help to planners and others determined to improve the forests in their community. Two, in particular, are widely used—CITYgreen and i-Tree. This sidebar presents a brief summary of each. Please consult the appropriate website to gather further, up-to-date information; they are www.americanforests.org/productsandpubs/citygreen/ and www.itreetools.org/, respectively.

CITYgreen is a GIS-based software tool that analyzes the ecological and economic benefits of tree canopy and other landscape features. The software calculates dollar benefits for ecosystem services (e.g., stormwater runoff, air and water pollution removal, and carbon sequestration and storage) provided by land cover within a specified geographic area. CITYgreen, developed by American Forests, is an extension to ESRI's (Environmental Systems Research Institute) ArcGIS and works with Windows-based PCs that have ArcGIS.

The analysis is based on a land cover dataset derived from either aerial photography or satellite imagery and data specific to the area such as soil type, climate, and rainfall. The dataset is first "classified" into various land cover features, such as tree canopy, open space, impervious surfaces, water, etc., before CITYgreen can analyze the data.

The analysis findings are summarized in easy-to-read reports that stratify each land cover feature (impervious surface, tree canopy coverage, open space, etc.) in acres and as a percentage of the total area. This information is very useful when communities are establishing tree canopy goals or managing their land use.

One of the most powerful features of CITYgreen is the ability to analyze alternate land cover scenarios. Starting with a current land cover map, users can calculate the effects of future land cover change before those changes are made. With land cover maps from earlier time periods, users can also compare how land cover has changed over time and how these changes affect the land's ecosystem services. This becomes an important decision-making tool. Communities can see how historic land cover change trends affected air and water quality and use this information to guide their land-use planning in the future.

i-Tree is a suite of programs that can be used by communities of all sizes to inventory, evaluate, and assess the benefits of urban and community forests. Developed by U.S. Forest Service Research, State and Private Forestry, and other cooperators, i-Tree is offered free of charge to anyone wishing to use it.

The i-Tree software suite includes the following urban forest analysis tools:

- *UFORE* (Urban Forest Effects Model) is designed to use standardized field data from randomly located plots throughout a community and local hourly air pollution and meteorological data to quantify urban forest structure and numerous urban forest effects and benefits.

- *STRATUM* (Street Tree Resource Analysis Tool for Urban Forest Managers) uses a sample or existing tree inventory to describe tree management needs and quantify the value of annual environmental and aesthetic benefits such as energy conservation, air quality improvement, CO_2 reduction, stormwater control, and property value increases.

In addition to the analysis programs in i-Tree, the following utilities are also included:

- *MCTI* (Mobile Community Tree Inventory) is a basic tree inventory application that allows communities to conduct tree inventories and analysis at various levels of detail and effort. Data can be collected and entered into the program using paper tally sheets or a Personal Digital Assistants (PDA) using new or existing inventories.

- The *Storm Damage Assessment Protocol* provides a standardized method to assess widespread storm damage in a simple, credible, and efficient manner immediately after a severe storm. It is adaptable to various community types and sizes, and provides information on the time and funds needed to mitigate storm damage.

- Hand-held Personal Digital Assistant (PDA) programs to collect field data.

- Plot selection programs to determine where to collect sample field data.

- Report writers to generate reports, graphs, charts, and tables to summarize data and results in an easily understandable format.

Technical and field manuals are available on the i-Tree website. Technical assistance and training (including volunteer training and regional training workshops) will be provided by the Davey Resource Group and other partners to ensure that users receive all the support that they need to successfully use i-Tree.

WHAT IS AN ARBORIST?

Arborists are trained professionals knowledgeable and equipped
to provide proper tree care. They
provide a variety to services to
maintain trees. The International
Society of Arborists (ISA) certi-
fies individuals who have at least
three years of experience and have
passed a comprehensive examination. They are also required to
continue their education in order
to maintain their certification. ISA
certification is a nongovernmental,
voluntary process. It is an internal
self-regulating device administered by ISA, and therefore cannot
guarantee or ensure the quality of
performance. Certification provides a measurable assessment of
an individual's knowledge and
competence required to provide
proper tree care.

Source: www.treesaregood.com/faq/faq02.
aspx.

org/cityparks/index.htm) documents many cities' efforts in this regard. The
CPF program also resulted in the publication of three PAS Reports on topics
related to city parks and open spaces (PAS Reports 497/498, 502, and 551).

How these three groups—arborists, urban foresters, and parks managers—work together or relate to one another is determined primarily by how
a local government organizes its own departments and work force, and
how lines of responsibility are established. The case studies in Chapter 3
highlight many of the different approaches local governments have used
with regard to urban forestry. Many, for instance, have placed the city arborist within their public works department. It is also possible, however,
to include an arborist within the planning department to review tree issues on proposed site plans and in other design review functions. In some
cases, a larger city may have an independent urban forestry department;
in others, urban forestry may be a function of the parks department or a
local environmental agency. As some of the case studies illustrate, two
or more departments may also share responsibilities for implementing
forestry programs.

The difference among arborists, urban foresters, and parks professionals
may seem clear, but the latter are nonetheless often involved in overseeing
the work of arborists in parks that either contain a forest or some significant
tree population. Parks are typically municipally owned open spaces used
for either active or passive recreation, as opposed to nature preserves with
more restricted public access. The work of a parks professional is typically
quite different from the work of an arborist or urban forester because it is
focused on public use of open spaces, including a great deal of program
design and management for sports, entertainment, and civic activities. Their
involvement is important because the spaces they manage often contain a
high percentage of the overall green space and tree canopy of the entire community. Moreover, in cities like Minneapolis, Minnesota, parks departments
are responsible for overseeing urban forestry programs, in which cases the
chief forester reports to the parks director.

The Second Tier: Allied Professionals

Urban forestry programs rely on urban foresters and arborists to plan, manage, and carry out an urban forestry program, but they also need programmatic support from other departments and professionals in order to thrive.
For most of these other groups, urban forestry is one of many concerns, but
one that they cannot ignore without risking local quality of life. Various
aspects of the programs they manage and the regulations they enforce create work and opportunities for urban foresters and arborists alike, and they
in turn often need the help and advice of foresters and arborists to make
their own efforts more viable. While this report focuses specifically on the
intersection between urban forestry and planning, it is worth reviewing
briefly the roles of some other allied professions as well, as the following
paragraphs make clear.

Planners. Large planning departments often distinguish between long-
term (or comprehensive) planning staff and short-term (or project-focused)
staff, the latter dealing primarily with permits and approvals for individual
development projects or rezoning requests. Like most other aspects of municipal environmental planning, development and implementation of urban
tree policy can take place at both levels.

At city scale, planners can interact with urban foresters in integrating
canopy cover and other tree-related data into GIS and analytic tools. Planners,
in fact, are typically in an excellent position as coordinators of input from
various city departments in the review of pending development applications

and overall policy development related to managing growth. A growing number of communities are establishing goals for percentages of the city's surface covered by tree canopy as a means of furthering various environmental objectives. These tools assist with documenting existing conditions and making clear the best means of achieving long-term forest sustainability goals. Those goals and objectives can then be included in comprehensive plan elements addressing green infrastructure issues.

Below the macro policy level, however, planners have numerous opportunities to work with their urban forestry staff to implement those goals. Matheny and Clark (1998, Ch. 3) provide a synopsis of this interaction in the development process. The success of tree programs tends to lie in the details, which can include collaboration between both groups on all of the following:

- Requirements for detailing tree-planting plans in site plan submissions

- Regulations regarding tree preservation procedures in the development process

- Management of tree issues arising in the public hearing process on proposed developments

- Review of site plans, which can include having an arborist check the plans for compliance on tree-related issues

- Establishment of tree-planting and tree-preservation requirements in subdivision regulations

- Development and enforcement of standards for tree planting and maintenance in parking lots

- Monitoring of tree protection and proper planting during site development

- Acquisition of open space or easements to preserve existing forest in urban areas

- Metrics to calculate the amount of pollution removed by urban trees and the associated improvement in air quality

Planning commissioners. Planning commissioners are appointed officials who sit on boards that develop and review plans and land-use ordinances for approval and recommendation to local legislative bodies, such as city councils or county commissions. As such, they are typically unpaid volunteers and not planning professionals, though some are often former planners, architects, or other design professionals, as well as developers. Many simply have a strong civic interest in planning issues. The planning staff supports the commission's decision-making process with professional analyses and recommendations. Planning commissions can thus be involved in urban forestry through their reviews of and decisions about all the areas involving planners listed above. Planning commissioners can play a vital role in mustering public support for a strong municipal urban forestry program and encouraging the strategic use of urban forests to meet local climate protection goals.

Landscape architects. Landscape architecture combines art and science. It is a profession that designs, plans, and manages land, encompassing the analysis and stewardship of the natural and built environments (American Society of Landscape Architects 2007). Landscape architects apply their skills to site planning, garden design, environmental restoration, town and urban

Growing numbers of communities are establishing goals for percentages of the city's surface covered by tree canopy as a means of furthering various environmental objectives.

As cities move away from their reliance on gray infrastructure, engineers will have new opportunities to collaborate with foresters to integrate green infrastructure into their package of solutions.

planning, urban forestry, park and recreation planning, regional planning, and even historic preservation. Landscape architects are licensed in all but three states. Because they help design parks, public spaces, and the exterior areas of many development sites, they are intricately involved in integrating forest cover into urban site development. Their work is also, or should be, acutely sensitive to the visual impacts of vegetation within the built environment (Miller 1997). At the macro level, they can integrate green infrastructure into design and connect it to other hubs and links in an overall development pattern. Many work with, or as, consultants to municipalities or developers. In a number of cities, such as Urbana, Illinois, landscape architects serve as managers of city forestry programs (see the case study in Chapter 3). Their education and experience tend to provide a perspective that bridges the perspectives of urban foresters and arborists, while their design skills are valued in development processes.

Public works departments. One of the recurring issues involving trees concerns their placement and root structure in municipal rights-of-way, particularly on residential streets, where the same space must accommodate water and sewer lines and perhaps underground utilities. This is why urban forestry programs are often placed within the public works department and why the city forester works under the direction of the public works director. One current advantage of such an arrangement is that the case for using green over gray infrastructure in public works for programs like stormwater management may become easier to promote. Even where that is not the case, public works officials clearly play a crucial role in facilitating the success of urban forestry, and urban foresters and arborists in such departments can point the way to new environmentally friendly public works programs. A distinct disadvantage is that in many cases urban foresters who work within a public works department must contend with the aftermath of poor planning. They are often engaged in clean up, repair, and damage related to the urban forest rather than making planning recommendations in the first place. For that reason, it is critical to have urban foresters engaged directly in planning decisions.

Architects. Most people understand what architects do. What may be less clear to them is how architecture relates to urban forestry. With rapidly growing public interest in green building design, accompanied by concerns about urban heat islands and climate change, not to mention the increased popularity of the Leadership in Energy and Environmental Design (LEED) standards for buildings (see www.usgbc.org), architects are currently in a position to lead the discussion about how a building is sited both on its site as well as in the greater pattern of urban design to incorporate the many benefits of urban forestry, including energy use, aesthetics, networks of green space, and even strategic placement to enhance site, block, neighborhood, and community green infrastructure programming.

Engineers. Public works departments are largely the domain of civil engineers. Other types of engineers can interact with urban foresters as well to achieve urban environmental quality goals. Transportation engineers have excellent opportunities in this regard because of the many ways in which trees and road design affect each other, such as sight lines, traffic calming, and safety. Miller (1997, 65, 77) details a number of engineering uses of urban forestry, such as air pollution reduction, noise buffering, erosion control, and stormwater management. As cities move away from their reliance on gray infrastructure, engineers will have new opportunities to collaborate with foresters to integrate green infrastructure into their package of solutions.

Engineers work in both the public and private sector in varying capacities. Utility companies, including energy companies, but also telephone, cable television, and other service suppliers, involve engineers in siting and designing much of this infrastructure. Whether these lines are overhead or underground, their siting and design have implications for nearby trees on both public and private property. Utility engineers should be aware of those issues and be involved in resolving conflicts between them.

Consultants. Every one of the professions noted so far includes some number of consultants working either independently or as large firms, particularly in the engineering and architectural fields. They can serve either to fill gaps in municipal staff expertise or to supply short-term needs for specific kinds of expertise. In situations where the community feels that developers should bear the expense of hiring an outside consultant to review or monitor some technical aspect of a development proposal, development ordinances can spell out what services must be provided (e.g., certifying compliance with particular standards) and who will pay for them.

Effective urban forestry depends ultimately on the public policy supporting it—financially, administratively, and legally.

The Third Tier: The Public, Developers, and Elected Officials

Citizen support has played a vital role in supporting urban forestry. Tree-related advocacy groups and trusts are now common. They marshal volunteer support and voice support for urban forestry programs to local officials. Homeowner organizations often lobby for more street trees and greenery in their neighborhoods. Many groups are founded at times of crisis—as reaction to the destruction of trees and other natural resources resulting from growth and development. They demand open space and tree protection through better planning, new regulations, and public acquisition. These alliances can operate on any scale. As Erickson (2006) illustrates in an impressive series of case studies, citizens often provide the glue to link open space networks in large metropolitan areas like Chicago, Seattle, and Vancouver. Tree-planting volunteers join professional arborists on the front line, or first tier, at times, while leaving the maintenance to professionals. Most importantly, however, citizens tend to provide the political backbone behind municipal efforts to sustain public investment in green infrastructure and the urban forest.

Developers have always looked for a marketing edge for their properties. The best developers understand that building green means not just structural design. Rather, it encompasses the entire development site and its relationship to surrounding sites. They also understand that building green adds value, improving the investment-to-return ratio. As Matheny and Clark (1998) point out, building green begins at the conception of the project, not at the construction phase, and should involve an arborist or forester to help determine what sort of trees and vegetation will have the best chance of thriving in the environment altered by construction. And arborists or urban foresters should continue to collaborate with the developer until the project is completed (Duerksen and Richman 1993).

Effective urban forestry depends ultimately on the public policy supporting it—financially, administratively, and legally. Mayors and council members shape the programs and lines of authority within departments under which urban forestry programs must operate. They determine whether such programs are unified and coherent, or function instead as a patchwork of programs and initiatives stitched together over time. Mayors who seize the opportunity to make the urban forest an issue in the community can leave their mark for decades to come—but it is also important that they be open to the advice of experts who can help ensure that their programs succeed now and over time.

CHALLENGES FOR URBAN FORESTRY PROGRAMS

Urban forestry is a relatively young profession. The widely acknowledged wake-up call for better municipal management of trees arrived in the mid-

Fortunately, much of the professional and scientific knowledge necessary for improving urban forest health and management is becoming more readily available and continues to grow. What are not always available are the resources and political will to support better management.

twentieth century with the massive destruction wrought by Dutch elm disease. But the term "urban forestry" did not arrive on the scene until 1965 when Eric Jorgensen at the University of Toronto applied it to the entire tree population in an urban area. The federal farm bill legislation of 1990 provided the first substantial appropriations ($21 million) for the Forest Service to provide grants to state and local governments as incentives to underwrite their own programs. The same law also created the National Urban and Community Forestry Advisory Council (NUCFAC) to help oversee that program (Fazio 2003, 12).

Because urban forestry is still an emerging discipline, its relationship to planning is still evolving. Consequently, citizens, developers, planners, and city officials need better education about the principles of urban forestry. The public, which is generally supportive of environmental programs, needs to be moved beyond its appreciation for the aesthetics of trees to a more specific understanding of the many functions they serve, not only individually but collectively, which we have detailed above. And it is not just that the public does not understand. Rather, it is because "these benefits are not realized due to poor health and management of the urban forest" (Duryea, Binelli, and Kohrnak 2000, Abstract, 1). Furthermore, it is only recently that communities have had access to new research and methods for quantifying the economic and environmental benefits of the urban forest.

Fortunately, much of the professional and scientific knowledge necessary for improving urban forest health and management is becoming more readily available and continues to grow. What are not always available are the resources and political will to support better management. When bad things happen to good programs in local government, it is most often because the public or its elected officials, or both, do not fully appreciate the program's value and benefits. In contrast, when public leaders "get it," adequate funding ceases to be a problem. The much-publicized passion of Chicago Mayor Richard M. Daley for green initiatives is a vivid case in point.

Consequently, the essential challenge, to borrow an old bromide, may be one of connecting the forest and the trees in the minds of both the public and decision makers. As noted above, not only has public awareness of the benefits of the urban forest ecosystem lagged behind what professionals have learned about the local influence of the urban forest, but the ecological influence of the urban forest that extends well beyond the boundaries of any individual city or metropolitan area has not been adequately explained to the public and public officials. This places added emphasis on the importance of multijurisdictional, regional planning and cooperation for effective resource conservation. Inherent in the global warming debate is the understanding that the ecological health of individual communities cumulatively affects the ecological health of the entire planet and its atmosphere. Indeed, scientists continue to find that we are changing climate in ways we barely understand. Yet every tree whose shade or wind resistance reduces building energy use contributes to that larger solution, even before we indulge in calculations about carbon sequestration.

We should not exaggerate those impacts. Urban forests in the U.S. currently remove about only 0.1 percent of world carbon dioxide output (Duryea, Binelli, and Gholz 2000), though their impact in reducing fossil fuel use is greater. But we should likewise not dismiss that impact or be unaware of it. The challenge for both urban foresters and planners is to convey the many benefits of urban forestry succinctly and clearly so as not to overwhelm the public. As noted above, people already think trees are good. How can planners and urban foresters capitalize on that inherent sympathy to produce programs that are far reaching and effective?

Trees are more than a welcome respite on a hot summer day. Public support of urban forests depends on conveying the tangible environmental, social, and economic benefits trees provide to communities.

ELEMENTS OF A SUCCESSFUL URBAN FORESTRY PROGRAM

In addition to technical tools, successful municipal tree programs incorporate the following elements:

- Tree and planning commissions with historical understanding of the importance of urban forestry
- A dedicated, educated governing body with continuity of support
- Long-term citizen support
- Professional assistance
- Education of planning commission members
- Management plans and missions
- Grant funds
- Dedicated, educated volunteers
- Ordinances and enforcement
- Awards and celebration

Source: Elmendorf, Cotrone, and Mullen 2003

That predisposition, however, does not mean that people or decision makers know what is required to make a local urban forestry program effective (see sidebar). It is not simply a matter of money, though adequate funding helps. Advocates and professional staff alike must establish a vision for the program that specifies the technical tools required as well as the conditions that must be created if the program is to be a success. Technical tools, for example, might call for the integration of a tree database into GIS, or analytical software like CITYgreen to quantify the air, water, and carbon benefits of trees. Another option is the i-Tree software suite developed by U.S. Forest Service researchers and partners, which is in the public domain (see www.itreetools.org/), to assess the structure, function, and value of urban forests.

If the program's vision, for example, calls for greater diversity in the tree population in order to avoid a "wipeout" of the tree population by bug infestations (e.g., emerald ash borer) or diseases (e.g., Dutch elm disease), such data analysis is not an option, it is a requirement. If the vision mandates greater legal control over development and the maintenance of adequate and proper tree populations, the database will allow an arborist to add conditions to development permits ensuring site development plans that support, rather than undermine, tree survival. If the vision is to change development policies that require tree canopy thresholds to help meet compliance for clean air and water regulations, an analysis of satellite imagery to quantify how the tree canopy has changed over time and the change in its contribution to ecosystem benefits would provide the tangible information needed to change public policies. The challenge then is to make certain that decision makers in particular (but also the voting public) are presented with a compelling argument for carrying out a program that meets both short- and long-term goals. Inevitably, decision makers and advocates (e.g., local environmentalists and tree trusts) will want and need to focus more on the structure of the program, while much of the public will more likely be satisfied to support the program because of the benefits it promises.

The challenge of creating a successful program may require even more effort than all this implies. Decision makers, for instance, may want to know

A thorough audit by an outside consultant may be able to determine where existing plans and regulations work against urban forestry, where regulations have failed, and what tools are needed for better spatial and environmental analysis.

why it is necessary to have all of these elements in a successful forestry program. They might ask, Who says that we need stronger development regulations in order to ensure that the right trees are planted, or that we needed sophisticated software to find out the species of trees we need? Urban forestry may be competing with numerous other worthy programs for a limited supply of time, attention, and funds. And it may not always be immediately clear that some existing regulations work against the success of the program. Planners and foresters working together may be able to provide concrete examples of flaws in the regulatory system that impede the program (e.g., parking requirements that restrict space for tree preservation or minimum lot size requirements that impede the possibilities for clustered development).

This issue has arisen before in other planning contexts. Once the objective is clear—in this case, the desire for urban forestry to succeed in its mission—one well-established mechanism is to audit local plans and regulations to determine their impact on the resource. What, for instance, has been the outcome of existing subdivision regulations regarding open space dedication and tree planting in rights-of-way? Do existing tree ordinances that mandate tree canopy goals actually help meet federal clean air and water regulations or comprehensive plan goals? Are existing regulations clear enough? Detailed enough? Strict enough? Too strict? Do enforcement personnel have enough time and expertise to monitor compliance effectively? Do planners and urban forestry staff have the tools and capacity to measure the quality of the existing urban forest, create accurate projections, and document their results?

A thorough audit by an outside consultant may be able to determine where existing plans and regulations work against urban forestry, where regulations have failed, and what tools are needed for better spatial and environmental analysis. (The same audit could also be conducted in-house if the appropriate expertise is present.) If elected officials are sold on the merits of urban forestry, but less certain about the best means for supporting it, such an audit may provide the compelling evidence they need to decide on a course of action.

PAS Report 512, for instance, described how smart growth audits can help communities achieve their objectives by identifying similar strengths, weaknesses, and gaps in the existing planning regime (Weitz and Waldner 2002). The report defined such an audit as a "systematic inquiry that seeks to evaluate existing plans, policies, and practices against accepted principles of smart growth," but the last two words could be replaced with "urban forestry" so that, using the same points as Weitz and Waldner, the audit examines whether planning for urban forestry is:

1. encouraged and facilitated by the community's plans and policies;

2. reinforced by internal consistency between plans and policies;

3. implemented effectively by employing regulations, programs, and budgets consistent with plans and policies; and

4. reinforced in all aspects of implementation by consistency between development regulations, programs, and budgets.

OPPORTUNITIES FOR URBAN FORESTRY PROGRAMS

If challenges exist in communicating fully the value and benefits of urban forests, built-in opportunities for advancing urban forestry in the context of existing community responsibilities also exist. For instance, some of them may be mandated by federal or state laws and programs. Since trees produce demonstrable benefits in reducing stormwater runoff, these measurable benefits can also be tied to federal environmental requirements for managing stormwater. Since trees help filter air pollution, communities can use the Clean Air Act as an incentive for enhancing their urban forest and achieving air quality compliance. Mayors across the country have signed on to the U.S. Conference of Mayors Climate Protection Agreement and are looking for best management practices to incorporate into their cities. Certainly, urban forestry programs touch a number of popular election issues for these mayors, only one of which may be promoting actions to mitigate the effects of climate change. Since the urban forest provides vital habitat for local wildlife, an urban forestry program may facilitate compliance with the Endangered Species Act. Because urban forests can help buildings use less energy, they indirectly help reduce carbon emissions from power plants. Even where mandates do not exist, better management of the urban forest may facilitate access to grants and other incentives from the state or federal government. In some cases, piggybacking urban forestry concerns on mandated environmental responsibilities, including stormwater management and the other myriad outcomes of effective urban forest management cited above, may make compliance more attractive because of the clear and popular aesthetic benefit of trees.

Help Wanted: Drivers

Planners who succeed tend to be opportunistic. Although many people associate that word with negative connotations, opportunism is a very positive trait in a public servant. It involves, at its best, noticing and seizing opportunities to advance a public goal by linking it with other goals and objectives driven by related considerations. It is, in a way, a creative awareness of the many linkages that exist among the variety of social, political, environmental, and economic issues that confront planners in their everyday work. Some of these involve external mandates from states or the federal government, some involve attaching policy objectives to new development or redevelopment, and some simply involve taking advantage of funding streams of any sort that may relate to the policy objective in question. In some cases, it may even be a crisis such as a natural disaster or the growing concern about climate change that triggers unexpected opportunities to advance urban forestry as a solution.

We call these "drivers" because they can "drive" an urban forestry program forward, either by responding to legal requirements or by generating new resources to support the program. Another appropriately descriptive term would be "stimulus."

In developing the case studies in Chapter 3, we directed authors, to the extent possible, to identify those drivers that have influenced each local program. This section also references some of those drivers in order to reinforce the critical point that problems create opportunities for building critical support for urban forestry programs.

Stormwater management. The federal Clean Water Act provides one of the clearest examples of an external mandate affecting local government, and urban forestry and other elements of green infrastructure can be effective tools in meeting its requirements. The act first targeted point source pollution, and later EPA established nonpoint-source pollution compliance standards in two phases: Phase I (for large communities) and Phase II (for smaller communities). The act's provisions concerning nonpoint-source pollution, along with the implementing regulations, have required communities to find ways to reduce stormwater runoff to combat the flow of pollutants it accumulates on its path to surface waters. Solutions or best management practices can be expensive. Green infrastructure can play a major role in reducing those costs, particularly when strategically located in stream buffers and floodplains, where it can help to minimize soil erosion.

Even where mandates do not exist, better management of the urban forest may facilitate access to grants and other incentives from the state or federal government.

The provisions of the 1990 federal farm bill that created the current urban and community forestry program also created a challenge cost-share grant program.

Air quality and climate change. The provisions of the federal Clean Air Act dealing with listed criteria air pollutants, such as sulfur dioxide, are directed largely at metropolitan regions, in large part because of the enormous impact of transportation systems on air quality.

Habitat protection. The federal Endangered Species Act represents a significant opportunity for local and regional planners to incorporate an urban forestry program as part of a habitat conservation plan. Despite criticism of and opposition to the act from some affected landowners, the public continues to support the act against repeated efforts at repeal. How much and what types of habitat are protected in any case depends on the species involved, whose habitat needs may range from a few acres to hundreds or even thousands of square miles. Often the habitat needs of larger non-bird species may involve some form of connectivity, or what are known as wildlife migration corridors, which for planning purposes tend to involve greenways and stream corridors. Whole books focus on the details of particular situations, which are too varied to address here. Among the case studies in Chapter 3, Salem, Oregon, cited the Endangered Species Act as a factor in its urban forestry program in combination with the Clean Water Act, because the salient issue was the protection of salmon habitat, the icon of the Pacific Northwest. In fact, this particular case tends also to illustrate the cross-cutting nature of many of these issues, such as the impact of water quality on prospects for species survival.

Habitat protection is not an issue limited to species protected by federal or even state law. Many compelling local issues can drive public support for green infrastructure and, more specifically, urban forestry, creating the opportunity for foresters and planners to collaborate on better management of greenbelts and forest remnants. As Agee (1997) notes, the perception of nature in urban areas is pretty broad, meaning that urban forest management might easily be dovetailed with sustainable species management in highly valued landscapes.

State and federal grants programs. Finally, state and federal grants can also be drivers for an urban forestry program. In this respect, the provisions of the 1990 federal farm bill that created the current urban and community forestry program also created a challenge cost-share grant program. NUCFAC, an advisory committee to the Secretary of Agriculture, provides criteria and recommendations for this grant program. These grants have provided numerous opportunities to jump-start local initiatives, including the master plan in Syracuse, New York. Among the case studies in Chapter 3, Olympia, Washington, cited a state grant in addition to federal funding as a stimulus to its program, particularly when the resulting study documented ongoing tree loss due to rapid development.

The Urban and Community Forestry Program also provides financial assistance and grants to local government, nonprofit organizations, community groups, educational institutions, and tribal governments through the individual state forestry agency urban and community forestry programs in 59 states and U.S. territories.

Other drivers. While the federal programs mandating clean air, clean water, and habitat protection are clearly potent drivers for urban forestry programs, there are more given within our 13 case studies. Among them:

- brownfields cleanup
- smart growth concerns
- state-level forest conservation
- natural disasters
- concerns about tree diseases and pests

Strategic Opportunities in the Planning Process

Given the opportunities that planners and forest advocates can use to advance urban forestry goals, the question arises as to where, when, and how to intervene most effectively in the decision-making process. The answer may depend to some degree on the size of the community and the scale of the decision-making process in which intervention is contemplated—watershed, region, county, municipality, or neighborhood. Each has its own strategic considerations, but overall there are several strategic points of intervention that are critical in almost any planning process (see diagram):

- Visioning and goal setting
- Comprehensive planning
- Subarea and functional planning
- Plan implementation

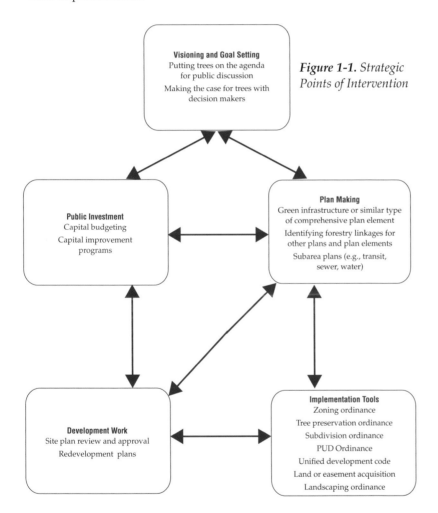

Figure 1-1. *Strategic Points of Intervention*

Addressing Urban Forestry in Local Plans

In an ideal planning process, the comprehensive plan should embody local policy, and provide the framework for implementing land-use regulations (e.g., zoning and subdivision codes). While much depends on state law and planning enabling legislation, this guiding role for comprehensive planning nonetheless introduces the final question for this chapter: What parts of that plan should address urban forestry, and how?

One straightforward answer is to include a specific element in the plan that addresses all aspects of green infrastructure. Rather than address the complexity of such an element here, we have included a model for a green infrastructure element in Appendix A. Note that the title "Green Infrastructure" is less important than whether the element addresses the appropriate issues. Many communities already have elements labeled "Natural Resources," "Urban Forestry," "Open Space and Recreation," or simply "Environment" that include much the same type of policy content.

It is also important that the plan establish meaningful links with urban forestry issues in other elements whenever possible. For instance, street trees may need to be addressed in a transportation element or an economic development element as well as in an environmental or green infrastructure element. In addition, urban parks often host arts festival and cultural events that draw tourists and strengthen the local economy. The APA City Parks Briefing Paper on Tourism (www.planning.org/cityparks/briefingpapers/tourism.htm) describes urban parks as the "engine" that drives tourism in many communities. All these elements should cross-reference one another and be consistent.

Cross-referencing the land-use element in a comprehensive plan may also be relevant because of the need to address the spatial composition of the urban forest and how development may affect it and because tree preservation during development may require a reexamination of conditions placed on both site plan and construction permits.

The infrastructure element and the community and economic development element also provide opportunities to strengthen an element addressing urban forestry. The reasons we have cited above (i.e., green infrastructure and increases in property values) apply.

The multidisciplinary nature of an effective urban forestry program may also afford opportunities during the planning process to bring together staff of affected departments (such as public works, parks, and planning) to discuss how their mutual efforts to implement the plan can complement one another.

Now that we have defined urban forestry, who plays a role in its planning and implementation, and why it is an important consideration for communities, the nation, and the world, we move on to a more specific discussion of how communities have successfully adopted urban forestry programs. We move from a discussion of principles that can be applied at the general, planning, and design levels to develop and manage successful urban forestry programs (Chapter 2) to a study of how individual communities and metropolitan areas have applied those principles to their specific circumstances and how well they have succeeded in pursuing their goals (Chapter 3), and finally, in Chapter 4, to a framework for analysis of a forestry program, as well as some conclusions and recommendations for moving forward.

The Principles of an Effective Urban Forestry Program

By James Schwab, AICP

In seeking to define the scope of its research for this project, the American Planning Association conducted a two-day symposium in March 2006, bringing nine invited experts to Chicago as well as staff representatives of the four partner organizations supporting the project—APA, American Forests, the International Society of Arboriculture, and the U.S. Department of Agriculture's Forest Service. In this wide-ranging discussion, one focus concerned the general principles that should guide planning for urban and community forestry. From a transcript of that discussion, APA's project team developed the set of principles described in this chapter. Participants then commented on the principles. We have divided the principles into general principles, planning principles, and design principles.

GENERAL PRINCIPLES

Urban and community forestry has transcended its original niche function in public policy as an aesthetic amenity to soften the urban landscape. It is increasingly perceived as a solution to many more pressing urban environmental problems and even as a tool for community and social development. Five general principles lay the foundations of a new planning agenda.

General Principle 1. Get Trees to the Forefront of the Planning/Visioning Process

Trees should not be an afterthought in the planning process. Besides the obvious beauty, breathing room, and value they add to communities, they play a vital role in helping communities solve numerous problems. They need high-priority attention in any community visioning or goal-setting process. Visioning is "a planning process through which a community creates a shared vision for its future and begins to make it a reality" (Ames 2006).

If this discussion of trees is advanced to the forefront of the visioning or goal-setting process, it is far more likely that citizens and stakeholder attention will focus on how trees can serve vital functions in better managing stormwater; improving urban air quality, human health, and property values; enhancing walkability and the quality of urban life; and lowering building energy demand, among other benefits. At the same time, a well-informed discussion can also avoid the pitfall of promising too much so that urban forestry does not find itself carrying an unrealistic burden in the quest for functional ecosystems.

A truly thorough examination of urban forestry in the visioning process would lead to a focus not merely on trees but on the entire ecosystem that supports the urban forest. As was noted in Chapter 1, urban forestry is really about the "forest," not just the "trees," and it is a big-picture approach. A visioning process must examine how this ecosystem supports urban life as well as the urban planning policies needed to support and maintain urban forest health.

One manifestation of this kind of visioning is the recent trend in some cities and communities toward quantifying goals for canopy cover, which entails establishing as a goal a certain percentage of canopy cover by a certain future date. There are some underlying assumptions in this type of goal setting. First is that current canopy cover is either not adequate, is declining, or could be improved in a way that would benefit the community. Second is that this increase is achievable in the projected time frame. Finally, there is the assumption that the entire enterprise involves a positive cost-benefit ratio—that the investment required will yield even greater dividends and value over time.

In April 2005, Baltimore, Maryland, for instance, began working with the Maryland Department of Natural Resources (MDNR) to identify the extent of existing canopy cover by land types and to establish a recommended tree canopy cover goal for the future. Notably, the driver for this joint effort was water quality improvement in the Chesapeake Bay, which has been the focus of an ongoing regional concern and a multistate cooperative agreement.

A report prepared by MDNR for the city (Galvin, Grove, and O'Neil-Dunne 2006) found that existing canopy cover—the percentage of land in the city that was beneath tree canopy—was 20 percent. The study recommended that the city adopt a 46.3 percent canopy cover goal to be attained by 2030–2036, recognizing that planting and maintaining the necessary forest to achieve that goal would take two or three decades. The recommended goal was derived from an assessment that 44.6 percent cover was the level associated with "good" stream health ratings, based on a study by

Goetz et al. (2003) of small watersheds in Montgomery County, Maryland. The MDNR study said achieving this tree canopy target would produce the gains in Chesapeake Bay water quality that were the ultimate goal. The study further recommended that the city develop a comprehensive urban forest management plan in order to implement this vision.

General Principle 2: Know Where You Came from to Know Where You Are Going

"If you don't know where you are going," wrote Lewis Carroll in *Alice's Adventures in Wonderland*, "any road will get you there." He could well have added that if you don't know where you have been, it is hard to know where you are going. It is truly critical with environmental issues like urban and community forestry to document the community's past experience in order to know what has succeeded or failed, and why, both to avoid the mistakes of the past and to understand fully where the most promising opportunities lie. New scientific knowledge of the functions and benefits of the urban forest cannot be fully used without this base of historical data. This information is also necessary for goal setting.

Professional planners have always documented a community's past and existing conditions in order to better inform public discussion in the visioning and goal-setting process. With regard to urban forestry, planners are likely to need substantial assistance from professional foresters, who will be more conversant with the technical details of species distribution and adaptation, soil conditions, stresses produced by development, equipment and personnel needs, and numerous other factors that can complicate the likelihood of success or failure for future forestry initiatives. Likewise, planners can seek GIS professionals who can conduct temporal analyses to answer the question, How has our urban forest changed over the past few decades? Public perception that trees are good is simply not enough to sustain a forestry program.

Urban foresters and arborists are professionally trained to assess the health of the urban forest ecosystem. Moreover, to the extent that urban foresters and planners work together to document the history of the local urban forest as an ecosystem, rather than just a collection of trees, that effort will advance public understanding of the interrelationships both of the parts of the forest in which people live and of the urban forest with the built

Systematic pruning and street tree maintenance have created an idyllic feeling in many of Urbana's residential neighborhoods.

Although the community may have more direct public control over municipal lands like parks, the urban forest would be sparse indeed if parks and rights-of-way were the only places where trees appeared.

environment. What is ultimately being driven through such documentation is the quality of the public debate that will result in a community vision about the urban forest.

In recent years, master plans for urban forests have begun with a detailed historical and quantitative assessment of the conditions in the community. This serves many of the same functions as the audit advocated in Chapter 1. Major examples include Syracuse (Nowak and O'Connor 2001), Savannah (Adler and Krawczyk 1995), and Baltimore (Galvin et al. 2006), as well as several of the case studies in Chapter 3. Fazio (2003) advises that conducting an inventory of trees in the community is the first step in creating attainable goals.

General Principle 3: Seek Out Private and Civic Partners

Urban forestry is an area of public planning where government need not tackle the job alone. In most cities, most of the urban forest canopy consists of trees on private property. Although the community may have more direct public control over municipal lands like parks, the urban forest would be sparse indeed if parks and rights-of-way were the only places where trees grew. Even development regulations affecting private property cannot cover the gap because they deal largely with preservation and planting but not long-term maintenance. Ultimately, true success in maintaining the urban forest depends on the continuing support of homeowners, businesses, and leagues of dedicated volunteers in organizations such as local tree trusts.

There may be no better way to stretch the value of limited public funding for urban forestry than through the largely uncompensated efforts of volunteers and property owners to plant and maintain trees. The cost-sharing program cited in the case study of Urbana, Illinois, in Chapter 3, for instance, taps the willingness of homeowners to do their part by splitting the cost of trees with the city while providing them with sound advice regarding planting and tree care.

Taken to the block or neighborhood level, such programs can enlist the active support of block clubs and community organizations interested in improving the livability of their city. Savannah is a great example of the power of such involvement not only to improve neighborhood forest canopy but ultimately to transform local public policy, in this case with the enactment of a new ordinance that, among other things, incorporated single-family residential development in its regulations (Adler and Krawczyk 1995).

Another example of involving property owners is Baltimore County's Rural Residential Stewardship Initiative. This program plants trees on lots with "excess" lawns in large-lot rural subdivisions where landowners typically use only a portion of lots larger than three acres. The Department of Environmental Protection and Resource Management provides design and installation of expanded riparian buffers in return for landowner monitoring and maintenance of reforested areas. Reforesting these underused lots helps provide the ecosystem services derived from trees and protects the Chesapeake Bay.

Business partners can be powerful contributors to the expansion and success of urban forestry through financial support, planting and maintenance of trees on commercial property, and active support of civic organizations involved in forestry. Some businesses clearly have a direct stake in urban forestry as a function of their own enterprises—including nurseries, home and garden suppliers, and tree care firms. Others may be interested in offsetting environmental impacts, an area that is likely to grow as carbon credits become commoditized as a result of climate change policy. On a much larger scale, business-driven civic leadership can incorporate urban forestry visibly into much broader planning initiatives and thus build its legitimacy as a public policy issue. A good example from a public-private partnership in this regard would be the chapter on urban forestry produced by Envision Utah (2002) in a statewide development plan.

One part of the business community that cannot be ignored is the media—in all forms. Print, broadcast, and electronic media all can play a part in disseminating information and cultivating public support, and it is important to understand their priorities and needs in order to work with them effectively. In the age of the Internet, the potential for creative use of all these media types is greater than ever before. While not always necessary, the strategic use of local or national celebrities can also help to bring attention to urban forestry projects and programs. Finally, educational institutions at all levels should be involved in any long-term communications strategy for urban forestry.

The most effective way to maximize the effectiveness of all private partners in combination is to develop and evolve a comprehensive strategy for programmatic relationships with them, knowing what strengths and capabilities each brings to the overall effort as well as their differences (Fazio 2003).

Children learn to plant trees through Olympia, Washington's NeighborWoods program.

General Principle 4: Investing in Trees Makes Economic Sense

Increasingly, it is possible to put hard numbers behind urban forestry, as was noted in Chapter 1. Some benefits contribute directly to property values as a result of the increased aesthetic appeal of home lots with trees, while others may contribute indirectly, as through increased retail sales in shopping districts with street trees. Environmental benefits, however, are also being quantified more accurately and more often in economic terms than even in

WORKING TOGETHER FOR CLEAN AIR

By *Susan Mockenhaupt, USDA Forest Service*

In Southern California, a coalition of organizations made history during "The Great Clean Air Tree Planting Project," planting 5,000 trees across Los Angeles, Orange, San Bernardino, and Riverside counties. United Voices for Healthier Communities coordinated and managed the effort with individuals, families, and organizations as diverse as community groups, arbor professionals, classmates, youth groups, and Boy and Girl Scout troops. Work was coordinated with the California Urban Forest Council, the Western Chapter of the International Society of Arboriculture, and California ReLeaf. The South Coast Air Quality Management District, Cal Fire (formerly the California Department of Forestry and Fire Protection), the USDA Forest Service Urban and Community Forestry Program, and the Britton Fund provided funding.

Thousands of volunteers planted trees in parks, schools, along sidewalks, medians, and in their own backyards. The project is believed to be the largest volunteer tree planting undertaken in the state. Participants also learned about long-term tree care, insuring that the thousands of trees planted will help clean the air for decades to come.

Using the i-Tree tools for assessing the value of the urban forests (see page 13), the mature trees will remove at least 840 tons of carbon dioxide and 24,160 pounds of pollutants from the air every year for decades to come.

the recent past (see, e.g., McPherson 1995, but also McPherson et al. 2005; Kollin 2004). Increasingly, communities are realizing that green infrastructure is an economical long-term investment that reduces the need for much greater expenditures in gray infrastructure.

These valuations are working their way into some local plans and planning activities. For example, Baltimore County's Department of Environmental Protection and Resource Management (DEPRM) has used capital funds with the USDA Forest Service to assess and value urban canopy function using the Forest Service's Urban Forest Effects (UFORE) model. The use of Urban Ecosystem Analysis in communities working with American Forests has produced local valuations of the ecosystem services provided by the urban forest.

General Principle 5: Urban Forestry Must Be Sustainable Financially

Urban forestry makes economic sense. Consequently, there is no reason not to put it on a sound financial footing. In the past, many tree programs have been viewed (and many still are) as cost centers, and the goal was to hold costs down while recognizing that such programs were politically popular because of their aesthetic value. The movement toward quantifying the economic benefits of trees at all levels (direct economic benefits but also indirect savings from environmental, health, and psychological benefits) suggests an entirely different model focused on trees as a wise public investment strategy—and through this lens, as a profit center.

The increasing use of the concept of green infrastructure also transforms the usual understanding of environmental costs into one of cost-benefit ratios. If the net benefits are positive, then it makes sense to invest the necessary resources to reap those benefits. Much as we are trained to see investment in traditional infrastructure, such as roads and bridges, as a means of spurring economic development, environmental investments including urban forestry are acquiring a new status as wealth generators rather than mere externalities.

Most urban forestry programs will probably always rely heavily on general fund allocations, but other options exist that can provide a revenue stream more clearly dedicated to the stewardship and management of urban forests. The case studies mention some of these options. For example, Olympia, Washington, uses a capital improvement plan fund derived from real estate excise taxes and utility taxes, with interest, to underwrite its program. Salem, Oregon, funds its care of street trees through the municipal portion of the state motor fuel tax, while funding some tree preservation through fines and donations. Urbana also uses fines to aid its program, particularly for motorists who damage trees in accidents. Urbana has also largely established a self-supporting yard waste recycling center by selling back to property owners the soil amendments and compost it produces from the waste it receives. This latter effort demonstrates the entrepreneurial approach that cities can use when their quest for sustainable funding becomes more creative.

Other cities have carved out a role for nonprofit organizations in supplementing tree funding. For example, the Sacramento Tree Foundation is substantially funded by the Sacramento Municipal Utility District.

Development fees (including impact fees where legal) can help underwrite tree programs in newly developing areas of a community. In this regard, development regulations can become a tool for supporting trees by establishing fees related to permit processing and enforcement. These fees can be written into zoning, subdivision, and landscaping codes, and then linked to those aspects of the program that benefit new development or redevelopment. Another option is to dedicate a portion of revenue from a

Much as we are trained to see investment in traditional infrastructure, such as roads and bridges, as a means of spurring economic development, environmental investments including urban forestry are acquiring a new status as wealth generators rather than mere externalities.

tax increment financing district to urban forestry improvements, following the rationale that such improvements add proven value to new economic development.

PLANNING PRINCIPLES

Successful urban forestry requires more than platitudes and good intentions. Planning increasingly is playing a major role. These six planning principles are designed to help usher the vision into reality.

Planning Principle 1: Incorporate the Tree Ordinance in the Development Code and Ensure Consistency with Other Codes

When a tree ordinance is adopted in isolation but never incorporated into the development code, do developers even know it exists? If this question sounds like an echo of the old riddle about a tree falling in the woods, that is the point. Tree ordinances need to be noticeable, so that if a tree falls on a development site, both planners and developers will know there are regulations that apply.

A major problem cited by participants at APA's symposium for the project that produced this report was that too many tree ordinances are stand-alone laws that are not incorporated into zoning, subdivision, or other development codes, and, consequently, go unnoticed by the development community. One reason cited for that practice is that it is often easier to include regulatory provisions for trees separately rather than amend the zoning code, but the consequence is an inherent loss of effectiveness. This was a lesson that Columbus, Georgia, took to heart in redesigning its 1972 tree ordinance to give it some teeth and to respond to public demands for better enforcement (Williams 2002). The ordinance includes provisions for landscaping plans, tree planting and protection plans, and inspections for compliance.

Chatham County, Georgia, has even older ties between development and tree ordinances, having passed its first Land Development Activities Ordinance in 1987, which established a system of tree quality points to encourage planting of hybrid species with the best prospects for surviving the development process (Adler and Krawczyk 1995). Among the case studies, Chapel Hill, North Carolina, has focused on protecting trees on development sites and included its Tree Protection Ordinance in the Land Use Management Ordinance it adopted in 2003.

One problem created by not having all tree regulations in one place is that it is potentially counterproductive to force users of the development codes to go to more than one section of the city's codes to find everything that relates to trees. Landscaping provisions, tree protection and planting requirements, street tree provisions relating to the right-of-way, and other tree-related regulations, if they cannot be kept entirely within the same chapter of the code, ought at least to cross-reference one another. The danger otherwise is that, as codes are revised over time, inconsistencies may creep into the newer requirements as a result of a lack of consolidation. One reason for this is that multiple professional and other interests are at stake in these ordinances, so that planners may not think comprehensively about the place of trees in the development code, while landscape architects and arborists may not even focus on the development code at all when seeking adoption of provisions they deem essential.

Planners must help overcome that tendency toward diffusion of tree requirements in local codes. Finally, planners, urban foresters, and elected officials must work to ensure that when ordinances are adopted, they remain consistent both vertically and horizontally with national and state environmental and development laws and other regional and local codes. Conflicting code provisions serve only to undermine the effectiveness of the community's original intent in trying to protect the urban forest.

PLANNING PRINCIPLES

Planning Principle 1: Incorporate the tree ordinance in the development code and ensure consistency with other codes.

Planning Principle 2: Collaborate with developers, environmentalists, and other stakeholders to draft ordinances.

Planning Principle 3: Planned Unit Development regulations should include an urban forestry evaluation checklist or guidelines.

Planning Principle 4: Ordinances must include provisions for enforcement personnel.

Planning Principle 5: Take an adaptive management approach to resources.

Planning Principle 6: Plan for long-term maintenance of trees.

Planning Principle 2: Collaborate with Developers, Environmentalists, and Other Stakeholders to Draft Ordinances

When Columbus, Georgia, drafted its new tree preservation ordinance, it did more than incorporate it into its land-use codes. It undertook a process of civic debate that, although at times raucous and contentious, involved broad segments of the community in forging an effective consensus about what would actually work. Local tree organizations that included retired and active attorneys debated issues with developers and real estate agents before the city council produced a remarkably strong ordinance that responded to public opinion, which strongly favored better tree preservation (Williams 2002).

As Rachel Buice, the city's deputy director of public services, noted at the APA symposium, "We had developers, we had the greenies, we had city staff, we had everybody. It was a large group which then came down to a smaller group to flesh out a very strong ordinance." As Buice also noted, this was followed by internal collaboration within her department among engineers and consultants on how to enforce the ordinance.

Her point underscored a second issue in collaboration: the need for interdisciplinary cooperation within the city staff to ensure that the resulting ordinance will succeed in producing its intended results. Planners do not need to know enough about trees to decide exactly what species is right in a particular setting or how best to preserve an entire grove on a development site. Urban foresters and arborists can supply that knowledge, but they likewise do not necessarily need to know all the fine points of site design. Landscape architects can serve as a bridge in many cases, but all these professionals, including engineers who must fit infrastructure into development sites, must collaborate to determine what each needs in the final decision in order to make the process of tree preservation and planting successful. The effectiveness of any tree ordinance within the development code is fundamentally a function of interdisciplinary teamwork.

Planning Principle 3: Planned Unit Development Regulations Should Include an Urban Forestry Evaluation Checklist or Guidelines

McHarg (1969) was the pioneer of conservation and preservation in planning and development. Mandelker (2007) notes that Arendt's *Conservation Design for Subdivisions* (1996) brought attention to conservation in land development considerations in new significant ways—ideas that have been expanded beyond subdivision design to the design of planned unit developments (PUDs). Eugene, Oregon, defines a PUD as "a comprehensive development plan intended to provide flexibility in design and building placement, promote attractive and efficient environments that incorporate a variety of uses, densities, and dwelling types, provide for economy of shared services and facilities, and protect natural resources (Mandelker 2007, 4).

Developers generally prefer clear guidelines if their work is going to be subject to stringent requirements. It is important that communities simplify the task of compliance by summarizing those requirements in checklists or visual design guides so that developers can more easily understand what is expected of them. The need for good PUD regulations has grown because, as Mandelker (2007, 1) notes, "more than 20 percent of the homes in this country are built by the nation's top 10 builders." The largest share of this development is in PUDs and master-planned communities, especially in fast-growing states like California and Florida. One noteworthy example of state planning legislation facilitating flexible and creative development for planned residential developments and traditional neighborhood development (TND) is the collection of articles in Pennsylvania's Municipalities Planning Code. The TND article specifically encourages preservation of trees and open space among its criteria.

Arendt's central innovation was the idea of using zoning, subdivision, and land development ordinances for site design that clustered development, in which the parts of a development site better endowed with natural resources are protected while housing and other structures are concentrated on smaller lots elsewhere within the site, thereby conserving nature and density simultaneously. Trees—especially an intact urban forest—constitute a natural resource worthy of such treatment within an ordinance. The essential calculations should determine the percentage of a site subject to the conservation regulations, including land set-asides for other environmentally sensitive areas, such as wetlands, floodplains, and hillsides. Planners then figure out how to distribute the allowed number of units elsewhere on the site.

Even without cluster development, PUD regulations can address tree protection on individual lots and certainly on public rights-of-way. As noted in Planning Principle 2, these regulations should result from collaboration among urban foresters and arborists, landscape architects, engineers, architects, and planners to maximize the likelihood of a successful outcome, and the proposal review process should include the earliest possible collaboration among planners, arborists, and the developer. Examples of plan specification requirements are included in Appendix D.

Forest buffers provide important environmental and quality-of-life benefits in dense urban areas such as the Owings Mills New Town.

Planning Principle 4: Ordinances Must Include Provisions for Enforcement Personnel

Urban forestry is a long-term proposition. Trees planted today will grow for years to come. Depending on the species and the local environment, some will probably live generations longer than the people who planted them. On the other hand, poor maintenance in a high-stress urban environment will greatly increase the prospects of a high death rate for the trees. Humans create the conditions under which trees will thrive, survive, or fail in communities. It is the responsibility of urban forestry programs to improve the success rate. If a community wants a program to truly work, it needs to give it authority. It needs an ordinance tied to the program, whether that be a tree preservation ordinance, landscaping ordinance, vegetation ordinance, or tree-related provisions embedded within a zoning or subdivision code.

One way to guarantee failure is to enact a program of planting and preservation of trees on development sites without incorporating the resources needed for effective oversight. Enforcement personnel are not a luxury for urban forestry, but a necessity. Planners, when drafting ordinances regarding trees and development practices, should advocate adequate budgeting to support the positions they feel are needed to implement and enforce those ordinances.

First, planners should ensure that some office or agency with qualified personnel is either created or assigned the duties of regulatory enforcement for the urban forest program. Inadequate staffing will mean a lack of responsibility and, consequently, a lack of effectiveness.

The ordinance can also include provisions for effective intervention points. For example, all tree, landscaping, and vegetative buffering requirements should be part of a checklist used in the final site plan approval process before a certificate of occupancy can be granted. Modifying the zoning ordinance to include such a provision can give enforcement personnel real power.

The case of Urbana, Illinois, highlights the difference such a choice can make. The arbor division, responsible for urban forestry management, is a separate division within the public works department. The city arborist directs a staff of urban foresters and arborists who care for the street trees. The city arborist is responsible for planning tree work as well as communicating with the public and coordinating the arbor division's activities with the public works department and other departments and divisions, such as community development and engineering. These activities include checking development proposals for compliance with tree provisions and inspecting development sites for compliance with provisions, including those for tree planting and maintenance in commercial parking lots. In effect, the duties of the city arborist have been built into those of the design team. In a similar vein, Chapel Hill, North Carolina, has incorporated such roles for the landscape architect or urban forester to ensure that tree protection and preservation requirements are followed. The bulk of the city's annual budget for urban forestry is invested in funding these positions and support staff.

Columbus, Georgia, again supplies an effective example here. According to Rachel Buice, the deputy director of public services, the city revisits development sites every two years after development is completed because developers and property owners are expected to keep trees alive "in perpetuity." The city also checks grading plans to ensure that trees are not badly placed or compromised by power lines, water mains, sanitary sewers, and other infrastructure on the site. The public works department includes an urban forestry and beautification division with 80 people handling both urban forestry and right-of-way maintenance. Of those, 20 are tree specialists.

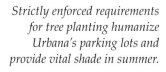

Strictly enforced requirements for tree planting humanize Urbana's parking lots and provide vital shade in summer.

Jim Schwab

Planning Principle 5: Take an Adaptive Management Approach to Resources

Scientists have learned a great deal about the urban forest in the last two decades. Because this learning process is ongoing, a way to incorporate new findings into best practices in managing the urban forest will always be needed. If anything, the pace of scientific research has quickened, rather than slowed, over time.

Adaptive management is the name for the application of new knowledge in updates and changes to a program. In this approach, notes Rowntree (1995, 57), "the best science, albeit incomplete, is brought to bear on an ecosystem, management is implemented under rigorously monitored conditions, and adaptations in management are made as the feedback from monitoring teaches us more about the way the ecosystem behaves." The very process of management yields new lessons as an urban forestry program moves forward (e.g., the ways in which trees respond to new stresses as well as new treatments for those stresses). Applying the new knowledge helps improve the accuracy in predicting how an ecosystem will respond to new managerial approaches.

Adaptive management is also a very interdisciplinary process. Various kinds of scientists, as well as design professionals and resource managers, must compare notes and share viewpoints in order to maximize the dissemination of new information and speed up its application in the field. The interaction among disciplines allows each to challenge the viewpoints of others and to avoid the intellectual stagnation that may result when a narrow group of professionals talk only among themselves (Benedict and McMahon 2006). One good example of interdisciplinary cooperation in developing appropriate guidelines for growing, installing, and maintaining healthy trees is the work of the Illinois Specification Review Committee (www.illinoisgreen.net). Their guidelines are the work of a task force representing various green industry organizations working through the Illinois Green Industry Association. Their stated goal is to reduce a frequent and troubling pattern in recent decades of tree failure.

Ultimately, the real benefit of adaptive management is that it allows incremental adjustments over time rather than requiring jarring change when conventional assumptions go unchallenged for too long. Regular review of ordinances and regulations with an eye to lessons learned helps to institutionalize this concept.

The other major benefit of adaptive management is that it allows resource managers a level of comfort with uncertainty (Bradley 1995). Too often, scientific policy in the public arena awaits definitive answers, a tendency shown all too tragically in the nation's response to climate change. Planners know they often cannot wait for absolute certainty to craft policy because the pace of change in urban communities does not allow it. On the other hand, allowing uncertainty, while embracing adaptation to new discoveries, allows both scientists and planners to make the best possible decisions knowing that some adjustments may need to be made over time.

Ultimately, the real benefit of adaptive management is that it allows incremental adjustments over time rather than requiring jarring change when conventional assumptions go unchallenged for too long.

Planning Principle 6: Plan for Long-term Maintenance of Trees

It bears repeating: The urban forest is a project that requires long-term maintenance. Short-term commitments to planting more trees beg the question of how those trees will be cared for and survive well into the future. One primary reason for General Principle 5, putting urban forestry on a sustainable footing financially, is that long-term success is undermined when such programs are subjected to short-term budget cuts. Deferred maintenance results in tree die-offs as the stresses of the urban environment take their toll. Preventive maintenance, on the other hand, increases the life span and the resulting benefits of trees, increases public safety by keeping trees stable

LIST OF DESIGN PRINCIPLES

Design Principle 1. Use urban forestry to support other planning goals.

Design Principle 2. Include a green infrastructure element in the local comprehensive plan, but link it to other elements in the plan.

Design Principle 3. The natural environment makes neighborhoods more livable.

Design Principle 4: Make the place right for trees and then pick the right trees.

in storms, reduces community conflict with government agencies, and decreases long-term work and costs associated with the program.

Long-term maintenance is more than a matter of convincing local elected officials to maintain urban forestry as a budgetary priority. Some of the case studies illustrate that planners and urban foresters can act creatively to stabilize their budgets for tree programs. They can also adopt long-term planning and investment procedures to stabilize maintenance over time, particularly in four specific areas described here.

Conduct an operations review. Putting General Principle 2 into practice, this means conducting an audit of past practices to determine what elements of the program have been successful and which are more problematic.

Review and maintain tree inventory data. Presuming your community has created a tree inventory already, this involves reviewing it periodically to see what has changed over a given period of time, determining why that change occurred, and deciding what implications these changes have for the future. If certain species are thriving better than others, are there specific conditions causing this to happen? Do they thrive more in certain parts of town, in specific soils, in different kinds of built environment? These kinds of information provide the road map for program managers to make adjustments and increase the likelihood of success.

Budget for equipment. Where do your funds come from, and how do they relate to your ongoing equipment needs? Are there gaps, and how can budgeting be adjusted to fill those gaps? While most equipment is itself a long-term investment, it too has long-term maintenance needs that cannot be ignored.

Maintain adequate personnel. Planning Principle 4 made this point already, but it too bears repeating: No ordinance should be enacted without providing for enforcement personnel. Long-term maintenance also requires appropriate staffing for street tree maintenance, removal of hazardous trees, and other tree functions involving city staff responsibilities. As R.J. Laverne, a symposium participant from the Davey Tree Resource Group, noted, "There is no easier way to fail than to plant a whole bunch of trees and watch them die."

DESIGN PRINCIPLES

In addition to the broad general and planning principles discussed above, successful urban forestry also requires creative and effective design at all levels, from metropolitan areas and regional ecosystems down to neighborhoods and individual development sites.

Design Principle 1. Use Urban Forestry to Support Other Planning Goals

Good community development practices include consideration of trees, parks, and green infrastructure. These practices include new urbanism, smart growth, low-impact and conservation development, walkable neighborhoods, multimodal transportation systems, and transit-oriented development. Trees and a broader metropolitan green infrastructure add lasting value and help to realize the goals of sustainable development.

Planners are already trained to be comprehensive thinkers. Instinctively, many planners are inclined to agree that "everything is connected to everything." Urban forestry lends itself to supporting so many other planning goals that establishing those connections is largely limited by one's own imagination. Among many other possibilities, trees can help:

- create a sense of place;

- promote aesthetics in the community;

- create walkable neighborhoods;

- improve traffic safety through planting in parkways;
- calm traffic by limiting fields of vision along residential and some commercial streets; and
- advance environmental goals for air and water quality and energy conservation.

Some of these points are already covered to one degree or another in the general and planning principles above, but the point here is that planners and landscape architects should actively seek these linkages when working on other issues and then use trees to support those broader public policy goals. Part of this involves recognizing and acting upon opportunities to develop the rationale for supporting urban forestry.

Meadowbrook Park provides for many Urbana residents an island of serenity, while incorporating iconic sculpture, bicycle and hiking paths, and activities for all ages.

At the same time, other planning goals can also support urban forestry through mutual reinforcement. For instance, if a community adopts the principle of preventing forest fragmentation, with all the losses of wildlife habitat (and habitat quality) that accompany that process, the logical corollary would be to adopt land-use policies that do not allow new development to cut up the forest, but instead consolidate urban growth in more compact, contiguous development patterns. In some places, this may also reduce threats to an otherwise viable forest products industry. One example of mutual reinforcement is an initiative by the Maryland Department of Forestry to persuade large lot owners to reforest their properties as a way of contributing to restoration of watersheds, which ultimately may result in water quality improvements in Chesapeake Bay (Maryland DNR Forest Service 2002).

Trees can be central to economic development. Fort Worth, Texas, included tree planting in its design guidelines for new downtown businesses as part of an effort to revive the central business district. The city also used this strategy in its Camp Bowie historic district, according to Melinda Adams, the Fort Worth city forester and a participant in the APA symposium for this report.

Design Principle 2. Include a Green Infrastructure Element in the Local Comprehensive Plan, But Link It to Other Elements in the Plan

Appendix A of this report describes the contents of a green infrastructure element for a local comprehensive plan, although such an element may have a

Far from empowering criminals, green vegetation has served to reduce stress, aggression, and violence, and produces a calming effect.

different title (e.g., "natural resources," "open space," "environment," or even "forestry"). There clearly are many ways to organize a comprehensive plan, as well as specific legal requirements in many states regarding the contents of a comprehensive plan. The important question is the nature and focus of the element's description of existing conditions and whether it reflects an understanding of the various benefits provided by green infrastructure within the community, such as improved stormwater management and water quality. As Benedict and McMahon (2006) note, "green infrastructure planning can fit in many places," of which the comprehensive plan is clearly one, along with budgeting, various functional plans (e.g., sewer system or parks), visioning, and land-use regulations.

Also important is whether those benefits and values are reflected throughout the rest of the comprehensive plan, with appropriate links to the one element that presumably pulls it all together. For instance, is roadside vegetation a part of the transportation element? Are trees and pocket parks in public housing developments discussed in the housing element? Is there a connection between natural resource conservation and the land-use element? Virtually any feature of the natural environment that provides ecological services to the community is a fit topic for a green infrastructure element. It is vital that the community have a full picture of the value and utility of its natural resources.

With that full picture in place, it is easier to envision the tools that can advance the integration of green infrastructure into the built environment, including provisions in zoning and subdivision codes and the permit approval and site plan review processes that implement them. These can include features such as stormwater retention, pedestrian and bicycle paths, greenways, and preserved open spaces. Using these procedures and regulations in concert with the comprehensive plan provides both short-term and long-term strategies for making green infrastructure an integral part of the community's overall planning. The green infrastructure element then becomes both a capstone and stimulus for those efforts.

Design Principle 3. The Natural Environment Makes Neighborhoods More Livable

What makes a place like Savannah, Georgia, appealing? In large part, it is the very sense of place created by its trees and their massive canopy cover, perhaps the best in the nation. It is hard to imagine Savannah without its urban forest, which, as symposium participants noted, owes a great deal to citizen activism through the Savannah Tree Foundation. Savannah is the quintessential walkable community because of its tree canopy and neighborhood parks. A look at APA's Great Places in America program (see PAS Report No. 552) indicates that many great streets and neighborhoods owe that designation to the beauty and quality of their streetscapes highlighted by wonderful trees.

The benefits of trees in making a neighborhood livable extend beyond creating pride and a distinct sense of place, as important as those may be. They also humanize the built environment by providing shade on hot summer days, cool places to relax on otherwise sunlit lawns, and filters for excessive heat buildup in many urban buildings.

In addition, there is the simple matter of the civility of the urban setting. Despite considerable urban mythology about the utility of trees for hiding lurking criminals, University of Illinois researchers Frances E. Kuo and William E. Sullivan (2001) have shown through studies in Chicago that greener surroundings for inner-city apartment buildings experienced crime rates generally at least 40 percent lower than in buildings with no greenery at all. They have argued that far from empowering criminals, green vegetation has served to reduce stress, aggression, and violence, and produces a

Even densely built neighborhoods, like this one in San Francisco, can be humanized with a modest amount of greenery in a small urban park.

calming effect. The clear line of sight produced by a total lack of trees may allow one to see attackers, but it also produces a sterile environment that may breed a greater sense of alienation. More work is needed in this area, but what Kuo and Sullivan have begun through their Human-Environment Research Laboratory is important to understanding the psychological impact of the urban forest.

Design Principle 4: Make the Place Right for Trees and Then Pick the Right Trees

Much of the discussion in this chapter has focused on the benefits of the urban forest and how to ensure that they are factored into the planning process. It is wise to conclude by cautioning that maximizing those benefits—and minimizing the costs and losses—requires some care in distinguishing which trees are right for which circumstances and locations. The wrong tree in the wrong place with inadequate care is almost doomed to failure, and its failure will often serve to undermine public support for urban forestry as a productive investment. Consequently, the final design principle is that communities must put the right tree in the right place in order to optimize their prospects of success. This means that they must be willing to support the work of tree professionals who can choose appropriate sites and soils for specific tree species. And they must support that work throughout all phases of the development process.

Following this design principle requires several important considerations in making tree-planting decisions:

- What is the nature of the local water supply, and what trees are best adapted to those conditions? Water-consuming plants in an arid landscape can be highly wasteful, but good design can use a "water budget" that still provides an attractive landscape (Perry 1995).

- What soil conditions and types of soil exist on the site that will affect the survival of particular tree species? In a given urban location, the soil may not entirely be the original soil, or it may be somewhat affected by site disturbance stemming from previous development or environmental degradation. How much room does a tree have to grow within the built environment? Matheny and Clark (1998) point out that lateral growth of roots is just as important as soil depth. Trees must be well matched to their available growing space. Planning for the underground needs of trees is as important, if not more important, than planning for the space above ground.

- What type of terrain is involved (hilly or flat, for instance), and what does that mean for both the ability of trees to hold the soil or to survive?

- Which trees are native to the area, which are not, and what is the impact of using non-native species? The urban environment is a significantly altered environment not replicated in nature. Like engineers specifying building materials, trees must be selected to perform under the stresses of specific situations, which often are harsher than what existed before settlement. "Plant Native" is a public relations phrase, not a planting specification; there is much more to selecting a tree than choosing one that is native.

- How does the planned or existing built environment affect the microclimate of the site on which trees will be planted?

By providing the proper location and growing conditions trees can thrive, grow to their full potential, and maximize the myriad of benefits they provide to the community.

Gary Moll, American Forests

Considering the site-specific nature of many of these decisions, it is nearly impossible to prescribe a precise solution in an ordinance. Performance standards or broad design guidelines are more likely to work, but enforcement will usually require the involvement of some sort of tree professional to review the site plans and monitor progress to ensure that the choices made for that site actually work. What works in a parking lot may be very different from what works in a residential yard, a right-of-way, or a corporate campus or industrial park. Each creates its own set of conditions, such as differences in soil depth or shade, in which some trees thrive and others may not. Many state universities, either through extension services or forestry or horticulture programs, can offer expert advice on which species are most likely to thrive in specific climatic and environmental conditions.

In the larger picture, however, planners and urban foresters must consider tree choices and locations in light of overall performance goals for the urban forest and more generally for the green infrastructure in their community. Different species contribute differently in terms of filtering air pollution or stormwater runoff, or adding to citywide tree canopy goals. The big picture can become quite complex, and learning as much as possible about how the pieces fit together underlies the adaptive management approach behind Planning Principle 5. We don't have all the answers, but new tools for scientific measurement of results from the urban forest continue to emerge and advance our understanding in this area. It is the role of good planning to make effective use of this new knowledge.

CHAPTER 3

Case Studies

One of the planning principles in Chapter 2 discussed using an adaptive management approach to natural resources. This is necessary because there is much that we still do not know or understand about the natural environment, particularly in terms of its response to and interaction with the built environment. The urban forest lives and grows in the built environment. Both environments evolve, respond, and adapt over time to changing demographic, climatic, technological, and other circumstances.

CASE STUDY SELECTION CRITERIA

After choosing case studies to provide a sample with geographic diversity (for climatic reasons), researchers examined the designees by asking the following questions.

- What public policy goals does the case study serve?

- What problems or external stimuli are driving the program?

- Is this a holistic approach or a single-purpose approach?

- Is this program part of a comprehensive plan? If so, how? Are there linkages to other plans or plan elements?

- What codes help implement the plan or program?

- What agency(s) is responsible?

- What are the innovative features, if any?

- How is the program funded? How well is it funded?

- When did the program start? How long has it been in existence?

- How much of this is transferable to similarly sized cities? (All, most, some, none?)

- Who is the best contact for a case study author to interview?

In a broader sense, because the welfare of the urban forest depends so heavily on human management, it is wise to suggest an adaptive approach to planning for the urban forest. Planning should always incorporate new knowledge, not only of the science of urban forestry, but also from on-the-ground experience. As we learn more about what works in mustering public support behind green infrastructure in the visioning process, for example, we should employ it, just as we should also employ the best lessons concerning financial support for urban forestry.

With such thoughts in mind, the American Planning Association (APA) enlisted its partners in a search for exemplary case studies across the U.S. In the end, using a variety of criteria highlighted in the sidebar, the project partners chose 13 case studies. This chapter presents those case studies, divided into three categories. First are those communities that take a predominantly holistic approach to urban forestry; that is, they seek to incorporate urban forestry in the planning process. Second are those that had more limited or single-purpose objectives in crafting their urban forestry programs, such as embedding tree preservation into the site plan review process, but without, for example, undertaking efforts to make forestry an integral element of the visioning process. Finally, two case studies involved regional efforts to plan for green infrastructure and thus did not focus on the regulatory capacities of individual communities. These efforts merited separate consideration because they rely much more for their success on larger planning scales and intergovernmental coordination and cooperation.

HOLISTIC APPROACHES

Baltimore County

By Donald C. Outen, AICP

Baltimore County has developed a comprehensive Forest Sustainability Program, building upon the county's 40-year tradition of growth management and environmental protection. The program incorporates the international Montreal Process Criteria and Indicators (MPCI) framework for measuring ecological and economic sustainability, defined generally as meeting the needs of society today without diminishing the ability of future generations to meet their needs. (See the sidebar on the following page for more about MPCI.) The county is implementing a three-part strategy to: assess forest health; protect remaining forests; and reforest priority lands including riparian buffers, reservoir watersheds, and urban communities by engaging landowners regarding stewardship of 75 percent of the county's privately owned forests. Because local governments directly influence land use and are responsible for pollution control mandates, Baltimore County's program provides an example of effective planning for urban and community forestry.

Growth and resource context. Despite intense development pressures in the Baltimore region, Baltimore County is successfully managing growth and protecting important natural resources. Baltimore County is Maryland's third-largest county in land area (610 square miles) and population (804,600). The county, which contains no incorporated municipalities, nearly surrounds the City of Baltimore, an independent jurisdiction.

Baltimore County's population increased from 155,825 in 1940 to 621,077 in 1970, and projections indicated continued rapid growth to more than 1 million by 2000. Aggressive application of land-use tools helped direct growth to existing communities surrounding the city and two growth areas designated in 1979, thereby protecting fertile agricultural soils, forest patches, and the region's three drinking water reservoirs from intensive development.

Nearly two-thirds of the watersheds for Baltimore's reservoir system, which serves 1.8 million people or one-third of Maryland's citizens, are located in Baltimore County. Growth management tools included adoption of master plan policies to protect farmland and reservoir watersheds and adoption in 1967 of an urban growth boundary, the Urban-Rural Demarcation Line (URDL). Starting in 1975, the county created Resource Conservation zones outside the URDL, downzoning and protecting more than 60 percent of the county's land area. The county continues to refine its conservation zones and to downzone rural lands as part of its quadrennial comprehensive zoning map process. Several land preservation programs have also permanently protected 50,000 acres, including about 15 percent of the forest cover. Some of the anticipated growth, originally over-projected, bypassed the county for surrounding counties in the region. Nevertheless, Baltimore County's 40 years of growth management progress resulted in 90 percent of its year 2000 population residing inside the URDL on only one-third of its land. Land cover (2000) for the county and the URDL are presented in Figure 3-1.

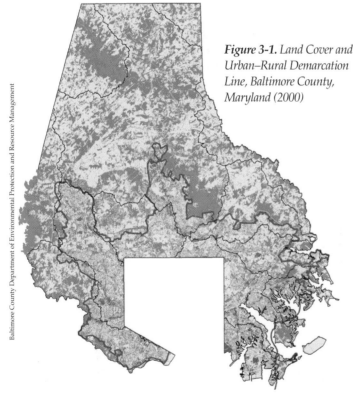

Figure 3-1. *Land Cover and Urban–Rural Demarcation Line, Baltimore County, Maryland (2000)*

Baltimore County Department of Environmental Protection and Resource Management

Forest management challenges. As Sprague et al. (2006) concludes, the bay watershed's forests are being converted to nonforest cover at more than 100 acres per day. Forest cover in Baltimore County was reduced from more than 90 percent at the time of European settlement to about 24 percent a century ago due to clearing for charcoal production, mining, and agriculture. With a decline in agriculture, forest cover increased until the mid-1900s, at which time development reduced forest cover to about 34 percent today. In Maryland, the Forest Conservation Act of 1991, the nation's first statewide forest protection law, was passed, requiring developers to retain forests on development sites in accordance with thresholds set for each zoning classification, or to mitigate for forest loss by planting on or off site, or by paying fees to counties. The act has resulted in the retention of 68 percent of all forests on development sites. Forest retention is also a priority within the 1,000-foot Chesapeake Bay shoreline under Maryland's 1984 Critical Area Act.

These protections aside, the sustainability of ecosystem services pro-

THE MONTREAL PROCESS

The Montreal Process Criteria and Indicators (MPCI) serve as a leading international protocol for measuring forest sustainability. MPCI originated with the 1992 Earth Summit, the United Nations Conference on Environment and Development (UNCED), which called on all nations to ensure sustainable development including the management of forest resources.

In 1993, an international group of scientists met in Montreal to develop forest criteria and indicators for a dozen nations that collectively comprise 60 percent of the world's forests and 90 percent of temperate and boreal forests. Five of the seven criteria address ecological sustainability, one addresses multiple socioeconomic benefits of forests, and the seventh addresses institutional, legal, and economic frameworks for forest conservation and sustainable management. The MPCI were used to prepare the first National Report on Sustainable Forests in 2003. Several indicators have since been modified and will be used for preparation of the 2010 National Report. Efforts are also under way to engage the broader community of forest stakeholders at multiple scales through the Roundtable on Sustainable Forests (RSF). For more information about the MPCI, see www.rinya.maff.go.jp/mpci/criteria_e.html, and see www.sustainableforests.net for information about the RSF.

vided by forests is threatened as a result of long-term patch fragmentation (the fragmentation or spatial break-up of large forest blocks into smaller pieces of forest when land is cleared for agriculture and development) and parcelization (an increase in the number of owners and the number of developed properties). More than 9,000 forest patches exist in the county with a mean patch size of only 14.6 acres and an edge-to-interior acreage ratio of 13:1. Parcelization of forest patches has resulted in an estimated 40,000+ owners who manage 75 percent of the forests in the county. The health of remaining forests is vulnerable as a result of invasive, non-native plant species, the deer population, and numerous forest pests and diseases.

Program framework and development. Baltimore County's Forest Sustainability Program was developed by its Department of Environmental Protection and Resource Management (DEPRM), created in 1987 to protect, enhance, and restore the county's natural resources. Having identified a green infrastructure framework for ecologically important forests in the mid-1990s with the Maryland Department of Natural Resources (DNR), DEPRM's work was introduced to the U.S. Forest Service (USFS) by DNR in 2001. The USFS, working with American Forests, invited the county to become a national case study for local implementation of MPCI, an international science-based approach for measuring the ecological and economic sustainability of forests. Under the "Linking Communities to the MPCI" program, DEPRM convened a stakeholder steering committee in 2003 to explore the MPCI framework and its utility for the county.

Baltimore County's forests protect many miles of natural trout streams in the Gunpowder River basin.

Donald Outen

The steering committee produced a *Forest Sustainability Strategy* in 2005 that included guiding principles, goals, recommended actions, and assessment and data needs for 15 ecological and economic sustainability issues (http://resources.baltimorecountymd.gov/Documents/Environment/Workgroup/Forest%20Sustainability/finalstrategy_110505.pdf). A memorandum of understanding among the county, DNR, USFS, and American Forests was then signed to guide cooperative implementation of the strategy. Five subcommittees are continuing to implement actions from the strategy following a 2006 "5E Forum" for forest Education, Ecology, Economics, Easements, and Environmental Indicators ("Endicators"). Baltimore County's Forest Sustainability Program became a key component of the county executive's Green Renaissance Initiative in 2005. It also supports the county's 2010 Master Plan, adopted by the county council in 2000, which recognizes the importance of forests for protecting air and water quality. Because forests are the most beneficial land cover for the protection of air and water quality, forest sustainability supports broad environmental programs.

In a region where restoration of the Chesapeake Bay has been a major intergovernmental commitment since 1983, forests play a major role in bay nutrient and sediment reduction strategies and sound land-use, land preservation, habitat protection, riparian buffer, and urban tree canopy goals. Forests are a strategic tool for federal Safe Drinking Water Act source water

Baltimore County's forests protect the Baltimore region's drinking water reservoirs.

protection requirements, Clean Water Act Total Maximum Daily Loads, and National Pollutant Discharge Elimination System municipal stormwater permits, and Coastal Zone Management Act nonpoint source control and coastal habitat protection priorities. Urban forests are also becoming recognized as part of Statewide Implementation Programs for attainment of air quality standards. Forest protection will be an important element for new sensitive area and water resource planning requirements in county and municipal master plans through Maryland's 2006 HB 1141.

Program implementation. In addition to the MPCI framework, the Forest Sustainability Strategy, and implementation partnerships, Baltimore County's Forest Sustainability Program includes other innovative features, especially forest assessment and monitoring programs, and citizen stewardship initiatives.

Using capital restoration funds (see sidebar on page 48) supported through bond referenda, DEPRM contracted for a forest health assessment and management plan for a 1,000-acre forested park using the USFS's North East Decision (NED) model, a software tool developed by the USDA Forest Service that uses field forest plot data to assist natural resource managers in developing goals, assessing current conditions, and producing management plans for forests in the eastern U.S.

Implementing a Chesapeake 2000 initiative, an urban tree canopy assessment and goal are also under development for areas inside the URDL with funding from USFS. DEPRM is also using its capital funds to contract with USFS to conduct an Urban Forest Effects (UFORE) model for forest canopy within the URDL to assess and value urban canopy function. The UFORE model, designed by USFS, uses field data from randomly selected plots and local meteorological data to quantify urban forest structure and to estimate environmental effects, such as carbon storage and sequestration, air pollution removal, and building energy use.

BUDGETING FOR FOREST SUSTAINABILITY IN BALTIMORE COUNTY

By Donald C. Outen, AICP

Baltimore County uses capital improvement funds supported by bond referenda. Its FY 2007–2008 budget to implement forest sustainability (assessment and reforestation programs) is $270,000. About five separate projects are funded through this at this time—the Oregon Ridge Forest Assessment (NED study mentioned), a coupon match for the Growing Home Campaign, some trees for Rural Residential Reforestation Initiative, a feasibility study for economic sustainability (probably a wood waste biofuels demonstration project), and rural forest health monitoring. The county does capital budgets on two-year cycles in conjunction with bond referenda. It also awards a small operating grant each year to the County Forestry Board.

Baltimore County also has a four-person year-round reforestation crew funded from fees-in-lieu of mitigation under the Forest Conservation Act for reforestation installation, monitoring, and maintenance (our Community Reforestation Program). A typical year might include about $150,000 for operations.

Operating budget support, which includes some of the author's work coordinating the forest sustainability program, GIS analyst work on data analyses and mapping, and other technical assistance from program staff, is more difficult to nail down as different staff contribute various amounts of time as part of doing the job (but no separate staff just doing forest sustainability). The total regulatory program for forest conservation was about $260,000 in FY 2006–2007. The DPW Bureau of Highways performs required removal and pruning on public lands and deals with street tree problems (sidewalks, etc.), as well as Christmas tree mulching and other operations. Recreation and Parks buys, plants, and maintains trees at parks. The Office of Community Conservation does streetscape projects with trees. Overall, the county qualified for the Tree City USA designation, exceeding the minimum $2/capita ($1.6 million for 804,000 pop.). In 2006 the county documented a total of $2.4 million on community forestry. The overall breakdown by agency was approximately:

$ 526,000	DEPRM
$ 270,000	Recreation and Parks
$ 1,419,000	DPW
$ 188,000	Community Conservation
$ 11,000	Community Colleges
$ 2,414,000	**Total (operating, not CIP)**

DEPRM is currently working with USFS scientists to develop a forest health monitoring network for rural forests using Forest Health Monitoring/Forest Inventory and Analysis (FHM/FIA) protocols, which use field-generated data to report on the condition and trends in health of individual forest tree species (growth rates, crown condition, decay, breakage, open wounds, etc.) and detection monitoring of forest area conditions (fragmentation, drought, fire, insects and disease, air pollutants, etc.). Exploration of the feasibility of a biomass energy project and several education partnerships with landowners and schools are also in progress.

Using capital funds, grants, and corporate donations, the county is working to encourage reforestation. New programs include the Growing Home Campaign and the Rural Residential Stewardship Initiative.

The Growing Home Campaign provides education and economic incentives to increase urban tree canopy by planting trees in residential yards. Thirty nurseries and garden centers provide point-of-purchase discounts to homeowners who bring in $10 coupons for the purchase of qualifying trees costing more than $25. The county reimburses retailers for half of each coupon submitted, in return for coupon data about the location, species, and cost of trees purchased. A three-month pilot in 2006 resulted in the distribution of 15,000 brochures and website downloads. Homeowners purchased 1,700 trees, and $50 of private sector investment was leveraged for each $5 coupon matched by the county.

The Rural Residential Stewardship Initiative targets reforestation of "excess" lawns in large-lot rural subdivisions where landowners typically actively use only a portion of lots larger than three acres. DEPRM provides design and installation of expanded riparian buffers in return for landowner monitoring and maintenance of reforestation areas. For the 2006 pilot program, more than 17 acres of new forest were added to 12 lots in two subdivisions.

Conclusion. Working aggressively with state and federal agencies, landowners, environmental organizations, and forestry professionals, Baltimore County is committed to the comprehensive management of its forest resources. The county's program emphasizes forest assessment, protection, and reforestation in urban and rural communities. The continued development and implementation of the Forest Sustainability Program are an attempt to improve the ecological and economic sustainability of Baltimore County's forest resources today and for the future.

And the county's efforts have been noticed:

- In 2006, the Chesapeake Bay Partner Communities gave the county its gold award.

- The county has been a Tree City USA for years, most recently continuing that designation in 2007.

- In 2005, the Maryland Department of Environment nominated Baltimore County for the Region 3 U.S. EPA Source Water Protection Award. Each state is allowed one recipient each year; EPA bestowed the award.

- Baltimore County was also featured in *Nature-Friendly Communities: Habitat Protection and Land Use Planning* (Island Press, 2005).

Minneapolis

By Janette K. Monear and Lorrie Stromme

On February 27, 2004, the Minneapolis City Council made a strong policy statement—it declared that the green infrastructure, the urban forest, is as important as the built environment. The new policy recognized that trees are an integral part of the city's infrastructure and its quality of life. The city has policies about sidewalk repair, bridge maintenance, street construction, and other types of gray infrastructure, but until the Urban Forest Policy was adopted, the departments that make up the City of Minneapolis lacked a comprehensive policy about their role in planning, protecting, and maintaining the city's trees.

The Urban Forest Policy contains standards and guidelines that help the departments work more effectively with the Minneapolis Park and Recreation Board (MPRB). Unlike most cities, Minneapolis has an independent board of park commissioners. Authorized by the state legislature on February 27, 1883, the park commission was given its own taxing authority. This would provide the needed funding to manage and maintain public trees, recreational facilities, and open space in Minneapolis, but it also created a conflict between infrastructure repair and trees. The Urban Forest Policy was the impetus to develop standards and guidelines to bridge the gap between the agencies that adversely affect the urban forest and those that protect and enhance it.

The city adopted two specific policy goals: (1) To adopt a citywide policy with guidelines and standards to ensure the continued protection, maintenance, replacement, and management of the urban forest in the City of Minneapolis; and (2) To establish an urban forestry policy that promotes and facilitates the communication and coordination among city departments, the Minneapolis Park and Recreation Board, the University of Minnesota, Minneapolis public schools, state agencies, public utilities, developers, tree-servicing companies, and other nongovernment organizations in their respective interactions affecting urban trees.

The process. In late 2002, Minneapolis City Council President Paul Ostrow and council members Dan Niziolek, Sandra Colvin-Roy, and Dean Zimmermann convened a meeting of stakeholders to identify the challenges to the city's urban forest and to make policy recommendations for its protection and preservation. In a series of subsequent meetings, the stakeholders worked collaboratively to identify problems and corresponding solutions. The Minneapolis Urban Forest Policy is a product of that collaboration. The policy was circulated among stakeholders. Comments were collected, and the policy was shaped around them.

The stakeholders. The city identified a broad spectrum of public and private agencies as stakeholders and invited them to participate in shaping the policy: city department heads and staff, Minneapolis Park and Recreation Board staff, public utility companies, Minneapolis public schools staff, the Minnesota Department of Natural Resources, the Minnesota Department of Transportation, the University of Minnesota, developers, landscape architects, private arborists, the Tree Trust, and interested residents. An unlikely collaborator was the Minneapolis Fire Department, which offered to water newly planted boulevard trees.

The outcome. The outcome of the dialogue among the stakeholders is an urban forest policy that includes best management practices to mitigate tree loss and tree damage caused by construction and infrastructure repair and to promote the long-term health of urban trees. The policy also included some illustrations and a link to an online field guide of best management practices. Past policies have not included graphics. The policy also includes a list of pertinent city and park board ordinances at its conclusion. We provide an excerpt from the policy statement here:

Section 3. Guidelines, Standards, and Recommended Practices
The following guidelines, standards, and recommended practices will help protect and preserve the Minneapolis urban forest:

3.1. Avoid conflicts between trees and public sidewalks or rights-of-way.

3.1.1. Public Works specifications will include removable sections of sidewalk to accommodate tree roots without having to replace an entire sidewalk panel.

The Urban Forest Policy contains standards and guidelines that help the departments work more effectively with the Minneapolis Park and Recreation Board (MPRB).

3.1.2. According to Public Works specifications, no living trees shall be removed without written permission of the Minneapolis Park and Recreation Board (612) 370-4900. Root removal for the purpose of installing sidewalks at the proper grade is subject to inspection and approval by the Park Board forester. The contractor may remove all roots within the area defined as 6.5 inches below the top of the new finished sidewalk grade, by severing them off cleanly with a sharp axe, or by grinding them off using a root grinding machine, instead of breaking them off with a backhoe or similar equipment.

3.1.3. Public Works specifications will include parameters for rings (aka arcs) around trees in boulevards and/or adjacent to sidewalks and rights-of-way.

3.1.4. Contractors shall follow specifications and policy and be held responsible for violating them.

3.1.5. The standard width for boulevard tree-planting space shall be 5.5 feet, with a minimum of four feet. Planted medians shall be a minimum of ten feet for tree planting. The MPRB already has discretion to refuse to plant or maintain a tree in a boulevard or median that does not meet an adequate width.

3.1.6. Public Works shall provide the Park Board Forester with a copy of the sidewalk improvement plan annually, prior to the commencement of construction of sidewalk improvements.

3.2. In accordance with Section 427.10 of the Minneapolis Code of Ordinances, open boulevards shall not be paved.

3.2.1. Developers and site plan proponents must obtain paving permits and encroachment permits in conformance with the City Code. [Note: Sections 3.1 and 3.2 will involve amendments to Section 427.10 of the Minneapolis Code of Ordinances.]

3.3. Tree grates are strongly discouraged. After the adoption of this Policy, tree grates may be installed, with the mutual consent of the MPRB/Forestry Division and Public Works, in the downtown Central Business District or within a full block east-and-west or a half block north-and-south of areas where community corridors intersect with commercials corridors or where commercial corridors intersect with one another. However, an open boulevard or alternatives to tree grates shall be considered first.

3.4. An applicant for a Tree Servicing license in Minneapolis must provide proof that at least one employee of the tree servicing business is currently recognized by the International Society of Arboriculture (ISA) as a Certified Arborist at the time of their license application or renewal. [Chapter 347 of the Minneapolis Code of Ordinances.]

3.4.1. Tree servicing companies must comply with American National Standards Institute (ANSI) Standard A300 when pruning or otherwise servicing trees on public or private property.

3.4.2. The practices of tree-topping and using spikes for anything other than tree removals or emergency rescues are prohibited as tree care practices on public or private trees.

3.4.3. This requirement shall be phased in to allow tree servicing companies time to budget for and obtain the Certified Arborist credentials.

3.5. Avoid construction damage to trees and their root systems.

3.5.1. Developers, other government entities, and contractors should have a pre-construction meeting that includes a representative from MPRB/Forestry, in addition to appropriate City staff. If there is any impact on existing trees, projects managed by the City will be handled by internal communications between the City and the MPRB. For projects built by the City, the MPRB will be notified.

3.5.2. Effective tree preservation must be integrated into site/design plans during the design and land development process. [*Editor's Note: See* Field Guide: A Resource for Builders and Developers to Follow When Preserving, Protecting, and Restoring Trees, www.ci.minneapolis.mn.us/cped/docs/field_guide.pdf]

3.5.3. For projects that require major site plan review, contractors/subcontractors, MPRB/Forestry, and others subject to site plan review are encouraged

The outcome of the dialogue among the stakeholders is an urban forest policy that includes best management practices to mitigate tree loss and tree damage caused by construction and infrastructure repair and to promote the long-term health of urban trees.

to enter into a Memorandum of Understanding (MOU) that establishes, at a minimum and where practical:

- a Tree Protection Plan with text and/or graphic illustrations indicating the methods that will be used to protect existing trees during construction;

- location of the protected root zone (PRZ) around each tree where construction equipment and materials cannot be placed or piled, to avoid soil compaction;

- location and installation of protective barriers, fences, and signage to designate the construction-free zone(s) near trees;

- depth of wood chip mulch in and around each impacted tree;

- geotextile fabric barriers shall be used to trap concrete debris;

- cement/concrete mixers, paint containers, and solvent containers shall not be rinsed out in the PRZ;

- construction debris shall not be deposited or left within a PRZ;

- no cars, other vehicles, or temporary structures shall be parked or placed on unpaved surfaces within a PRZ, excluding street or parking pavement areas;

- amount of the fine for each violation of the MOU, pursuant to MPRB specifications and ordinances.

3.5.4. Appropriate MPRB/Forestry personnel shall be allowed in the construction site at any stage of the construction project to monitor the work's impact on the trees that are within the MPRB's jurisdiction.

3.6. Structural or engineered soil should be used in planting pits, continuous trenches, and in other areas as necessary in order to provide a sustainable growing environment for public trees. [Planting pits and continuous trenches are defined in the Glossary section of this policy.]

3.6.1. Exceptions to using structural or engineered soil and the volume of soil for trees on public property may be approved by the MPRB Forestry Section.

3.7. The recommended size of an in-ground planting pit shall be a minimum of 300 cubic feet (*e.g.*, 10 feet x 10 feet x 3 feet deep).

3.7.1. The surface opening shall be no less than 5' x 5' or the size obtained in Section 3.1.5 of this report (meaning that paving can go up to the surface opening, leaving the surface opening smaller than the width and length of the pit underneath.).

3.7.2. Shared planting trenches for trees are encouraged, forming a copse of trees, provided that the 300-cubic-foot minimum is met for each tree.

3.8. Development proposals that are subject to Site Plan Review shall submit landscaping management plans as part of the Site Plan Review process.

3.8.1. The landscaping management plan will detail how trees, turf, and other landscape features shall be watered and maintained for the first five years after installation.

3.8.2. The use of structural or engineered soil or other healthy growing media in planting islands in parking lots is encouraged for the long-term vitality of trees and other plant materials, heat-island mitigation, and stormwater-runoff reduction.

3.8.3. The use of salt- and heat-tolerant plants in parking lots is encouraged.

3.9. Whenever below-grade conduit work is performed in the vicinity of trees, contractors and city staff are encouraged to use directional boring at a minimum depth of 24 inches instead of trenching procedures by tree roots.

3.9.1. During excavations, when it becomes necessary to expose or cut tree roots that are greater than one (1) inch in diameter or are within the PRZ of any tree, the contractor has a duty to protect the roots in accordance with City and MPRB policies and specifications.

3.9.2. Any exception to the use of directional boring by a private contractor must have the permission of the MPRB Forestry Section. Excavators shall consult with the MPRB regarding the feasibility of alternatives to directional boring.

3.9.3. The contractor is subject to the MPRB ordinances that pertain to tree protection.

3.9.4. For notification purposes, Public Works shall provide the MPRB with a copy of its underground utility and conduit installation and/or maintenance plans for areas in the PRZ 2 weeks prior to construction.

3.9.5. Public Works shall install its utility and conduit installations as close to the curbside edge of the boulevard as possible, in order to leave maximum open boulevard space for plantings.

3.10. Public Works is encouraged to look for cost-effective ice- and snow-melting products or methods that will minimize the impact to trees, turf, and other vegetation.

3.11. Residents and property owners are encouraged to plant and maintain trees on their own private property, but especially in areas where public boulevards are too narrow (i.e., under 4 feet wide) to sustain a mature shade tree.

3.12. Site Plans shall be stamped with a notice that requires the owner and/or contractor to contact the MPRB Forestry Section prior to the start of any on-site construction that may have a tree-related impact.

3.12.1. All applicable permits are required from the MPRB, pursuant to Chapter 10 of Park Board ordinances. Failure to obtain such permits may subject the owner and/or contractor to monetary penalties.

3.13. The City's Housing Inspection Services Division shall maintain a process for identifying high-risk trees on private property. High-risk trees on public property are monitored by the Minneapolis Park and Recreation Board.

3.14. Public Works is encouraged to contact the MPRB Forestry Division prior to planning street-lighting projects, in order to coordinate tree-planting/spacing standards with lighting designs and layouts in boulevards and public rights-of-way.

3.15. The Fire Department is encouraged to continue assisting with watering public trees, as this activity was very beneficial to the urban forest during the drought of 2003 and is also a useful training activity for firefighters.

Relevant ordinances:

Minneapolis City Code:
- Chapter 347 – Tree servicing companies (licensing). The Minneapolis City Council amended this ordinance in August 2007 by establishing professional certification and performance standards for tree-servicing licensees, effective December 31, 2008. All licensees shall employ an individual who possesses current certification as an arborist from the International Society of Arboriculture (ISA) or a post-secondary degree in urban forestry, arboriculture, or an equivalent area of study from an accredited institution of higher learning before a license will be issued to the applicant. Licensees shall comply with all American National Standards Institute (ANSI) standards.

Results. The city achieved a number of noteworthy results through its urban forestry program. The most prominent are listed here.

- The Minneapolis Park and Recreation Board voted to support the Urban Forest Policy.

- The city council has directed city departments to support MPRB efforts. As described in the following bulleted paragraphs, the departments cooperated.

- The fire department has entered into a Memorandum of Understanding with the park board to water newly planted boulevard trees during the growing season. During drought, the fire department will water young trees.

- The public works department has assisted the Park Board Forestry Division in providing work crews, equipment, and emergency assistance to

The comprehensive plans that are being prepared by the city and the park board are being integrated and aligned, and sustainability indicators for the Minneapolis urban forest will be incorporated into both plans in 2008.

help remove trees that blow down during storms and block sidewalks and roadways. Public works crews also helped to haul elms that were removed during an upsurge in Dutch elm disease in 2004.

- The planning division arranged a site which the park board can use as a staging area to deal with storm debris and diseased elms that are cut down.

- The environmental division has assisted with the development and promotion of the City Trees tree-distribution program and has included the urban forest in the City Sustainability Plan.

- Mayor R.T. Rybak has been an advocate for urban forestry and instrumental in the creation of the Urban Forestry Task Force with the U.S. Conference of Mayors.

- A park board resolution to authorize the Minneapolis Tree Advisory Commission was passed on March 17, 2004. This commission represents designees from the Minneapolis City Council and mayor's office and a commission delegate from the park board, citizens representing four quadrants of the city, Minnesota Shade Tree Advisory Committee (Minnesota State Urban Forest Council), University of Minnesota, and a developer. The commission's goals are to:

  - coordinate issues related to trees across city jurisdictions;

  - coordinate fiscal resources and explore new ways to acquire funds to increase support for urban forest establishment and management; and

  - evaluate issues related to trees and report annually to the Minneapolis Park and Recreation Board and City Council.

- The Minneapolis Tree Advisory Commission helped to educate the public about Dutch elm disease during a dramatic resurgence among city elms in 2005.

- The Minneapolis Tree Advisory Commission is working with Minneapolis Public Works and the Park Board to establish streetscape standards and guidelines to minimize adverse impacts on trees during construction and renovation.

- Park board foresters are now included in the city site plan review process for new development and redevelopment.

- Minneapolis has set a goal, through its Sustainability Initiative, of no net loss of tree canopy.

- The comprehensive plans that are being prepared by the city and the park board are being integrated and aligned, and sustainability indicators for the Minneapolis urban forest will be incorporated into both plans in 2008.

- The mayor recommended and the city council approved $400,000 for tree planting on both public and private lands in 2005–2006 after 12,936 trees were lost to Dutch elm disease and severe storms.

- 7,413 trees were replanted.

- The park board increased funding to the Forestry Division for stump removal.

- Minneapolis was chosen to become the first city to test the data collection and analysis applications of the i-Tree software (see page 13 for a description of the software). These data quantified the benefits of the urban forest to demonstrate its value to policy makers, which included $24.9 million each year in improved air quality, reduced stormwater runoff, increased energy savings, and increased property values.

The Minneapolis Park and Recreation Board currently has a $9 million annual budget for forestry, which equates to approximately $38 per capita. The City of Minneapolis continues to fund planting on private lands. Together, the city and park boards are creating, protecting, and managing the urban forest that will be a growing asset and an investment in the community.

The trees in the urban forest are the unpaid engineers in the City of Minneapolis. Trees serve the public every day by reducing stormwater runoff, slowing global warming, and reducing energy costs. Trees for the City of Minneapolis are a necessity, not a nicety, and the Minneapolis Urban Forest Policy will guide and define how its green infrastructure is built and maintained not only for its utility benefits, but also for the quality of life of Minneapolis residents and visitors.

This curbside landscaping for a new housing development on Lyndale Avenue in Minneapolis features continuous open planting beds and concrete curbs, which direct salt-laden snow-melt away from planting areas.

Urbana, Illinois

By James Schwab, AICP

"One thing people value about our community," says Robert Myers, the planning manager for the city of Urbana, Illinois, "is that, although our land is flat and the surrounding farmland has few trees, we have a wonderful tree canopy in our city. What we have here is what we create. And part of that consists of street trees."

This college town of approximately 38,000 people, which shares the honors with neighboring Champaign of hosting the University of Illinois and its 41,000 students, places a high value on the quality of life it associates with the resulting urban forest.

Public policy goals. In addition to "quality of life," Urbana's other policy goals for its urban forestry programs are "public safety" and "public education." City arborist Mike Brunk notes that the federal Occupational Safety and Health Administration (OSHA) requires hardhats for forestry workers, but citizens walk under the tree canopy every day without such protection. It is the job of the forestry program to prune and remove trees on a systematic basis to ensure that danger from hazardous trees is minimized.

Greening a city can be more than just planting trees. Here, the city of Urbana has planted native prairie grasses on the median at the Cunningham Avenue entrance to the city.

Public education results from continuing outreach by the city arborist and his staff to remain in frequent contact with citizens about the planting and care of trees through meetings, high-quality publications, and other outlets. Brunk even appears on a local Illinois Public Broadcasting System garden show and regional radio program. Urbana, he notes, is one of 13 charter members of Tree City USA (launched in 1975) still in the program.

Problems driving the program. In 1975, when Urbana was first designated a Tree City USA, its urban forest was not well balanced: 30 percent of its trees were silver maples, and 50 percent consisted of species deemed undesirable. The city worked to diversify its street tree population, and today no individual species makes up more than 10 percent of the total. This diversification serves to reduce the vulnerability of the urban forest to the sort of devastation wrought by Dutch elm disease and Emerald ash borer.

However, the city's tree pruning was long driven by citizen complaints. After being appointed city arborist, Brunk sought to drive down the costs of the program by instituting a systematic schedule for pruning, putting street

Establishing species diversity and a long-term cycle of pruning and maintenance have helped Urbana's neighborhoods support its Tree City USA designation.

trees on a 13-year rotation, with the highest priorities going to areas with trees posing an imminent public hazard, based on a thorough inventory. The first cycle began in 1995 and ended in 2008, to be followed by a second cycle in which costs are expected to be lower because a new pattern will have been established with a focus on prevention rather than response to crisis.

To accompany this approach, the city also created a tree commission composed of seven members appointed by the mayor, four of whom represent allied professions. This commission serves as a good release valve for those wishing to contest decisions made by the city arborist.

Holistic forestry and the comprehensive plan. Overall, Urbana's approach to its urban forestry program has been a fairly holistic one. Tree preservation and care have become a clearly stated aim of the city's 2005 Comprehensive Plan:

Goal 14.0. Increase Urbana's inventory of trees.

Objectives

1.1. Maintain the City's status as a [Tree City USA] through the arbor program and arbor commission.

1.2. Promote appropriate tree plantings in new development to contribute to the urban forest.

In addition, under Goal 6.0, "Preserve natural resources," Objective 6.2 states, "Protect sensitive areas, such as wooded areas, major drainageways, and areas of topographic relief." Consequently, there is an institutional awareness in the planning process of the role of trees in protecting critical elements of the urban environment. These themes are repeated in the plan's implementation program, which specifically recommends the following strategies:

- Amend the zoning code concerning landscaping and screening

- Construct an inventory map of environmentally sensitive areas

- Continue the "Share-the-Cost" tree planting program to increase tree planting in the right-of-way

- Amend the subdivision code to require tree plantings in the right-of-way for new residential development

Tree plantings and maintenance are required in Urbana commercial parking lots, and the city arborist is responsible for monitoring compliance.

Jim Schwab

While cyclical pruning was not itself an innovation, having been tried and proven elsewhere, what is more noteworthy is the highly proactive approach that Brunk has taken toward public education and outreach.

Implementing the plan. Chapter 25 (Vegetation) of the Urbana code, Article 2, offers specific details about the city's variety of trees, plants, and shrubs to help do appropriate planning. In addition, the city's *Arbor Specifications Manual* serves as a guide for tree maintenance. The zoning code requires tree planting for screening and in parking lots. The ordinance stipulates that contractors who wish to remove trees in the right-of-way for commercial development must get city approval, remove them at their own expense, and replace the value of the tree according to standards developed by the Council of Tree and Landscape Appraisers (2000) and published by the International Society of Arboriculture (ISA).

Myers noted in September 2007 that the city was "rewriting and updating the subdivision code," which he described as "very solid but outdated." One key issue has been a reduction from 31 to 27 feet in the minimum pavement width required for new local streets, and, consequently, how the potential crowding of underground infrastructure and tree roots may affect tree survival.

Program responsibilities. The city arborist's staff, the arbor division, works within the Urbana Department of Public Works. The public works director meets weekly with the department of community development, which handles planning and passes questions related to street trees in proposed new development on to the arborist. Brunk noted that the arborist has had a formal role in reviewing development plans since the mid-1970s. Moreover, recent arborists, including Brunk, have also been landscape architects by profession. Specifically, the arborist must approve landscape designs and tree planting in commercial parking lots.

Upon assuming the post of city arborist in 1992, Brunk convinced the incoming public works director that cyclical pruning, as opposed to responding to complaints, was the best way to improve the city's urban forest for the least amount of labor, thus cutting costs.

Innovations and funding. While cyclical pruning was not itself an innovation, having been tried and proven elsewhere, what is more noteworthy is the highly proactive approach that Brunk has taken toward public education and outreach. Brunk realized at the outset that a public accustomed to "calling and getting a response" would require a lengthy explanation at times of why the city was now insisting on adhering to a long-term schedule. Brunk spent a great deal of time on the telephone and in neighborhoods making his case, and "calls started to decline noticeably after three years." In Brunk's experience, selling the program to elected officials, given its cost efficiencies, was much easier than selling it to citizens. As noted above, winning that battle has included his aggressive use of broadcast media to spread the message.

Brunk's program has also sought to "plant the seed" of forestry in newer areas of the community by targeting the parkways in these areas as back-up planting sites for unclaimed or extra trees. The city's Share-the-Cost Tree Planting Program charges $95 per tree and $20 for a required tree watering bag that improves the tree's chances of survival. Replacement trees are free, but the city still charges $20 for the required watering bag.

The city has also created a Landscape Recycling Center for processing countywide yard wastes into mulches and composts, which are then sold to help support the center's operations. Because the center is self-supporting, it is treated as a special fund and separated from the general budget. The Landscape Recycling Center fund, however, does support one-third of the arborist's salary and provides up to $15,000 in outreach funds for promoting landscape recycling.

Urbana's forestry program has also benefited from innovative funding sources, such as the "URBANa Greenscapes Program," which was developed through grant dollars and enables officials to seek and channel outside funding to green-space-related programs and projects. These outreach initiatives, along with the use of grants, have been made it possible to enhance components of the arbor division's program, such as educational publications and tree planting. Publications funded through these additional funding sources include a pamphlet about how to use compost, a Landscape Recycling Center mailer with information about products and a coupon for purchases, a self-guided tour booklet for the State Street Tree Trail, which gives walkers a map and tree descriptions for the 20 species of trees along the two-hour tour of the State Street neighborhood, and a very popular publication, *Tree Growing Guide: The Selection, Planting, and Care of Community Trees,* developed with input from the cities of Champaign, Bloomington, and Decatur. Due to the success of the *Tree Growing Guide* and its popularity around the state, Brunk recently completed a new publication that expands upon this how-to information, *Under the Canopy, A Guide to Selecting, Planting and Caring for Trees in Illinois.* More than 80,000 copies have been purchased by communities, universities, and extension offices across the state.

Chosen by the Sustainable Urban Forests Coalition from a national pool, Salem, Oregon, is one of 14 localities exhibiting leadership in the field of urban and community forestry.

Overall, the funding is a mixture of tax dollars, donations, parking fees, and capital improvement funds. The total budget for the program in 2005 was $331,857, nearly $9 per capita. Greenscape Program donations have generally ranged from $2,000 to $5,000 per year but have resulted in pulling together as much as $35,000 for specific projects, such as the *Under the Canopy* publication. One should note to drive safely in Urbana, which charges citizens for the tree damage if they hit one by driving off the road. And if the tree is damaged beyond repair, the culpable party must also pay for the removal and a replacement tree.

Salem, Oregon

By Jan Staszewski, Florence Davis, Kat Conley, and Peter Gutowsky

Chosen by the Sustainable Urban Forests Coalition from a national pool, Salem, Oregon, is one of 14 localities exhibiting leadership in the field of urban and community forestry. As demonstrated below, the approaches implemented in Salem offer municipal planners, foresters, water quality and stormwater managers, and public officials examples for developing an adaptive urban forestry management program. Salem is working on programs that demonstrate the interrelationship between healthy natural environments and the economic benefits they provide in terms of air quality, stormwater retention, water quality, and aquatic and terrestrial habitat. Salem officials are committed to maintaining and enhancing an urban forest canopy as well as providing clean, ecologically viable urban streams. Using resources stemming from an urban forestry management program, the federal Endangered Species and Clean Water Acts, and, most importantly, informed and active citizenry, Salem is fostering partnerships that create livable communities and healthy ecosystems.

Located in the center of the Willamette Valley, Salem serves as the hub of both state government and the surrounding farm communities. Salem is the third-largest city in Oregon, with a population of 152,290 and a land area covering 46 square miles. There are more than 50 perennial streams in Salem, the most notable being the Willamette River. Salem has been designated as a Tree City USA for 31 years, the longest in Oregon.

Salem's population growth in the 1990s had drawn development into forested hillsides. After hearing vocal concerns from neighborhood associations, watershed councils, and other concerned citizens, Salem's City Council in 1999 embarked on a 12-month process that led to the adoption of an interim tree preservation ordinance to prevent clear cutting on these hillsides and to provide heightened protection for trees located within riparian areas. This local action was further substantiated in the summer of 2000 as federal actions, dictated by the federal Endangered Species Act and Clean Water Act, required Salem

A WORD ABOUT SATELLITE RESOLUTION

Satellite imagery is very different from the aerial photography that was commonly used for land-use planning just a few years ago. A satellite image is a digital product, whereas a traditional aerial photograph is a picture (a continuous stream of colors and shades). Because the two are very different products, their accuracy is recorded much differently.

An aerial image or picture is described by the ratio of the number of feet per inch of the photograph (e.g., 1:10,000 means one inch is equivalent to 10,000 feet in scale). Satellite accuracy is measured by the pixel size (e.g., each pixel depicts a four-meter-square area). High-resolution satellite images can portray data at a fine-grain scale (e.g., four meters or less) versus a moderate-resolution satellite (e.g., Landsat satellite images, which provide a 30-meter scale).

The satellite collector averages all the data in the pixel and produces a color value for that pixel. If a tree dominates the pixel, it registers as a "tree" while a parking lot will register as a "gray" pixel.

to take a comprehensive approach to protecting fish habitat and preserving water quality.

Taking the first holistic step. In 2001, the City of Salem partnered with 10 other jurisdictions in a regional study that analyzed forest canopy from Eugene, Oregon, to Vancouver, Washington. Salem received regional as well as local data from American Forests to estimate changes in its urban forest canopy. The city separated itself from the other jurisdictions by obtaining high-resolution, four-meter, Ikonos satellite imagery.

Integrating CITYgreen software (see page 13 for a description of the software) with Ikonos imagery enabled staff to generate detailed land cover classifications and canopy benefits for Salem's entire Urban Growth Boundary, a boundary required by law for all Oregon cities and metropolitan areas that limits growth outside the boundary and requires a 20-year supply of developable land within the boundary, which is reviewed for necessary adjustments every 20 years. Staff also delineated detailed land cover classifications according to watershed boundaries. Twelve sub-basins within Salem, including riparian areas measured at 50 feet and 200 feet, were further distinguished. This sub-basin and tributary data provided Salem officials with another indicator of the relative health of Salem's watersheds, since canopy cover and impervious surface directly relate to watershed function. This comprehensive analysis ultimately gave Salem the distinction of having the most comprehensive canopy report in Oregon.

Relationship to the comprehensive plan and statewide planning goals. Salem's comprehensive plan is guided by the Statewide Planning Goals (www.lcd.state. or.us/LCD/goals.shtml). Oregon provides planning direction in the development of local comprehensive plans through 19 Statewide Planning Goals. These goals can also be used in the development of policy documents and ordinances. The city has recently adopted a tree protection ordinance that was guided by Statewide Goals 5 (Natural Resources, Scenic and Historic Areas, and Open Space), 6 (Air, Water, Land Resources Quality), and 15 (Willamette River Greenway).

The Urban Forestry Management Program. In April 2003, the pivotal step towards taking a systematic approach to urban forestry occurred with the hiring of Salem's first urban forester. Besides providing technical expertise over the programs listed below, this individual is responsible for managing tree crews responsible for more than 100,000 street trees, and 35,000 park trees.

Willamette River Protection Program. The City of Salem is one of 27 local jurisdictions bordering the Willamette River. For more than 25 years,

The Willamette River passes through Salem, coming from Eugene and flowing approximately 187 miles north to join the Columbia River in Portland. The Willamette River is one of the American Heritage Rivers.

Oregon's statewide planning goals have required each bordering jurisdiction to preserve the Willamette River's scenic, historic, and natural values. In 2004, the Salem City Council adopted an ordinance that provides an appropriate balance between allowing future urbanization along the Willamette River's riparian fringe while preserving and enhancing its sensitive ecological areas (www.cityofsalem.net/export/departments/slegal/codes/ch141.pdf).

Staff used CITYgreen to raise public awareness and model stormwater management options that place a higher reliance on pervious surfaces for development taking place near riparian areas. After a series of workshops, stakeholder meetings, and ultimately public hearings, the staff presented code amendments, recommending vegetated riparian buffers and mitigation measures with demonstrable water quality benefits. The preservation and enhancement measures stress a two-pronged approach: (1) Protecting a minimum riparian buffer area; and (2) Implementing one water quality mitigation measure from five options, when development or redevelopment occurs.

Staff used CITYgreen to raise public awareness and model stormwater management options that place a higher reliance on pervious surfaces for development taking place near riparian areas.

Mitigation measures include restorative plantings, larger building setbacks, and alternative stormwater treatment facilities, which, if they retain runoff on site, can receive a reduction in stormwater system development charges. Another option requires tree plantings as impervious area reduction techniques for parking lots. Replanted trees must result in canopy cover of not less than 50 percent of the impervious area within 15 years after planting. Finally, developers have the option of installing pervious pavement.

The long-term tree preservation ordinance. Using group consensus, a 32-month work program culminated in a citizen advisory committee drafting tree preservation code amendments. In 2005, the Salem City Council adopted their recommendations, creating one of the most progressive tree preservation ordinances in Oregon (www.cityofsalem.net/export/departments/slegal/codes/ch68.pdf)

Public policy and regulatory components include the following:

- Purchasing high-resolution imagery every census to monitor Salem's evolving tree canopy

- Evaluating tree canopy every census year to determine the effectiveness of tree preservation and replanting ordinances

- Establishing a fund for purchasing tree stands

- Protecting heritage trees and significant Oregon white oaks

- Protecting trees and native vegetation within riparian areas

- Prohibiting clear cutting on residential parcels greater than 20,000 square feet

- Requiring the following for new residential subdivisions:
  - Tree conservation plans
  - Tree planting regardless if the area contains existing trees; and
  - Street trees

- Developing a program to consistently administer and proactively enforce the tree and vegetation protection ordinance.

The Free Streamside Tree Program. In 2003, Salem instituted the Free Streamside Tree Program through its stormwater services division, in order to provide shade and to increase the amount of native vegetation bordering Salem's streams (www.cityofsalem.net/export/departments/spubwork/operations/swater/sw_freetreeprog.htm). During the annual program,

City of Salem

Shelton Ditch is one of many waterways in Salem. Citizen can enjoy the views along the waterway as it passes through city parks.

streamside property owners may order native trees and shrubs to plant near a waterway. Over the past four seasons, homeowners have planted more than 2,100 native trees and shrubs. Stormwater staff also provide planting assistance for those who require it. The program currently includes eight native species.

The role of the Trust for Public Land. The Trust for Public Land (TPL) has aided the city in the development of the Parks' Master Plan. In the plan, TPL assisted the city by studying the current state of the park system, stakeholder outreach, and undertaking *Greenprinting* (a TPL-developed GIS analysis; see www.tpl.org/tier3_cd.cfm?content_item_id=10648&folder_id=175) that provides an approach for analyzing parks and conservation goals and identifies areas not currently protected. The result was a map identifying areas to focus resources for acquisition of land for conservation and recreation.

The downtown tree plan. Salem recognized that its downtown faced a unique challenge in preserving and showcasing historic buildings while still softening the streetscape. This required a flexible tree ordinance to balance the desire for open views to buildings and the need for a green canopy. The element that provides the flexibility and balance is the review of downtown conflicts by the Salem Shade Tree Advisory Committee. This committee represents a broad spectrum of interests, including members that represent downtown businesses.

Salem's Revised Code (www.cityofsalem.net/export/departments/slegal/codes/ch86.pdf) authorizes the committee to handle controversial tree issues and make recommendations to staff and city council. In addition, the committee is used as a sounding board on tree issues before the city council, other boards and commissions, and city departments.

Wetlands operations. In other efforts that protect and enhance the urban forest, the city has developed an in-house program to restore and protect wetlands. Since 2003 the city has worked to bring existing wetland sites into compliance with the Oregon Department of State Lands and the U. S. Army Corps of Engineers permits. City staff install and maintain plants as required by permits. Currently, the city manages 15 wetland mitigation and stream bank restoration sites totaling 75 acres. This has resulted in the planting of more than 13,000 tree and shrubs, and 25,000 small plants.

Intragovernment coordination. A tree conservation plan is required for residential subdivisions. Tree conservation plans are first reviewed by the planning department for compliance with tree preservation requirements. The parks department reviews them for compliance with replanting standards. The public works department ensures that street trees are planted along new roads. All three departments attend subdivision review conferences with property owners to review proposed plans and coordinate implementation of tree standards.

If trees or vegetation are to be removed from a riparian corridor, the planning, public works, and parks departments work together to share information, review replanting plans, and coordinate responses to property owners. These same departments also work closely with code enforcement officers and the city's legal department when code violations occur. In addition, environmental mapping, master planning, and education programs are routinely coordinated across intrajurisdictional boundaries.

Donations and volunteer efforts resulted in a globe made up of more than 86,000 tiles.

Funding. The preservation and care of street trees is funded through Salem's portion of the state motor fuel tax. However, elements under the Long-Term Tree Preservation Ordinance are tied to fines and donations. The city is exploring this novel approach in an attempt to pay for the many environmental enhancements and studies as directed under the new preservation ordinance. Substantial fines have been levied under this ordinance but have yet to make their way through legal review and appeals. The donations generated under this code may be used in lieu of site amelioration requirements when there is a violation of the requirements but the site allows no room for a substantial replanting.

Olympia, Washington

By Megan Lewis, AICP

Olympia began its urban forestry program in 1989 when the city received a grant from Urban and Community Forestry Program of the Washington State

Department of Natural Resources to do an urban forest inventory conducted by volunteers and administered by the city's long-range planning division. From the survey results, the city realized that it had experienced significant tree loss. In 1992, the city hired an urban forester and then included a chapter on urban forestry in the 1994 comprehensive plan. In fact, a statement in that plan says that Olympia seeks to become "a city of trees."

This view of Legion Way provides an iconic image of the kind of neighborhoods Olympia wants to maintain.

Program drivers. The program came about primarily as a result of significant tree loss from 1980 to 1990. During that time, Olympia lost approximately 430 acres of wooded areas to development. This loss of trees caused significant citizen concern, which then captured the interest of the city council.

Another factor was a significant federal funding increase for urban forestry programs. The 1990 federal farm bill included provisions that required every state to hire an urban forestry coordinator and provided funding for this position. The farm bill also provided grants for local communities. Olympia acknowledges that without the support of the federal and state urban forestry programs and the grant funds they provided, it would not have been able to develop its highly acclaimed programs.

These two events along with public concern regarding significant tree loss from development and federal dollars for urban forestry worked together to create Olympia's program.

Management. The city's community planning and development department is primarily responsible for the urban forestry program. The program is located in the community services division of the department, which also includes Community Development Block Grants and housing, code enforcement, and historic preservation. The parks, recreation, and cultural resources department provides tree maintenance services to the urban forestry program, has two full-time arborists on staff, and meets on a weekly basis with the forester. Also, the public works department assists with tree removal related to storm events, as well as tree plantings related to capital improvement projects. To support the public works department, the urban forester provides technical assistance, advice, and inspection of new tree plantings, and also advises on tree issues with sidewalk repairs.

Primary program responsibilities. The program has five primary responsibilities:

1. Implement and enforce the Tree Protection and Replacement Ordinance (OMC 16.60), which ensures that trees are preserved and planted when property is developed. Approximately one full-time employee from the urban forestry team is required to administer and enforce the ordinance.

2. Operate the NeighborWoods program, started in 1998, which provides free trees to residents to plant along or adjacent to city streets. The urban forestry program has one staff person who is dedicated to administering this program, which has trained approximately 1,000 citizens and planted 500 to 1,000 trees a year since its inception. It also operates a tree nursery capable of growing up to 1,000 trees each year. To receive the free trees, citizens must undergo mandatory training (www.olympiawa. gov/cityservices/urbanforest/neighborwoods/and www.olympiawa. gov/NR/rdonlyres/74E8AEF7-8027-4DEC-8CD8-26A37275603E/0/ free_trees_app.pdf).

3. Conduct the Hazard Tree Abatement Program, which responds to reports of trees of concern by inspecting, pruning, or removing dangerous trees growing within the city's rights-of-way (www.olympiawa. gov/NR/rdonlyres/8825122E-5317-4DBC-9611-B3FA697160A4/0/ WoodWasteRecyclingReport.pdf).

4. Design, plan, and manage major street tree planting projects through the Streetscapes Program (www.olympiawa.gov/cityservices/urbanforest/ specialprojects/ and www.olympiawa.gov/NR/rdonlyres/DBF805F3- 2838-4DA3-9F20-66-F9B1322CF/0/StructuralSoil.pdf).

5. Produce educational outreach programs in partnership with schools and nonprofit agencies. All the urban forestry programs have an education and outreach component; however, this program has focused recently on an "anti-topping" campaign to promote the correct way to prune trees.

Teaching proper tree-planting techniques is part of Olympia's outreach program in its NeighborWoods program.

City of Olympia

Program approach. Olympia's program takes a holistic approach to urban forestry. It considers both public and private forests in its efforts. Its primary focus is on tree preservation; where preservation is not feasible, tree planting is then allowed. Under Olympia's ordinance, all properties under development are required to meet a minimum tree density of 30 tree units per acre (one tree unit equals one planted tree), regardless of their predevelopment condition. Built-in incentives, such as giving credits for preserving existing larger trees, encourage property developers to preserve trees. These credits

Diameter at Breast Height (inches)	Tree Units
1–6	1
6–12	1.5
14	2
16	3
18	4
20	5
22	5
24	7
26	8
28	9
30	10
32	11
34	12
36	13
38	14
40	15
42	16
44	17
46	18
48	19
50	20

City of Olympia, Washington

Table 3-1. *Tree Density for Existing Trees.*

are determined by existing tree trunk diameter, with larger tree trunks granting more credits for an equivalent number of newly planted trees against the requirement to maintain 30 planted trees per acre. As designed, this program also requires existing "noncompliant" (previously cleared or nonforested) properties to plant trees. See Table 3-1 for the tree unit sliding scale.

In addition to the urban forestry chapter in the comprehensive plan, the urban forester noted that nearly every other plan element discusses street trees in some capacity, often as an element to offset impacts from other actions, such as the loss of green space due to the city's requirement to increase density to seven dwelling units/acre to support transit, or the desire to create more pedestrian-friendly corridors. This observation led to developing the Master Street Tree Plan as a mechanism to achieve these other goals.

Connections to the comprehensive plan. Street trees are mentioned more than 80 times in the comprehensive plan, and 29 policies were developed specifically for trees. (Some goals in the comprehensive plan are connected to the joint plan with Thurston County for the unincorporated areas of Olympia.)

Urban forestry is addressed in a separate element in the comprehensive plan (Chapter 10, Urban Forestry). The comprehensive plan was adopted in 1994 and is amended annually. (For more on creating an urban forestry element for the comprehensive plan, see McFarland 1994 and Appendix A of this PAS Report.) The focus of the urban forestry element is on tree protection and replacement, with an emphasis on protecting Olympia's tree legacy. It includes:

- background on urban forestry in Olympia;

- a vision statement that details how trees are woven into the urban fabric, thus providing numerous benefits and creating character;

- a description of the value of an urban forestry program;

- goals, and policies to achieve those goals; and

- a list of the elements of an urban forestry program.

This last section provided the initial foundation for Olympia's program; however, not all the items suggested here have been implemented (www.olympiawa.gov/NR/rdonlyres/D968D8DE-0402-4136-AC3F-1B24CC85C182/0/CPChapter10.pdf).

Other comprehensive plan elements. Two other elements, Land Use, and Utilities and Public Services, include specific policy language related to urban forestry practices. In addition, as noted above, several other elements address street trees and streetscape generally (see www.olympiawa.gov/cityservices/zoning/advanceplanning/CompPlan.htm).

Regulations. The Tree Protection and Replacement Ordinance (OMC 16.60) implements the goals and objectives of the comprehensive plan. It ensures that trees are preserved and planted, and mandates that a tree plan be prepared to obtain a tree removal permit. A tree plan is also required for any land development on property with a tree density below the minimum required, which the ordinance states is 30 tree units per acre on the buildable area of a site. See Table 3-2 below for the required minimum tree density and replacement tree requirements for various activities.

The *Urban Forestry Manual* provides more detailed guidance on the ordinance's requirements, covering the tree plan standards, tree protection standards, tree planting and maintenance standards, tree density calculations, and specimen tree evaluation. A pdf of the manual is available at www.olympiawa.gov/NR/rdonlyres/340189DA-8F6D-4BA6-9440-B7358D4B2B93/0/UrbanForestryManual.pdf.

Proposed Activity	Tree Replacement Requirements	Required Minimum Tree Density for the Parcel
New Development	30 tree units per acre	30 tree units per acre
Developing Single Family (multifamily up to four units)	30 tree units per acre	30 tree units per acre
Developed Properties	30 tree units per acre	30 tree units per acre
Developed Commercial/ Industrial/Multifamily (more than four units) proposing an addition or other site disturbance	One tree unit for every 500 square feet disturbed and three tree units for every one tree unit proposed for removal	30 tree units per acre
Developed Commercial/ Industrial/Multifamily (more than four units) proposing tree removal	Three tree units for every one tree unit proposed for removal	30 tree units per acre
Option Harvest	Site must remain at a minimum tree density of 200 tree units per acre	200 tree units per acre

City of Olympia, Washington

Table 3-2. Required Minimum Tree Density and Replacement Tree Requirements per Activity

The city also developed two handouts to assist citizens in complying with the ordinance: one for residential builders (www.olympiawa.gov/NR/rdonlyres/443D32DD-DF1D-4EB9-9FCA-95F585F67647/0/BuildersGuideto-theTreeProtectionOrdinance.pdf) and one for homeowners (www.olympiawa.gov/NR/rdonlyres/BD8D615A-92F4-4383-9B67-D2C81262B663/0/HomeownersGuidetoTreeProtectionOrdinance.pdf). Each document briefly addresses the required number of trees, tree species, minimum tree size, minimum tree quality, and tree preservation guidelines. These handouts have been quite successful, especially in simplifying the program for the residential property owners. While the overall number of trees preserved under this initiative is relatively small, the volume of inquiries from this population group was high enough to warrant these specific documents. The forester notes that tree preservation on these properties is strictly on a "self-compliance" basis, but these documents help to encourage it.

In addition to these regulations, other ordinances are in effect that address tree planting and protection, all of which can be found at www.olympiamunicipalcode.org/. Specifically, they include the following.

- The Landmark Tree Protection Ordinance, OMC 16.56, protects landmark trees, defined as trees that are irreplaceable either because they are associated with historic figures, events, or properties; are rare or unusual species; or have aesthetic value worthy of protection for the health and general welfare of the residents of this city. The ordinance also establishes a register of these trees.

- The Public Trees Ordinance, OMC 16.58, encourages responsible management of public tree resources within the city, primarily because of the many benefits they provide the public at large. The ordinance addresses planting, pruning, maintenance, and removal. It focuses on trees located on property the city owns on a fee simple basis. One of the main issues addressed in this ordinance is deterring the cutting of trees planted by volunteers in public areas to create views for new development.

- The Landscaping and Screening Ordinance, OMC 18.36, is located in the Unified Development Code (UDC). It refers to OMC 16.60 with regard to

OLYMPIA, WASHINGTON, PUBLIC POLICY GOALS

The comprehensive plan element includes 29 policies, organized into eight goals (each identified as "Goal Tree #" in the comprehensive plan):

1. To recognize and use trees in the city to help achieve our other land-use goals.

2. To make Olympia a beautiful place to live in or visit by lining our High-Density Corridors and our entry and exit corridors with trees.

3. To bring a sense of natural beauty into the Downtown, our most urban area, by planting trees.

4. To recognize the special requirements for preserving and enhancing the urban forest so that the human environment can exist in harmony with nature. This goal includes policy 4.1: An urban forestry program should be established to provide education, encouragement and assistance for planting and preserving trees on private property and street frontages.

5. To take advantage of the economic value contributed to the City by its trees.

6. To manage the urban forest to maximize its contribution to wildlife habitat and recreational opportunities.

7. To manage the urban forest in a way that recognizes its effect on wise energy use.

8. To maintain strong and healthy neighborhoods by planting and protecting trees.

tree-planting requirements as part of a landscaping and screening plan. Of particular note is the requirement for minimum 12-foot-wide islands in parking lots for trees.

- The Critical Areas Ordinance, OMC 18.32, focuses on wellhead protection areas, important habitats and species, streams and important riparian areas, wetlands and small lakes, and landslide hazard areas, and addresses trees in relation to these areas.

- Other regulations, such as the subdivision ordinance's design standards section on trees, 17.48.040, require a tree protection and replacement plan and defer to Section 16.60 for the details.

Implementation. The Master Street Tree Plan is a 10-year plan, adopted in 2001. It is the primary implementation tool to carry out the broader policies outlined in the comprehensive plan. This plan identifies and analyzes the street tree resources in Olympia and provides a strategy for enhancing and managing these resources. Developed by the city to achieve the goal of tree-lined streets described in the comprehensive plan, it has five primary objectives:

1. Create a usable tool for the design of future street-tree-planting projects

2. Provide clear direction and priorities for the maintenance of our street trees

3. Identify and document our existing street tree resources to track and measure our implementation efforts

4. Estimate planting and maintenance costs to assist in the budget process

5. Perform as a marketing tool to solicit grants and other funding

The Master Street Tree Plan describes five programs related to the planting and maintenance of street trees (see also Figure 3-2):

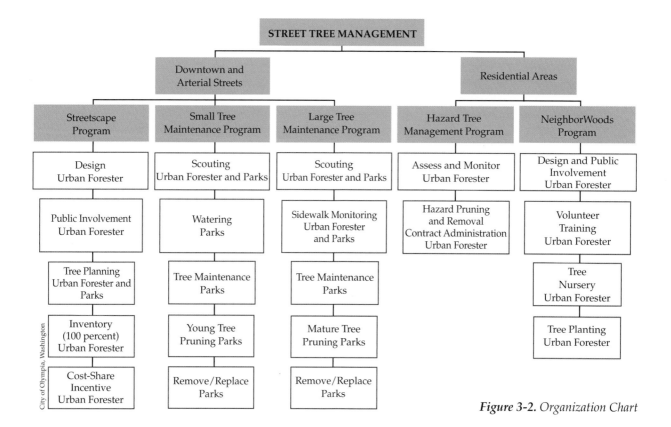

Figure 3-2. Organization Chart

1. The Streetscape Program focuses on planting new street trees in downtown and along major arterial streets, using streetscape improvement and downtown beautification funds.

2. The Small-tree Maintenance Program trains staff to provide maintenance and pruning for small or young trees (generally less than 12 inches in diameter).

3. The Large-tree Maintenance Program provides that the urban forester and parks department staff survey large trees, conduct sidewalk monitoring of them, and perform annual maintenance.

4. The Hazard Tree Management Program requires management on an as-requested basis by the public works department, assisted by the urban forester.

5. The NeighborWoods Program is a volunteer tree-planting program of city-grown trees, described in more detail above.

Funding. One of the primary funding mechanisms for the urban forestry program is the capital improvement plan fund. The money is derived from the real estate excise tax, interest, utility tax (1 percent), and the year-end cash surplus.

	2007	2008–2017	Total
Contract Tree Removal and Pruning	$40,000	$200,000	$240,000
Program Management	$60,000	$300,000	$360,000
Total	$100,000	$500,000	$600,000
CIP Budgeted Amount	$100,000	$500,000	$600,000

Table 3-3. Ten-Year CIP for Tree Management, Olympia, Washington.

According to the forester, program funding is sufficient for all functions except for the streetscape program. While funds are available through public works for small-scale tree planting in the rights-of-way, large-scale tree planting is not sufficiently funded. This is somewhat offset through the NeighborWoods program, which involves planting city-owned trees in or adjacent to rights-of-way.

To support the urban forestry program, the community planning and development department charges tree plan review and tree removal permit fees, the schedule for which is at OMC 04.36.010. Like the rest of the development review team (permit and planning services), this portion of the urban forestry program has sought to be a fully funded program. When the program began in 1992, the goal was to be half-funded, with the remaining funding from the city's operating budget to support public outreach and program development efforts. In 2006, increases in development activity required an entire full-time employee to administer the code; this function is almost fully funded, with permit fee revenues approaching $110,000 in 2006.

Grant funds are also received periodically; this funding is not as regular as the capital improvements program funding. On average, the city of Olympia has received small state and federal grants (i.e., $5,000 to $7,000) nearly every year of the urban forestry program's existence.

Since 2000, the city has received three state grants for approximately $30,000 each. For example, in 2001 the grant was for a structural soil demonstration project (www.ci.olympia.wa.us/NR/rdonlyres/DBF805F3-2838-4DA3-9F20-660F9B1322CF/0/StructuralSoil.pdf). Another grant project in 2005, Healthy Urban Forests for Everyone, funded a low-income and underserved population outreach campaign (www.olympiawa.gov/NR/rdonlyres/19A30529-3AB1-4CA3-AE4A-36BE973D989B/0/FinalTitleVIIIGrantReport1606.pdf). The third and most recent (2006) grant was focused on an anti-topping campaign, which

INNOVATIVE PROGRAM FEATURES

The Master Street Tree Plan proposes a level of service to achieve street tree planting, tree maintenance, and hazard tree abatement objectives. Joe Roush, Olympia's forester, created this concept, and it has subsequently been used by leaders in the urban forestry field.

The plan includes five areas to measure level of service (LOS) for enhancement and maintenance of street trees. Note that the 2001 LOS is in italics; the current level of service is in bold; bold italic text indicates that the 2001 LOS is the current LOS. Improvements in LOS are the direct result of increased city council funding for urban forestry.

1. Hazard tree abatement
   - *LOS 1 - Remove hazard trees on a request basis, eliminate hazard trees in 20 years*
   - **LOS 2 - Eliminate hazard trees in 15 years**
   - LOS 3 - Eliminate hazard trees in 10 years
   - LOS 4 - Eliminate hazard trees in five years

2. Tree planting (downtown and arterial streets)
   - *LOS 1 – Plant 60 percent of available planting spaces in 20 years*
   - LOS 2 – Plant 60 percent of available planting spaces in 15 years
   - LOS 3 – Plant 60 percent of available planting spaces in 10 years
   - LOS 4 – Plant 60 percent of available planting spaces in five years

3. Tree planting (residential streets)
   - LOS 1 – Plant 60 percent of available planting spaces in 20 years
   - LOS 2 – Plant 60 percent of available planting spaces in 15 years
   - **LOS 3 – Plant 60 percent of available planting spaces in 10 years**
   - **LOS 4 – Plant 60 percent of available planting spaces in five years**

4. Tree pruning (downtown and arterial streets)
   - LOS 1 – Provide no pruning for street trees
   - LOS 2 – Only hazard prune street trees
   - *LOS 3 – Prune street trees approximately once every eight years (no more than 10,000 trees per arborist)*
   - **LOS 4 – Prune street trees approximately once every three to five years (no more than 4,000 trees per arborist)**

5. Tree pruning (residential streets)
   - **LOS 1 – Provide no pruning for street trees**
   - LOS 2 – Only hazard prune street trees
   - LOS 3 – Prune street trees approximately once every eight years (no more than 10,000 trees per arborist)
   - LOS 4 – Prune street trees approximately once every three to five years (no more than 4,000 trees per arborist)

included a comprehensive education campaign to stop the practice of topping trees in the community (www.ci.olympia.wa.us/cityservices/urbanforest/ specialprojects/Anti-Tree+Topping+Educational+ Campaign.htm).

This yard sign distributed by the city of Olympia helps spread the message about the destructive impact of tree-topping practices, in which top branches are simply lopped off at a certain level.

Transferability. Olympia's program has several transferable aspects:
- Policy focus through an element in the comprehensive plan
- Connections to other elements in the plan that have overlapping policy areas
- Funding connection to the capital improvements program
- Creation of full-time staff person in planning department with connection to parks department
- NeighborWoods volunteer program
- Focus on providing trees in underserved neighborhoods

Awards and special recognition. In 2006, the city received the "Tree City USA" award for the 14th consecutive year. It also received National Arbor Day Foundation Growth Awards in 1994, 1997, 2001, 2004, and 2006. In 1997, it received an award from the state urban and community forestry councils, and in 1998, it received the 1998 Association of Washington Cities municipal achievement award.

Limitations. The city lacks adequate funding for a full-scale streetscape program, despite its inclusion as a major policy initiative throughout the comprehensive plan.

Future of the program. Olympia is 15 years into its program, and its main goals have been to administer the tree ordinance and develop the program. The city is now there, and the focus is on running the program and "tweaking" it as necessary. As the city continues to face development pressure, it will continue to have a well-funded program but may ramp up its tree preservation requirements.

The city is making a stronger connection between tree preservation and stormwater management, specifically through the creation of separate standards for a special district, the Green Cove Basin, which has been rezoned for low-impact development. In that area, the tree density requirements are 220 tree units per acre, which translates into preserving 60 percent of the site as forest, compared to 5 to 10 percent in other zones. This higher standard may ultimately be applied in other parts of the city that have a stormwater management problem.

When the comprehensive plan is updated, the city will be looking at how it can grow the program. The key to the program operating as it does today is the 1994 comprehensive plan; according to the forester, without that document, none of the program elements would be where they are today.

Ithaca, New York

By Nina Bassuk

Ithaca, New York, has commonly been referred to as the "Forest City" for more than a century. That description holds true today as the traveler enters Ithaca from atop any of its three hills. The traveler sees a canopy of trees looking very much like a natural forest, broken only by its tallest buildings. Arriving downtown, the traveler sees tree-lined streets even in the central business district. Ninety percent of Ithaca's "planting spaces" are planted, and 432 tree species are represented on those spaces, making Ithaca's forest one of the most diverse urban forests in the country.

Ithaca is situated at the southern end of Cayuga Lake, one of 11 Finger Lakes created by the retreat of the last continental glacier. The downtown area sits on an alluvial floodplain with glacial till underneath, and the surrounding hills have Devonian shale as bedrock with occasional outcroppings of Tully and Onondaga limestone.

Ithaca falls within the USDA hardiness zone 5a. This means its average lowest winter temperature is –15 to –20 degrees Fahrenheit. The downtown area is a slightly warmer zone 5b with –10 to –15 degrees Fahrenheit average minimum temperatures. Ithaca receives an average annual precipitation of 35 inches, with 67.3 inches of average seasonal snowfall. Most weather is influenced by the prevailing westerly winds. Cayuga Lake moderates the downtown weather, the hills often being 8 to 10 degrees cooler. The average temperature is 21.5 degrees in January and 68.5 degrees in July.

Ithaca's downtown greenery is part of its overall effort to create a "forest city."

The native vegetation in and around Ithaca is a mixture of eastern deciduous hardwood and northern conifer forests. In the city's 80 miles of roadway, there are 8,400 street trees and 3,300 park trees for a total of 11,700 managed trees. There are also 700 acres of forested watershed and numerous riparian corridors corresponding to the gorges that run throughout the city, as well as 22 parks, a public golf course, city cemetery, and several natural areas within city boundaries. Ithaca also has a successful landscaped pedestrian area called the Commons.

Located in central New York, Ithaca has a population of about 30,000; the greater Ithaca area has about 45,000 residents. Its primary industry is education given that it is the home of Cornell University and Ithaca College.

City departments and committees in the urban forestry program. The mission statement of Ithaca's government states that it "deliver(s) high-quality services to preserve and enhance the well-being of our community."

Given that Ithaca's green spaces contribute significantly to the well-being of Ithaca residents, many city departments, boards and committees work to enhance them.

Several city departments directly influence the health of Ithaca's urban forest, notably public works and planning. Within the department of public works lies the division of parks and forestry, where the city forester and crew manage all vegetation on public land. Numerous boards and committees including the board of public works, planning and development board, parks commission, shade tree advisory committee, natural areas commission, conservation advisory council, and common council, Ithaca's elected officials, advise the parks and forestry staff.

Ordinances and policies. Aside from these committees, several ordinances and guidelines inform the protection, placement, and enhancement of Ithaca's urban forest. Foremost is the Ithaca Tree and Shrub Ordinance (Chapter 306 of City Code), passed in 1990, which "regulates the planting, maintenance, protection and removal of trees and shrubs on public streets, parks and other city-owned property; provides for a shade tree advisory committee and establishes the office of a city forester in the department of public works. This chapter also provides for the issuing of permits for the planting, maintenance, protection and removal of trees and shrubs in city-owned places."

This law gives the city forester oversight into any actions from private or public persons or agencies that affect Ithaca's public vegetation. Notable with this ordinance is the discretionary right of the city forester to approve or disapprove the removal of trees and require caliper inch tree replacement where it is warranted.

In 2007, Ithaca's Shade Tree Advisory Committee revised Ithaca's *Master Plan for Public Trees and Parks*, which was adopted by the board of public works in March 2007. This document defines the vision and policies that guide the city's actions regarding tree planting and site selection, tree removal, tree maintenance, and protection as well as updates the tree inventory that has been in place since 1987.

Master plan vision statement. Ithaca has a vision for its urban forest, as expressed in the master plan:

> By the year 2015, Ithaca's community forest will be multi-aged, diverse, fully stocked, healthy, and safe. It will contain a wide variety of appropriate species and be maintained on a regularly scheduled basis. It will contribute to the general welfare of our residents by reducing energy costs, increasing property values, providing homes for wildlife, beautifying all neighborhoods, and projecting an image of quality to visitors and prospective businesses. Care of public trees will be used as a means to educate and inspire residents to care for trees on private property.

The City of Ithaca will cooperate in urban forestry research with Cornell University and other agencies to ensure that it will lead the nation in developing and utilizing better methods in its urban forestry program. The citizens of Ithaca will have an important role in community forestry by participating in programs such as Citizen Pruners and Ithaca Tree Works, a volunteer-based bare root tree planting method, or by serving on the Shade Tree Advisory Committee. The City of Ithaca Forestry Program will be accredited by the Society of Municipal Arborists and will be an annual recipient of the National Arbor Day Foundation Growth Award.

The department of planning and development provides a broad range of services to city residents, property owners, business owners, developers, elected and appointed officials, and other city departments. Among the areas in which the department is active are: housing; economic development; information management (i.e., mapping); neighborhood planning; transportation and parking; recreation and open space; environmental management; long-range planning; historic preservation; community design and amenity/quality of life; and grants development and administration.

Foremost among the legal instruments influencing Ithaca's urban forest is the city's Site Plan Review (SPR) Ordinance (Chapter 276, adopted 1999). The purpose of SPR is to promote the health, safety, and general welfare of the residents of Ithaca by ensuring that the development or redevelopment of private land is appropriate and compatible with the development of adjacent or neighboring lands. It is further intended to ensure the conservation and enhancement of natural and human-made resources within the city through a process of review and approval of site development plans. It is not intended to prohibit development otherwise permitted under applicable zoning laws; rather, it is intended to improve the design, function, aesthetics, and safety of projects and site plans that otherwise conform with zoning regulations. Development area thresholds trigger the site plan review process. Individual residences are not to be subject to site plan review, but a single lot and all commercial developments are reviewed.

Review criteria relating to vegetation. The parts of site plan review most closely applicable to vegetation in Ithaca follow.

- Avoidance or mitigation of any negative environmental impacts identified in the environmental review. The following shall be emphasized in particular:
  - Erosion, sedimentation, and siltation control
  - Protection of significant natural features and areas, including, but not limited to, trees, views, watercourses or bodies of water, and landform, on or near the site
  - Protection of, and compatibility with, other nearby features and areas of importance to the community, including but not limited to parks, landmarks, and historic districts
  - Compliance with all other regulations applicable to the development of, or development on, the subject site. These include, but are not limited to, the Zoning Ordinance, Sign Ordinance, Subdivision Regulations, Landmarks Preservation Ordinance, Environmental Quality Review Ordinance, and the State Environmental Quality Review Act.
  - Spatial and visual cohesiveness of the site plan through perceivable form and order in the basic layout of the major landscape elements and the application of landscape architecture techniques such as the proper and effective use of plantings, landform, water features, paving, lighting, etc., and color, and texture of buildings and other site improvements.
  - Open space for play areas and informal recreation, as appropriate, in the case of a residential development.

- *Criteria for parking area design.* The general criteria (above) shall also apply to parking area development. Additionally, in determining the adequacy and appropriateness of planting and screening of parking areas, zoning regulations and the following guidelines shall be considered:

- In parking areas with fewer than 20 parking spaces, adjacent uses and public ways should be protected against emissions, light, and glare from the parking by screening with planting or fences.

- In parking areas with 20 or more parking spaces, planting should be installed both on the periphery and within the lot. Plantings within such lots should be located so that no single row of spaces, or any two adjoining rows, or two rows separated by an aisle, would contain more than a total of twenty spaces unrelieved by planting.

- Interior planting islands should be a minimum of 80 square feet with at least six feet on one side. The planter should also be curbed and have a minimum three-foot excavation.

- High-branching shade trees should be considered for planting within the parking area, whereas woody shrubs with a dense growth habit should be considered for peripheral planting. The selected species should be tolerant of salt injury, soil compaction, and other adverse urban growing conditions. The city forester or the Shade Tree Advisory Committee should be consulted in plant species selection.

Innovation in urban forestry. The city has been in the forefront in the use of innovative techniques to enhance urban forestry. It was the first

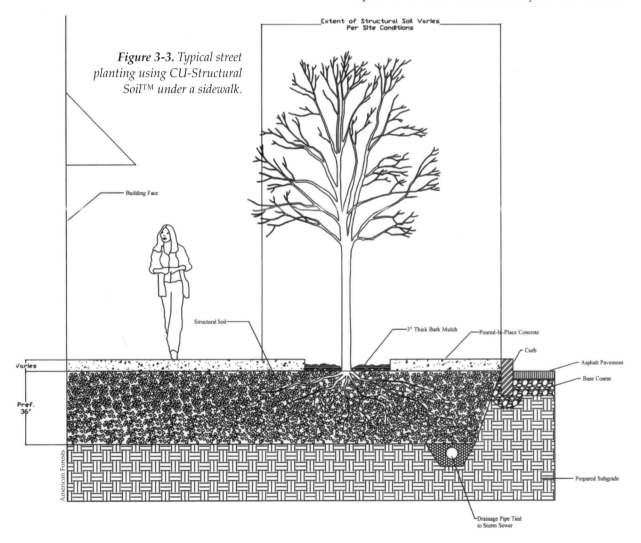

Figure 3-3. *Typical street planting using CU-Structural Soil™ under a sidewalk.*

municipality to use CU-Structural Soil (see www.hort.cornell.edu/uhi/outreach/csc/) under sidewalks and parking lots to enhance tree growth. It has recently combined the use of structural soil with porous asphalt to install the first parking lot that incorporates trees and reduces storm-water runoff. The city collaborates with Cornell University researchers to evaluate tree species better able to adapt to difficult growing conditions and has pioneered the use of bare root trees to decrease costs while planting more trees.

Palm Beach County, Florida

By Cheryl Kollin

Palm Beach County is part of the Everglades ecosystem, which stretches from the numerous lakes in Central Florida south to the Florida Keys. This unique U.S. ecoregion is characterized by its flooded grasslands and the rich wildlife that resides within the county's one-half-million-acre natural areas. These areas are critical for protecting the county's drinking water as well as for providing agriculture and promoting tourism. West Palm Beach, for example, depends on natural water catchment areas to filter surface water used for drinking. The county is also subject to annual tropical storms and hurricanes that destroy property and the very green infrastructure that protects its shorelines. Humans have further changed the land with drainage projects, waterway channels, and agriculture practices that have exacerbated flooding to the detriment of people and property.

Prompted by a significant tree canopy loss from Hurricanes Francis and Jeanne that battered the region in September 2004, Palm Beach County

Figure 3-4. Palm Beach County Study Area

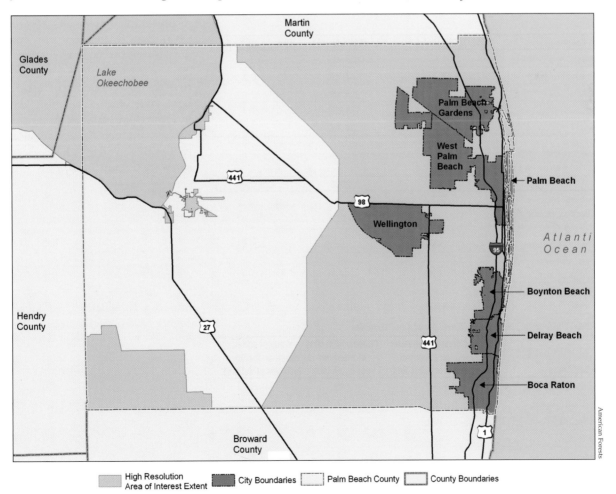

| High Resolution Area of Interest Extent | City Boundaries | Palm Beach County | County Boundaries |

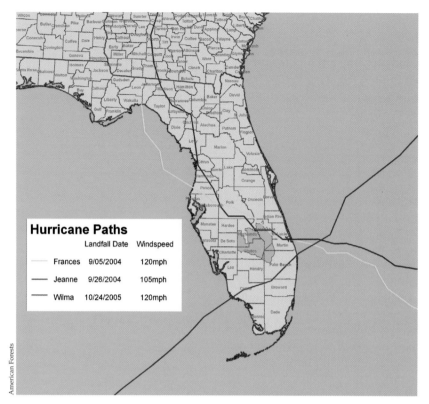

American Forests

Figure 3-5. Florida Hurricanes with Path Shown

Land Cover	1996 (acres)	2006 (acres)	Change (percent)
Trees	204,366	183,914	-10
Grass/open space	412,305	412,132	0
Bare soil	8,613	5,865	-32
Urban	111,522	134,873	21
Water	34,265	34,369	0
Total acres	771,082		

Lost Air Pollution Benefits

	1996	2006	Change
Pollutants removed (millions of pounds)	23	20.8	-2.3
Dollar value (millions of dollars)	58.4	52.5	-5.8
Carbon stored (millions of tons)	8.79	7.91	-880,000
Carbon sequestered (pounds)	68,400	61,600	-6,800

1996–2006 Change in Stormwater Runoff and Lost Benefits

Selected Areas	Additional stormwater volume to control (millions of cubic feet)	Construction cost of retention (per cubic foot)	Value of added retention facilities (millions of dollars)
Palm Beach County	157.8	$2	315.5
West Palm Beach	8.5	2	17
Wellington	10.1	2	20.2
Boca Raton	7.2	2	14.3
Delray Beach	3.9	2	7.8
Palm Beach Gardens	9.3	2	18.7

American Forests

received a grant from the Federal Emergency Management Agency (FEMA) to conduct an Urban Ecosystem Analysis. This case study presents how Palm Beach County leaders will use this study's findings and tools as a baseline for urban forestry restoration and, more broadly, to connect future land-planning decisions to green infrastructure.

Urban Ecosystem Analysis. The Urban Ecosystem Analysis provided the county with a GIS data layer that quantifies the benefits of land cover for slowing stormwater runoff, reducing water and air pollution, and storing and sequestering atmospheric carbon. American Forests conducted the analysis at two scales. The first analysis used moderate-resolution, 30-meter, Landsat satellite imagery (Digital Orthophotography Quarter Quadrennials) from 1996 and 2006. The second analysis used high-resolution 2.5-meter DOQQ and SPOT data to compare pre- and post-hurricane land cover from 2004 to 2006. Table 3-4 summarizes the 10-year trend changes in land cover and the resulting loss in ecosystem benefits. American Forests conducted the analysis at two scales, using its CITYgreen software (Figure 3-6).

Table 3-4. Palm Beach County Land Cover Changes

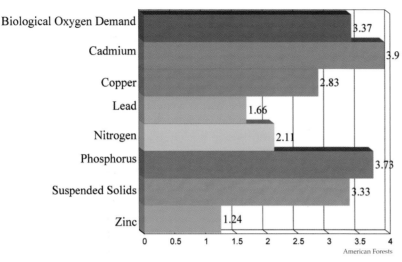

Figure 3-6. *Palm Beach County Water Contaminant Loadings from 1996 to 2006 Due to Land Cover Change*

The temporal changes in land cover during this time were most likely due to urbanization as viewed from tree canopy changing to urbanized areas. The change also reflects the county's aggressive removal of invasive tree species in areas that changed from tree canopy to grassland/open space. Palm Beach County will use its current 27 percent tree canopy cover data as a baseline to establish countywide tree canopy goals. Individual municipalities can devise their own tree canopy goals from this county-established goal.

Pre- and post-hurricane analysis. At a higher 2.5-meter resolution than the Landsat data described above, the land cover is more accurately represented and an analysis of pre- and post-hurricane land cover pinpoints areas that had the greatest tree canopy destruction.

A countywide comparison of land cover from 2004 and 2006 shows that tree canopy decreased by 42,000 acres or 17 percent while open space/grasslands increased by 9 percent. This change from canopy cover to open space suggests that Hurricanes Francis and Jeanne caused this land cover change. Urban areas also increased by 6 percent; this change was most likely due to urban development. This tree canopy loss increased stormwater runoff. An additional 146 million cubic feet of stormwater, valued at $292 million, must be managed. Air quality also declined with the loss in tree canopy: without these trees, there are 4.7 million more pounds of pollutants. The loss of air quality services is valued at $11.9 million annually. Water pollution, as measured in percent change in pollutant loading, increased as well (see Table 3-5).

Land Cover	2004 (acres)	2006 (acres)	Change (percent)
Trees	249,741	207,811	-17
Grass/open space	383,024	416,086	9
Bare soil	7,922	6,890	-13
Urban	92,454	98,209	6
Water	37,910	42,0469	11
Total acres	771,082		
Lost Air Pollution Benefits			
	2004	**2006**	**Change**
Pollutants removed (millions of pounds)	28	23.5	-4.7
Dollar value (millions of dollars)	71	59	-12
Carbon stored (millions of tons)	10.7	8.9	1.8
Carbon sequestered (pounds)	83,666	69,619	-14,047

American Forests

Table 3-5. *Palm Beach County Land Cover Changes per High-resolution Data*

This digital GIS land cover map will help county planners prioritize their reforestation efforts and tree giveaway programs, and aid in determining best species selection for future planting. For example, Hurricane Jeanne affected the more northern part of the county. Many sand pine trees toppled outright during the storm. Slash pine resisted the initial path of the damage, but the county now sees massive die-off from subsequent bark beetle infestations attacking the stressed trees. In contrast, Hurricane Wilma went straight through Palm Beach County. This time, the densely populated southern part of the county was most affected. Unfortunately, a lot of trees in the south are exotic to the region and as such were ill-adapted to hurricane conditions. Local experts recommend planting live oak as a replacement because it is one of the best native trees for withstanding hurricanes.

The county can also use the data in public education programs to extol the tangible benefits of urban forests. Tangible data are especially important in disaster-prone areas. Citizens are often fearful of replanting trees, believing them

Figure 3-7. Palm Beach County, Florida (2004–2006)

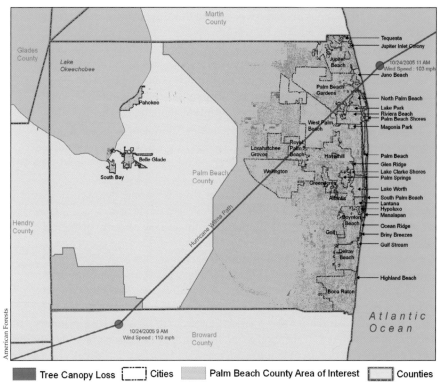

to be more of a hazard than of benefit in hurricane zones. When benefit data are combined with information about the best species and planting locations for hurricane-prone areas, citizens are more apt to support reforestation efforts in their communities.

A policy framework for conservation. The Urban Ecosystem Analysis ties ecosystem benefits of the county's natural areas to its regulatory mandates. Palm Beach County's comprehensive plan addresses several conservation issues in a separate conservation element of the plan, including: wetlands and conservation areas; air quality; water quality and quantity; estuarine systems; lakes; rivers; native vegetation; and wildlife habitat. The comprehensive plan details ordinances and regulations for the purpose of protecting and conserving natural resources.

Using green infrastructure. Created in 1987, the Palm Beach County Department of Environmental Resources Management (ERM) is responsible for a majority of the codes and programs that protect and conserve natural resources of the county. The comprehensive plan outlines 18 codes (see sidebar on the following page).

The county has an exceptional Natural Areas Program. In the early 1990s, voters approved state bonds to purchase environmentally sensitive natural areas. To date, the county has purchased more than 30,000 acres of natural areas. Now that most of the large tracts have been acquired, the Palm Beach County staff has shifted its task to linking these areas together and augmenting them. Their priorities are to reforest adjacent lands, to plant riparian buffers, and to create trails for wildlife and recreation.

In the 2004 image taken (above), there is a dense tree canopy in this neighborhood. By 2006 (below), the trees had been replaced by homes.

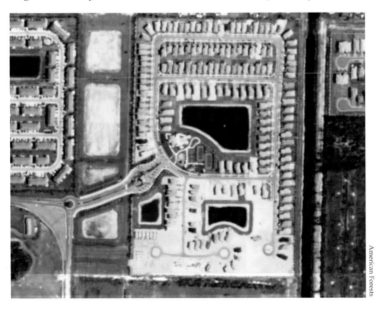

In 2003, the county passed an ordinance to assist property owners with the removal of invasive non-native vegetation from private properties. In addition, the county started a grant program to assist municipal governments with their own invasive vegetation removal programs. As part of these programs, the board of county commissioners also approved the creation of a Tree Canopy Replacement Program, which is currently under development. Although the county does not have an urban tree management plan, it takes a holistic approach with regard to preserving and replacing tree canopy and environmentally sensitive natural areas.

PALM BEACH COUNTY, FLORIDA, ORDINANCES AND CODES ADDRESSING NATURAL RESOURCES

1. Biological Waste Incineration Facility Ordinance

2. Excavation Ordinance

3. Environmental Control Rule I

4. Environmental Control Rule II

5. Irrigation and Water Conservation Ordinance

6. Landscaping and Buffering Ordinance

7. Lot-Clearing Ordinance

8. Natural Areas Ordinance

9. Natural Areas Stewardship and Endowment Fund Ordinance

10. Petroleum Storage Systems Ordinance

11. Petroleum Cleanup Ordinance

12. Sea Turtle Protection/Sand Preservation Ordinance

13. Stormwater Pollution Prevention Ordinance

14. Unified Land Development Code

15. Vegetation Protection and Preservation Ordinance

16. Wellfield Protection Ordinance

17. Wetlands Protection Ordinance

18. Invasive Non-native Vegetation Removal Incentive Program Ordinance

While land planning is primarily done at the municipal level, regional-scale planning can best address ecosystem issues, even when the coordination can be challenging, as it is in Palm Beach County, which has 38 municipalities.

Through its role in development regulation and permitting, the county is able to mitigate losses due to development activities. ERM has an active program in restoring and creating shoreline habitats, as well as mangrove systems. In unincorporated areas, ERM mandates that developers or owners who clear lots for development must revegetate and in some cases set aside areas as preserves. In addition, the Palm Beach County Planning, Zoning and Building Department regulates new development landscaping. Under Article 7 (Landscaping) of the county's Unified Land Development Code, developers are required to plant a specific number of trees, of which currently 60 percent must be native.

Restoring green infrastructure for water quality. Improving and restoring water quality is critical to the region's vitality and economic well-being. Since trees slow down stormwater runoff and filter pollutants, they significantly contribute to water quality. The county has acquired large tracts of natural vegetation to safeguard this resource. County planners and managers have also targeted specific areas for restoration, increasing tree canopy cover as a best management practice. Examples include:

- Using vegetation to filter agricultural and equestrian-generated phosphorus out of the water in popular horse communities like the Town of Wellington.

- Adding trees to ranchettes (i.e., the 1.25-acre residential lots that contribute to sprawl development)

- Restoring historic mangrove reef areas along the beaches (97 percent have been destroyed)

- Replanting hurricane-damaged slash pine trees. These trees were ill-adapted to urban, suburban, and ranchette environments, and as a result the stressed trees were subsequently killed by pine bark beetle. In contrast, slash pine trees growing in healthy, natural areas are well-adapted to their environment and have thrived. ERM will couple a tree giveaway program with an education program to teach homeowners how to make their properties habitable for slash pine.

Most of these programs are funded through general funds or through bonds. In addition, the county has actively sought grants (such as the FEMA grant for the Urban Ecosystem Analysis) for enhancing several of these programs.

In addition to the county's restoration efforts, the South Florida Water Management District has designated hundreds of thousands of acres of land as Stormwater Treatment Areas (STAs). For example, the county designated the Loxahatchee Wildlife Reservation Natural Area and planted its northern area to filter pollutants before they enter the Loxahatchee River.

A regional framework. While land planning is primarily done at the municipal level, regional-scale planning can best address ecosystem issues, even when the coordination can be challenging, as it is in Palm Beach County, which has 38 municipalities. Water and air quality issues, for example, cross political boundaries. The headwaters of the Everglades begin hundreds of miles to the north, in Orlando, and meander south through Palm Beach County, to terminate at the southern tip of Florida in Everglades Bay. The water picks up urban pollutants along the way.

Palm Beach County works with the South Florida Water Management District, the Florida Fish and Wildlife Commission, Florida Department of Environmental Protection, U.S. Army Corps of Engineers, the Treasure Coast Regional Planning Council, local municipalities and surrounding counties, and numerous other local, state, and federal agencies on shared land management issues. The classified land cover data and analysis tools provided to Palm Beach can be used in conjunction with regional and statewide data, such as the Florida Natural Areas Inventory.

By analyzing a statewide network of protected natural areas in combination with other data layers such as land use, transportation, and routes of commerce, planners can begin to think more comprehensively—from a systems perspective. In doing so, the county and the region can make their restoration and future development decisions in tandem, making them both even more effective.

SINGLE-PURPOSE APPROACHES

Chapel Hill, North Carolina

By Carrie Fesperman

This college town's urban forestry program started in 1989 when the town amended its charter to authorize the adoption of tree protection regulations upon recommendation of a Tree Protection Task Force. The task force was created, in part, to respond to developers' unsuccessful efforts to design around trees and to protect them during construction. The developers were protecting tree trunks without taking appropriate measures to also protect the root zones from compaction during construction. Consequently, trees "saved" during construction were dying within a few years after building occupancy.

The resulting Tree Protection Ordinance required the identification of rare and specimen trees as well as the preparation of a landscape protection plan that distinguished tree protection zones for most development projects. An urban forester position was created in the early 1990s to help implement the ordinance. In 2003, the city enacted its Land Use Management Ordinance, which included the Tree Protection Ordinance. At that time tree protection requirements were expanded to regulate certain single- or two-family dwelling projects.

In recognition of the town's urban forestry program, the town has been designated a Tree City USA for eight consecutive years by the National Arbor Day Foundation. (To qualify to be a Tree City USA, the city must spend at least $2 per capita on their urban forestry program; Chapel Hill spends $3.12 per capita.)

Public policy goals. The town council of Chapel Hill felt the Tree Protection Ordinance served a number of public policy goals. The diversity and abundance of trees and shrubs, as well as their appearance from public ways and the wooded setting they created, were felt to contribute to the town's economic prosperity by creating an enjoyable place for residents to live and visitors to stay. From an environmental protection standpoint, trees and other green landscape elements were seen as a way to moderate climate and mitigate flooding, erosion, noise pollution, and airborne pollutants. Trees and other vegetation were also considered to be valuable assets in protecting the health, safety, and welfare of citizens. As growth and development increased, the town wanted to avoid the diminution of these natural resources and considered their protection a necessity.

Primary program responsibilities. The purpose of the ordinance is five-fold:

1. Regulate the protection, installation, removal, and long-term management of trees, shrubs, and soils

2. Encourage the proper protection and maintenance of existing trees, shrubs, and soils on all public and some private lands

3. Charge the town manager to prescribe procedures for the proper protection, installation, and long-term management of landscape elements on all developing, all public, and some private lands

Chapel Hill's Tree Protection Ordinance requires the identification of rare and specimen trees as well as the preparation of a landscape protection plan that distinguished tree protection zones for most development projects.

Trees along East Franklin Street help shade and beautify the Chapel Hill shopping district.

The Chapel Hill town forester inspects a tree on a construction site to determine compliance with tree protection requirements in the permit.

4. Establish a system of permits to ensure the correct planting, maintenance, protection, and removal of trees and soil on public and private property

5. Establish penalties for violation of its provisions

Program approach. Chapel Hill's program is primarily single-purpose, addressing tree protection and preservation through a comprehensive site planning approach. Currently, tree preservation is mostly done through site plan review, focusing on protecting rare or specimen trees on developing land through a landscape protection plan, on-site supervision, protective fencing, and enforcement. Standards are also set for planting and removing trees on public land and in street rights-of-way.

Management. The town manager is responsible for dictating the proper measures to protect, install, and manage trees, shrubs, and other landscape elements over the long term. Afterwards, the town's planning and public works departments share responsibility for managing the rest of the urban forestry program. The planning department receives and processes applications for building permits submitted by developers and residents. Planners then forward the development plans to the public works department, where a landscape architect or urban forester reviews the site plans for all proposed commercial, multifamily, institutional, single- and two-family residential, and downtown plans. After approval of the landscape protection plan, the landscape architect or urban forester inspects the site once tree protection fences are installed and throughout construction to ensure that tree protection areas are not violated. The landscape architect or urban forester also oversees the design and construction of improvements on town property of pedestrian areas, sidewalks, lighting, and landscaping, including street trees and downtown streetscape.

Connections to the comprehensive plan. The Natural Environment Element states, "The quality of Chapel Hill's natural resources—soil, air, water, flora, and fauna—is a barometer of the health of the community." The goal and objectives from this element outline a plan for the protection and preservation of open spaces and natural areas (see sidebar below), specifically citing several tree preservation and protection strategies. The comprehensive plan also directly references the Tree Protection Ordinance as being designed to protect environmentally sensitive resources. Consequent amendments to strengthen the ordinance have been proposed, quoting language in the comprehensive plan as justification.

CHAPEL HILL CASE STUDY:
FROM SECTION 9.0—NATURAL ENVIRONMENT

9.2 Goal
Identify, protect, and preserve open spaces and critical natural areas and enhance the community's air quality and water resources

Objective
Natural Resources: Implement regulations, policies, incentives, and programs to conserve valuable natural resources, including trees, woodlands, and habitat areas; stream corridors and floodplains; sensitive soils and steep slopes; and air and water quality.

Strategies
9A-1. Evaluate the effectiveness of Chapel Hill's environmental regulations in protecting natural resources
While the existing environmental provisions of the Development Ordinance provide a good regulatory foundation, they should be evaluated for opportunities to strengthen protection of sensitive resources

Action: Develop and adopt improved tree preservation and planting provisions as part of Strategy 9A-1 (Town staff, Planning Board, Town Council)

Action: Develop and adopt tree planting and preservation standards for the rights-of-way of Town entranceway corridors and adjacent private properties as part of Strategy 9A-1 (Town staff, Planning Board, Town Council, NC DOT)

9C. Tree preservation and planting: Residents and visitors alike consider Chapel Hill's wooded setting to be an essential part of the Town's special community character. In addition to their aesthetic contributions, trees afford many environmental benefits such as maintaining air and water quality, providing natural habitat, minimizing erosion, and ameliorating climactic extremes.

9C-1. Improve tree preservation and planting efforts along entranceway corridors. Trees are important to the character of the Town's entranceway corridors such as US 15-501, Airport Road, and NC 54. Tree preservation and planting should be pursued along public rights-of-way throughout the Town, with entranceway corridors constituting a special focus of these efforts. Specific recommendations include:
- Implement the tree preservation and planting recommendations of the Master Landscape Plan for Entranceway Corridors
- Designate entranceway corridors as "special character" corridors with provisions for tree planting and preservation

9C-2. Review and improve tree planting provisions in Chapel Hill's Development Ordinance. In addition to incorporating new provisions for entranceways, the Development Ordinance should be reviewed for opportunities to improve tree planting requirements. Possibilities include:
- Improve standards for tree plantings in surface parking lots
- Incorporate requirements for street tree plantings into the Subdivision Regulations

Source: www.ci.chapel-hill.nc.us/documentview.asp?DID=246

Regulations, implementation, and enforcement. The Tree Protection Ordinance is a section within Article 5: Design and Development Standards in the Land Use Management Ordinance. The latter ordinance is designed to outline the rules and expectations of applicants trying to gain approval for land development, while the Design and Development Standards article establishes the criteria for designing a lot, a development, or a site. The Tree Protection Ordinance requires the identification and protection of trees and other vegetation from incompatible development, describes what trees require protection (e.g., all trees of at least 18 inches in diameter; uncommon species, such as the long leaf pine or live oak) and how the critical root zones and other features should be protected, including lot layout, building or paved surface placement, or location of utilities. Fencing is used to protect vegetation during all construction activities (e.g., storage of equipment, building material) as well as right-of-way clearing during the subdivision process. The ordinance also outlines plans for tree plantings and maintenance to be performed by the town.

In order to accomplish these goals, the ordinance requires that a landscape protection plan (see sidebar on the following page) be approved and a preconstruction conference with the town staff be arranged prior to any development of a site. Permit applicants must prepare a landscape protection plan and get it approved before a zoning compliance permit will be issued. A landscape architect or urban forester is available for assistance in plan preparation, and a brochure is provided with a list of information that needs to be shown on the plans. A certified landscape protection supervisor must be designated and responsible for supervising all construction activities on nonresidential and multifamily residential sites. Once the zoning and building permits are issued, and the tree protection fence installed, the landscape architect or urban forester has to inspect and approve the fence before any work or site disturbance can start.

Throughout the construction process, the landscape architect or urban forester regularly inspects sites to ensure that fences remain in place and vertical and that the tree protection area is not violated. If construction does not conform to the agreed protection measures or the landscape protection supervisor is not present during critical development activities, a stop work order may

This Chapel Hill building site uses fencing around a tree to protect it until construction is completed.

Emily Cameron, with permission of Town of Chapel Hill

CHAPEL HILL LANDSCAPE PROTECTION PLAN EXCERPT

5.7.4 Permitted Activities and Standards Applicable to Developing Land

(a) Landscape Protection Plan Required

(1) A Zoning Compliance Permit shall not be issued for development covered by provisions of this Section unless a Landscape Protection Plan is first approved by the Town Manager.

(2) No person shall spray, prune, remove, cut above ground, or otherwise disturb any tree or the soil within the critical root zone of any tree on developing land without first obtaining a Zoning Compliance Permit and approval of a Landscape Protection Plan from the Town Manager.

(3) All development activities on a site, including installation of public and private utilities, shall conform to the provisions of an approved Landscape Protection Plan.

(b) Landscape Protection Plan

(1) The Town Manager shall prescribe the contents of Landscape Protection Plans and information that may be reasonably required to determine compliance with this Article, with sufficient copies for necessary referrals and records.

(2) The Landscape Protection Plan shall:

A. describe the existing soil types, trees, vegetation, and other landscape elements of the development site;

B. identify areas where trees, vegetation and soils are to be protected and preserved and areas where trees, vegetation and soils are to be removed or modified; and

C. address measures of tree, vegetation and soil protection and management that will be used before, during and after all construction activities to promote the survival of such elements.

(3) If vegetation identified for survival in the Landscape Protection Plan is dead or dying as determined by the Town Manager at the time of the issuance of a certificate of occupancy and is part of a required buffer, replacement of such vegetation shall be required if the Town Manager finds the buffer to be inadequate.

(4) Otherwise, compliance with the Landscape Protection Plan shall establish a presumption that the requirements of this Section have been met.

(c) Surveying

No tree greater than six (6) inches in Diameter at Breast Height (DBH) shall be removed for the purpose of surveying without a permit issued by the Town Manager approving such action.

(d) Pre-Construction Conference

Prior to the commencement of any activities requiring a permit (see Section 5.7.2(a)), a pre-construction conference shall take place to review procedures for protection and management of all protected landscape elements identified on the Landscape Protection Plan and to designate one or more persons as Landscape Protection Supervisor(s) as described in Section 5.7.4(e).

(e) On-site Supervision

For all development other than that related to single-family and two-family dwellings on individual zoning lots, the following on-site supervision is required:

(1) The applicant shall designate as Landscape Protection Supervisors one or more persons who have completed instruction and examination in landscape protection procedures with the Town and have received a Landscape Protection Certificate.

(2) It shall be the duty of the Landscape Protection Supervisor to ensure the protection of new or existing landscape elements to be preserved, as defined in the Landscape Protection Plan. At least one identified Landscape Protection Supervisor shall be present on the development site at all times when activity is taking place that could damage or disturb such landscape elements. Such activities include:

A. clearing and grubbing;

B. any excavation, grading, trenching or moving of soil;

C. removal, installation or maintenance of all landscape elements and landscape protection devices; or

D. the delivery, transporting and placement of construction materials and equipment.

(3) The approved Landscape Protection Supervisor(s) shall supervise all site work to assure that development activity conforms to provisions of the approved Landscape Protection Plan.

Source: www.ci.chapel-hill.nc.us/index.asp?NID=149

Emily Cameron, with permission of Town of Chapel Hill

Emily Cameron, with permission of Town of Chapel Hill

Fencing aims to protect street trees in Chapel Hill during construction projects.

be issued until the nonconformance issue has been resolved. Those in noncompliance can also be fined.

Landscape protection plans are required for more than just new development projects. Currently, they must be provided for new construction or the expansion of single- or two-family dwellings when renovations require a building permit and cause a land disturbance of 5,000 square feet or more. In addition, development activities on or adjacent to public land, including construction, excavation of tunnels, or utility or pavement repair require the approval of the town manager and a landscape protection plan.

Funding. Chapel Hill's urban forestry program is funded as part of the town's annual operating budget, including salaries, staff training, new trees, vehicles, and equipment (Table 3-6). Its estimated expenditure per capita for the program in 2006 was $3.12.

Future changes to the tree protection ordinance. Because the type of development is changing in Chapel Hill, the town council began to consider ways to further regulate tree protection on existing single-family lots. The number of buildable lots within town limits is shrinking, focusing attention on infill development and redevelopment. Consequently, in January 2006 the council endorsed the idea of expanding current tree protection regulations. Expansive changes to the current policy could take place as the council considers

Table 3-6. Chapel Hill, North Carolina, Funding for Urban Forestry Program

2006 Budget	
Salaries	*$149,421*
—including Urban Forester (½ annual salary); Landscape Architect (½ annual salary); Arborest (¾ annual salary); and portion of 5 Groundskeeper II and III salaries	
Training	$501
Professional Licenses and Membership	$665
New Trees	$7,753
Equipment and Supplies	*$7,828*
—including maintenance and fuel for aerial bucket truck and chipper machine, mulch, chainsaws, chaps, gloves, and planter bars for seedlings	
Total	**$166, 168**

the adoption of a vision statement calling for no net loss of canopy cover and an increase in trees proportional to population growth.

In the spring of 2007, the town council endorsed a two-phased approach The first phase took effect in June and put in place interim changes to the ordinance to provide more protection to trees by (1) regulating land disturbance and tree-cutting activities taking place without a building permit on single-family and two-family lots, and (2) lowering the size diameter threshold for trees required to be shown on all landscape protection plans. The town has identified a consultant to assist with the second phase, which is to develop more substantive changes to the regulations based on the vision and principles recommended by the planning board and to incorporate strategies consistent with the goal of increased tree protection. This phase also includes a study that will focus on the staffing implications and the effects of the ordinance on single-family homeowners. While this PAS Report was being prepared for print, the town council was holding public hearings on proposed changes to the ordinance. The council had already opted to increase public awareness of the issues through a multimedia strategy, so the outcome of the public hearings should be interesting.

Emeryville, California

By Max Eisenburger

Originally dominated by heavy manufacturing, Emeryville (population 7,600; 1.2 square miles in area) grappled with enormous changes wrought first by industrial decline in the 1970s, then by surging demand for housing, office space, and high-tech industry from the early 1980s to the present day. Emeryville's industrial bust and post-industrial boom posed a number of unique challenges for city officials: widespread contamination deterred redevelopment, while increasing land values made it difficult to expand a parks and recreation system that was not meeting the needs of existing, much less new, residents.

In the face of these enormous challenges, the city's public officials and relatively small staff have displayed extraordinary creativity by turning apparent disadvantages and threats into opportunities. Together, they are leveraging brownfield grants and a hot real estate market to expand parks and open space, create a more pedestrian-friendly streetscape, and meet stormwater management goals.

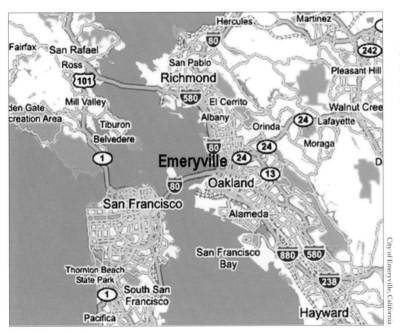

Figure 3-8. Emeryville, California, Location (East End of San Francisco–Oakland Bay Bridge)

City of Emeryville, California

Trees are playing a central role in accomplishing all three of these goals. Though Emeryville has no overarching urban forestry plan to speak of, it is evident that, through these various initiatives, city residents, officials, and staff recognize the urban forest's importance, both as a means to accomplish various policy objectives and as a goal in itself.

Public policy drivers. Efforts to expand Emeryville's urban forest have been driven by a unique combination of circumstances arising from its post-industrial legacy and rapid redevelopment.

With redevelopment well under way in the 1990s, Emeryville quickly went from industrial decline to high-tech boom. Film companies, such as Pixar Animation Studios, and biotechnology and software firms set up company offices, and retail and housing development followed closely. The city's resurgence was a welcome development, but open land was already at a premium: In 1984, the city had just 7.7 acres of parks and open space, and vacant and underused parcels that might have been assembled to increase recreational area either were being snatched up by developers or were contaminated from years of industrial pollution.

Emeryville's industrial heritage also posed a challenge to the creation of a vibrant, pedestrian-friendly community. Streets in formerly industrial areas were designed almost exclusively for trucks and vehicle traffic, with narrow sidewalks, frequent curb cuts, little shade, and wide setbacks. This made for an inhospitable pedestrian environment and discouraged the development of successful retail districts and residential neighborhoods.

Controlling stormwater runoff in order to comply with National Pollutant Discharge Elimination System (NPDES) permit requirements was another major concern for the city. Given its density and industrial history, a high percentage of Emeryville's surface is impermeable, but improving infiltration of runoff directly into groundwater is problematic because of widespread soil contamination. In fact, in 1995, approximately 213 acres (55 percent of Emeryville's designated Commercial, Mixed Use, and Industrial proper-

Poplars lining Temescal Creek are part of an effort in Emeryville to preserve existing species in new and retrofit projects.

Community Design + Architecture

ties) were known to have soil or groundwater contamination, while many more untested sites were assumed to be contaminated as well (Emeryville, California, 2005b, 14).

Public policy response. In reaction to these issues, the city pursued a number of goals, chief among them the enhancement of the pedestrian environment and an aesthetic upgrade of streetscapes, containment and mitigation of soil contamination, and improved stormwater management. In 1976, the city council convinced the state of California to designate the entire city a redevelopment area. This allowed the council, acting as the redevelopment agency, to issue bonds and act toward its goals with more flexibility. In some ways, the city has benefited from its small size, which enables different departments

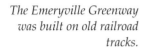

The Emeryville Greenway was built on old railroad tracks.

Peter Schultze-Allen, City of Emeryville

and the city council to work together closely. Staff members from public works and planning meet with the city council often to coordinate action, and the latter also acts as the redevelopment agency. In each of the policy responses discussed below, all of these actors played a significant role.

The city council recognized the shortage of open space and pedestrian amenities and laid out recommendations for improvement in the 1993 General Plan. The plan identified several sites for future park development and recommended creation of a new linear park with bicycle and pedestrian paths, which would be planted with large trees "to emphasize the linear form of the corridors."

As efforts came together later in the decade to implement the planned greenways, the city's post-industrial legacy proved a mixed blessing: An abandoned rail spur on the Santa Fe line was well-situated and available for purchase, but it was also badly contaminated. In 2000, the city acquired funding for planning and remediation through the EPA Brownfields Assessment Demonstration Program, and used the grant to leverage additional funding from California state park and bicycling bonds, Union Pacific Railroad, and municipal sources. Ground on this first, publicly funded phase of the Emeryville Greenway was broken in February 2004. In a unique twist, the remainder of the greenway will be constructed with private money. Emeryville has taken advantage of the powers granted to its redevelopment authority to require that developers build sections of the greenway abutting their properties as part of the conditions of development approval.

EMERYVILLE FUNDING

Park Avenue District Plan: $820,200 out of a total budget of $6.9 million budgeted for street tree planting.

Sources of funds: Redevelopment Area Bonds; general capital improvement funding

Street Tree Program: $100,000 annually for planting and maintenance; unspecified amount from street trees planted by developers under redevelopment conditions of approval.

Sources of funds: 100% funded by general capital improvement funds.

Emeryville Greenway – Doyle Street Portion: $1,000,000 total remediation and construction cost; specific cost of tree installation component not available

Sources of funds: EPA Brownfields Assessment Demonstration Pilot Program, City of Emeryville funds; California State Park and Bicycle Bond Bonds; Union Pacific Railroad; Pulte Homes (developer)

When finished, the Emeryville Greenway will provide pedestrian and bicycle connections from Berkeley in the northeast all the way through to Oakland in the southwest, with trees helping to define the path and buffer it from vehicle traffic.

Echoing the general plan and working at a subcommunity level, the city's 2006 Park Avenue District Plan devotes considerable space to street trees as pedestrian enhancements, identifying areas in which more trees are to be planted as well as offering locations with existing mature plantings as pedestrian-friendly. The district plan budget includes $820,200 for street tree planting at an estimated cost of $1,000 per tree, suggesting that the plan will result in an additional 820 street trees if the plan is fully implemented and costs are accurate. In its implementation guidelines, the plan also notes that tree coverage could and should also be increased by ensuring that all parking lots meet existing tree requirements in the zoning ordinance.

The Park Avenue sidewalk contains roses on one side and London Planes on the other. The roses belong to Pixar, the animation studio, which used structural soil for these trees, so their roots could get to the lawn inside the fence; the trees have grown fast.

Peter Schultze-Allen, City of Emeryville

Implementation and codification. According to Emeryville's 2007 Capital Improvement Program, "the city has an inventory of 3,500 street trees," and this number will only grow with completion of the Emeryville Greenway and Park Avenue District Plan. Areas of the city that do not abut the greenway are also being redeveloped, and the city has limited capacity and funding to expand its street tree inventory as much as it would like. Consequently, it has looked to further harness redevelopment by shifting the burden onto developers, incorporating street tree planting in the general requirements for commercial and industrial development.

Where a commercial or industrial property abuts a right-of-way, the zoning ordinance's site standards stipulate a minimum of one tree per 25 feet (for commercial) or one per 30 feet of frontage as part of screening and buffering requirements. If the property includes a parking lot with more than 35 stalls, further tree plantings are required at a rate of one tree per 7.5 stalls (see excerpt in sidebar).

The intent of these requirements is to break up the parking lot and avoid the appearance of a continuous expanse of vehicles. The public works department ensures that these requirements are met, and advises developers on tree well design (the tree well is part of the aeration system around the tree and its root system, created when the soil grade is raised) and species selection. Once installed, the trees are subject to preservation and maintenance requirements established by the city's Urban Forestry Ordinance.

Stormwater management. Taking advantage of new county rules that require new developments to implement onsite stormwater treatment and detention measures, the city hired consultants to prepare a set of guidelines that would encourage developers to use vegetative stormwater management techniques. The resulting document, *Stormwater Guidelines for Green, Dense Development,* was adopted by the city council on December 15, 2005 (www. ci.emeryville.ca.us/planning/stormwater.html). While it consists primarily of a set of suggestions and examples meant to inspire developers, all new developments and redevelopment resulting in more than 10,000 square feet of impervious surface (as of August 15, 2006) are required to implement onsite stormwater treatment and detention measures under Alameda County's NPDES permit, and the city has made clear that it strongly prefers vegetative to mechanical treatments.

These London Plane trees are on a fairly new street built on an old railroad right-of-way, next to the Besler Building, which was converted from a factory to lofts.

City of Emeryville

Among the vegetative measures addressed, trees and the urban forest are the first to be extensively discussed. The guidelines catalog the various ways in which trees reduce and slow down runoff, as well as remove pollutants through root uptake. It also notes that trees provide additional benefits beyond stormwater control, including an improved pedestrian environment and heat island effect reduction. The section then outlines site planning and development guidelines relevant to trees. In particular, it recommends the preservation of significant stands of trees during the pre-site planning phase, stresses the need to protect trees during grading

EXCERPTS FROM TITLE 9:
PLANNING AND ZONING, EMERYVILLE MUNICIPAL CODE

ARTICLE 2. IMPROVEMENTS

9-3.201. Required.

No subdivision, parcel map, or other division of land contemplated by the provisions of this chapter of the Map Act shall be approved unless the following improvements are constructed or required to be constructed in order to serve the lots being created:

(a) Grading and the installation of curbs, gutters, sidewalks, street lights, *street and sidewalk trees,* and roadway surfaces (p. 9)

9-4.54.5. General Requirements for Commercial Districts.
...

(4) Boundary Areas. A minimum of one tree per 25 linear feet of each property line abutting a street is required, unless it is determined by the Planning Director that this is not feasible. Required trees may be grouped or clustered and shall be in addition to required ground cover and shrub material.

(5) Parking Areas. One tree per each 7.5 parking stalls, which may be clustered or grouped, shall be installed in each parking area containing 35 or more spaces. Boundary planting cannot be counted towards this requirement. Trees should be placed so as to give relief to the monotony of rows of parked vehicles. (p. 87)

9-4.54.6. General Requirements for Industrial Districts.
...

(3) In all front and street side yards, the equivalent of one tree per 30 linear feet of property line shall be planted in either a linear or grouped manner.

(4) In all rear and side yards abutting residential neighborhoods, one tree for each 30 linear feet of combined rear and side property lines shall be planted in either a linear or grouped manner.

(5) Trees equal in number to one per each 7.5 parking stalls, either grouped or clustered, shall be installed in all parking areas containing 35 or more spaces. Said trees shall be placed on the lot so as not to interfere with interior industrial parking lot circulation. Trees shall be placed so as to give relief to the monotony of rows of parked vehicles.

and construction, and emphasizes continual maintenance post-construction. In addition, the guidelines encourage the use of structural or engineered soil for street trees where wide tree wells are not feasible.

Conclusion. At the time of writing, Emeryville is in the process of updating its general plan, and workshop and community survey results reveal that the pedestrian environment, open space, and other issues friendly to the urban forest are among the top concerns of citizens. Moreover, the Emeryville Department of Public Works is considering adoption of "bay friendly" landscaping guidelines that would promote the use of native tree species.

This compact Bay Area community may not yet have a single mission statement on urban forestry to unite its many disparate initiatives that incorporate trees, but that has not stopped it from formulating a variety of tree-friendly policies that, in aggregate, are leading to both widespread revitalization and the emergence of a healthy urban forest. Along the way, city officials have employed some creative methods, requiring developers to install street trees and build the greenway as part of the redevelopment conditions of approval, and using NPDES requirements to integrate trees and stormwater management. In many ways Emeryville presents a unique case, and some strategies may not be applicable to every community: relying on development exactions to construct a greenway would not work in areas without strong development pressure. However, many local authorities could learn from Emeryville's simultaneous pursuit of stormwater management and urban forestry goals.

Flagstaff, Arizona

By Paul Summerfelt

Flagstaff is ranked as Arizona's most at-risk wildfire community. The area averages roughly 400 ignitions per year, split between those caused by lightning and those caused by humans. With a brisk wind, low humidity, and high temperature, any single fire, or a combination of fires, could rapidly overwhelm response agencies.

As evidenced in other affected communities, wildfire can disrupt or damage wildlife habitat, recreational opportunities, watershed and scenic values, spiritual or emotional beliefs, ecosystem health, and property and other improvements, as well as threaten public safety and induce panic. Protecting the community from these effects is a priority of government.

The San Francisco Peaks form a dramatic backdrop to the community.

Courtesy Flagstaff Fire Department

Flagstaff is the largest metropolitan community in northern Arizona. Sitting at 7,000 feet elevation on the south flank of the San Francisco Peaks, the community resides in the midst of a dense Ponderosa Pine forest. The forests offer a cool respite from the nearby desert heat and are an important factor to those living in and visiting the area. Promoting and maintaining this green, sustainable environment is of key importance to city leadership.

Problems driving the urban forestry program. Low-intensity wildfire is both natural and necessary for southwestern Ponderosa Pine forests. Such fires reduce fuel accumulations, recycle nutrients, and invigorate grasses, forbs (i.e., herbs that are not grasses or grasslike), and flowers. Prior to settlement in the 1870s, such fires burned frequently—every two to five years on average—and evidence suggests that trees occupied only 5 to 10 percent of the overall area with an average density of 30 to 50 trees per acre.

Today, the forests are heavily overcrowded: Trees now occupy 95 percent of the area with a common density of 500+ trees per acre. Complicating the challenge of wildfire mitigation are issues of persistent patterns of drought, ongoing outbreaks of insect infestations, and increasing numbers of people.

The Woody Fire, which burned within the community in June 2006, dramatically reinforced awareness of the risk from destructive wildfire.

Courtesy Flagstaff Fire Department

Nationally, there has been a disturbing escalation in historically uncharacteristic dangerous, destructive, and costly wildfires during the past few decades. The 1996 wildland fire season saw numerous large and destructive wildfires both adjacent to and within the city, effectively shattering the illusion that a "green" forest was a "healthy" forest, or that what existed now was and always would be the same.

One other motivating factor driving the urban forestry program is economic: A study completed in 2003 by the Flagstaff Fire Department (FFD) and other community organizations shows that a single large fire that damaged or destroyed 300 homes would have a first-year negative economic impact in excess of $60 million.

Approach. The Federal Emergency Management Agency (FEMA) defines "hazard" as a source of danger, and "risk" as a possibility of loss or injury. Traditional fire prevention programs employ the standard "Three-E" approach: Education, Engineering, and Enforcement. However, because wildfires occur in an ever-changing natural environment, the addition of a 4th "E"—Ecosystem—is required.

Flagstaff's approach focuses on five core areas:

1. Public Preparedness: Motivate and assist individuals to prepare themselves, their families, homes, properties, and neighborhoods to survive wildfire.

2. Strategic Development: Shape direction of program to meet overall mission, while engaging with partners.

3. Response: Develop and sustain capacity to deliver effective, efficient, and safe community protection, and to provide assistance to partners at every level.

4. Land-Use Planning: Create and maintain FireWise neighborhoods. (See www.firewise.org/ or PAS Report 529/530, *Planning for Wildfires*.)

5. Hazard Mitigation: Manage wildland fuel regimes (condition, amount, type, and location) to reduce likelihood of destructive wildfire and create sustainable forests.

Relation to comprehensive plan. During the past decade, both the city and Coconino County have worked together on numerous plans to improve quality of life in the greater Flagstaff area. They include, among others, Open Space and Greenways, Regional Land Use and Transportation, Growth Management, Flagstaff 2020, Multi-Hazard Mitigation, and Emergency Operations.

While each recognizes the current state of the natural environment and speaks to public safety, recreation, watershed protection, and economic vitality, none is specific to community wildfire protection and forest health and sustainability. Like many issues that transcend ownerships and jurisdictional boundaries, a collaborative partnership approach is a must. The city is actively and successfully engaged in three such efforts:

1. The Greater Flagstaff Forests Partnership (GFFP) represents environmental, business, and land/resource management agencies whose three-fold purpose is to:

   - restore the Ponderosa Pine ecosystem,

   - protect communities from wildfire, and

   - test and demonstrate key ecological, economic, and social aspects of forest restoration.

   GFFP, along with the Ponderosa Fire Advisory Council (an area emergency agency coordination group), co-authored the Greater Flagstaff "Community Wildfire Protection Plan" (CWPP). The plan encompasses nearly 900,000 acres, and seeks to promote:

   - an educated and involved public,

   - implementation of forest treatment projects designed to reduce wildfire threat and improve long-term forest health, and

   - use of FireWise building techniques and materials.

   Development of the CWPP was authorized by passage of the Healthy Forests Restoration Act (HFRA) by Congress in November 2003 and subsequently signed into law by President Bush. The plan encourages collaboration on both public and private lands by identifying local protection priorities, mitigation practices, and other needed actions.

2. The Northern Arizona University Centennial Forest is a joint effort between the Arizona State Land Department and the university's School of Forestry to

manage 50,000 acres of state forest land southwest of the community. Because any large fire in this area will likely move into the community, the city is an active member of the advisory board and was involved in the development of the overall land-management plan and annual operating plans for the site.

3. The Arizona Forest Health Council was originated in 2003 by Governor Janet Napolitano. The council culminated its effort with the completion of the Statewide Strategy for Restoring Arizona's Forests, which the governor adopted by in 2007. The city was an active member of the council and assisted with the development of this plan.

Codes that implement the program. The city has adopted the Uniform Fire Code, and FFD has both enforced it and added various supplementary regulations. In the early 1990s, the city developed a Land-Development Code (LDC), a portion of which is geared toward resource protection, including tree preservation and landscape requirements.

As wildfire and forest health awareness grew, the earlier community paradigm of "saving every tree" began to change. FFD and the Flagstaff Community Development Department worked cooperatively to develop an administrative solution to the need to aggressively manage forests while preserving the natural character of the community. Flagstaff was the first community in Arizona to require selective tree removal and debris disposal, as well as incorporation of FireWise construction materials and techniques, throughout all new developments: The concept is now overwhelmingly embraced by the development community.

Program origin and responsible agency. Begun in late 1996, the program remains a branch of FFD's Prevention Bureau. Originally a single-person effort, the program now has six permanent full-time staff, augmented by a year-round seasonal crew (eight in summer, three in winter). Volunteers and student interns round out the organization.

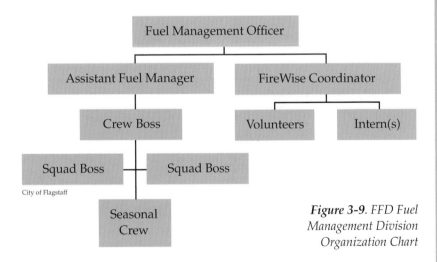

City of Flagstaff

Figure 3-9. FFD Fuel Management Division Organization Chart

Four of the full-time staff have B.S. degrees (or higher) in natural resource management fields, and all staff possess other professional qualifications and certifications (e.g., arborist, National Wildfire Coordinating Group Fire Management positions, Emergency Medical Technician, etc.).

Innovative features. Hazard mitigation treatments are highly visible to community members, encouraging interaction and participation. Projects are planned and implemented in a partnership environment, provide job experience and career opportunities for crew members, and foster promising biomass and wood-use efforts.

ADDITIONAL INFORMATION: FUEL MANAGEMENT STRATEGIC PLANS

- **FFD FUEL MANAGEMENT**
  www.flagstaff.az.gov/fuelmanagement

- **COMMUNITY WILDFIRE PROTECTION PLAN**
  www.gffp.org/PDF_Pages/CWPP_Report.htm

- **NAU CENTENNIAL FOREST PLAN**
  www.for.nau.edu/CentennialForest

- **AZ STATEWIDE STRATEGIC PLAN**
  www.governor.state.az.us/FHC/

- **MULTI-HAZARD MITIGATION PLAN**
  www.flagstaff.az.gov/common/modules/documentcenter2/documentview.asp?DID=1078

- **EMERGENCY OPERATIONS PLAN**
  www.flagstaff.az.gov/common/modules/documentcenter2/documentview.asp?DID=1609

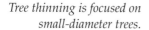

Tree thinning is focused on small-diameter trees.

Courtesy Flagstaff Fire Department

Thinning dense stands of trees—focusing on small-diameter material—does more than reduce the risk of devastating wildfire and improve forest health. It also increases residential property values. A recent study in the area documented that market value increased an average of $200 or more for each quarter-acre of thinned land surrounding a home or property.

Use of prescribed fire immediately adjacent to structures and improve-

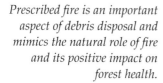

Prescribed fire is an important aspect of debris disposal and mimics the natural role of fire and its positive impact on forest health.

Courtesy Flagstaff Fire Department

ments is commonplace. It is an important component of debris disposal and mimics the natural role of fire and its positive impact on forest health.

Funding. During the early, formative years, the budget for the program was relatively small (≤ $100,000 per year) and funded largely by various state and federal grants. Over time, the program has grown—both in staffing and services offered—and funding sources have shifted. Today, funding has stabilized (± $500,000 per year). Approximately 80 percent of the funding comes from the city's general fund and 20 percent from grants, contracts, and donations.

Flower Mound, Texas

By Cheryl Kollin

Flower Mound, Texas, a 43-square-mile community located 28 miles north-west of Dallas, experienced rapid growth in the 1990s (Figure 3-10). The town was the nation's tenth-fastest growing community during the 1990s, growing by 226.54 percent, from 15,527 to 50,702.

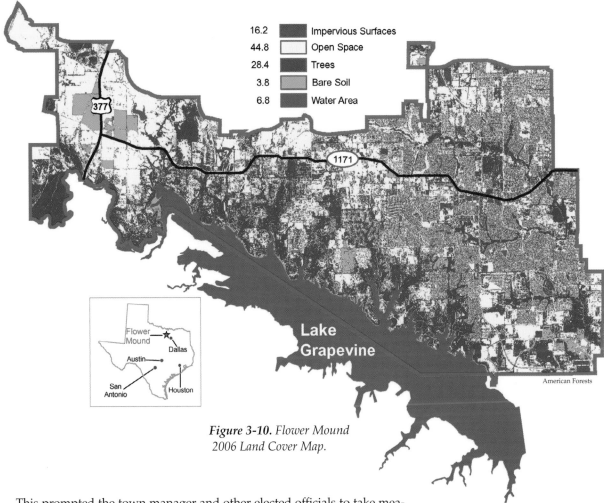

16.2	Impervious Surfaces
44.8	Open Space
28.4	Trees
3.8	Bare Soil
6.8	Water Area

Figure 3-10. *Flower Mound 2006 Land Cover Map.*

This prompted the town manager and other elected officials to take mea-sures to preserve the rural, open space character of the town and its unique landscape features. While the town's overarching public policy was to preserve its open space, the driving forces for this policy were rapid development and the resultant impacts on stormwater and water quality. The town council ad-opted a smart growth approach of preserving natural open space and forest lands and incorporated specific policies into the 2001 Flower Mound Master Plan. This case study serves to demonstrate how a community can quantify the environmental benefits derived from conservation development.

Flower Mound's commitment to smart growth began with the adoption of a Smart Growth Program in January 1999, as part of its master plan review process that began during the prior year. A Smart Growth Management Plan was adopted in February 2000, and the town's Master Plan was amended and adopted in 2001. Amendments to the Smart Growth Program were adopted in July 2002 with the following goals:

- Mitigate the ill effects of rapid and intense urbanization. Ensure growth is served with adequate public infrastructure, services, and facilities.

- Ensure growth contributes to the attainment of the community character and quality-of-life objectives established in the town's Master Plan.

- Preserve open lands, natural landscapes, farmland, sensitive ecological resources, and scenic vistas on the urban fringe.

- Integrate the built and natural environments and contribute to a sense of place.

- Ensure growth does not occur at the expense of environmental quality, community character, or quality of life.

Flower Mound's Environmental Resources Division adopted an innovative approach to quantifying the environmental and economic benefits of conservation development, Urban Ecosystem Analysis.

The Smart Growth Program, the 2001 Master Plan, and its land development regulations operate together to create a development framework for the town.

The town council created a conservation development provision within the town's Code of Ordinance, Chapter 98–Zoning Plan. They designated two conservation developments in the undeveloped southwest part of town. A conservation development is defined as a residential development project that does not increase net density and clusters dwelling units on smaller lots than are currently zoned in order to protect and preserve open space. Its desired benefit: "to preserve open or natural lands as an integral component of the development" (Flower Mound Master Plan 2001).

Conservation development provides development options in order to preserve the natural functions of floodplains and riparian corridors and protect significant contiguous tree stands to prevent habitat fragmentation. New development must "respect the existing natural topography, waterways, and viewsheds. Conserved lands are placed in a voluntary conservation easement, which then permanently limits development or subdivision of the property."

While conservation development is currently voluntary, developers and homeowners have incentives to build and live in these designated areas. Developers can sell their lots at a premium and can increase their marketability by promoting their homes in open space and forested settings. Their infrastructure costs decrease because homes are located closer together. Conservation developments are given a higher priority for review, so the approval process is shortened. From a homeowner's perspective, residents enjoy living next to open space and home values are greater in conservation developments.

Urban Ecosystem Analysis. The Environmental Resources Division adopted an innovative approach to quantifying the environmental and economic benefits of conservation development, Urban Ecosystem Analysis. American Forests developed the analysis so that communities could quantify the benefits of their green infrastructure. Flower Mound recognized its application for quantifying the benefits of conservation development. Urban Ecosystem Analysis uses scientific and engineering models to quantify the value that tree canopy and other land cover provide for stormwater management and air and water quality. American Forests conducted initial analyses with 2006 high-resolution (one-meter), four-band (blue, green, red, and near infrared) satellite imagery. A GIS-based digital data map was produced from the imagery. These data, along with American Forests' CITYgreen software (see description on page 13), were used to quantify the ecological and economic benefits of land cover. The Environmental Resources Division will continue to use the analysis to aid in conducting environmental site assessments and development review.

Sanctuary, an 89-lot conservation development on 100 acres located in the south-central part of town, was used to demonstrate the ecosystem benefits of conventional versus conservation development land planning. The lots are approximately one-half acre in size, in an area that conventionally would be one acre. No net increase in the number of lots is permitted on the site. The reduced lot size allowed 40 percent of the site to be preserved

The Sanctuary conservation development.

as open space. This also preserved contiguous hardwood tree stands and riparian and wildlife corridors.

Two land development options were modeled using CITYgreen software. The first compared lot size (one-half acre versus one acre) to the ecosystem benefits of the preserved open space and tree cover when the number of lots remains the same.

A second series of analyses examined the built lot, to address how the proportion of tree canopy, open space, and impervious surface affects the ecosystem benefits to the site as a whole. Each of these scenarios was then extrapolated to the Cross Timbers Conservation Development District, a 2,792-acre area in the western, less developed side of town, to show the magnitude of ecosystem benefits when applied to a larger area.

Table 3-7 summarizes the conventional versus the conservation lot size analysis. The table lists the percent land cover under each scenario and the corresponding added costs of stormwater management in post-development

Development scenario	Percent tree canopy of site	Percent open space of site	Percent impervious of site	Percent lots** of site	Additional stormwater management (cubic feet) and costs over predeveloped site
Predevelopment site	45	55	0	0	not applicable
Residential (one-acre lots)	0	0	5	95	152,543/$305,000
Residential (half-acre lots)	31	12	10	47	125,622/$251,000

American Forests

Table 3-7. *Flower Mound Sanctuary Lot Size Modeling and Storm Management (100 Acres)**

* Percentages may not add up to 100 percent due to rounding.

**Land cover on one-acre undeveloped lot scenario is assumed to be 80 percent vegetated and 20 percent impervious. On the half-acre-lot site scenario, it is assumed to be 75 percent vegetated and 20 percent impervious. The figures are taken from the Natural Resource Conservation Service's TR–55 stormwater model.

Table 3-8. Sanctuary Lot Size Modeling Water Contaminants Increase Over Predevelopment Conditions (100 Acres)

Water Pollutants	One-half-acre development (percent)	One-acre development (percent)
Biological Oxygen Demand	28	34
Cadmium	37	44
Chromium	49	59
Chemical Oxygen Demand	53	64
Copper	21	26
Lead	10	12
Nitrogen	14	17
Phosphorous	34	40
Suspended Solids	28	33
Zinc	7	9

American Forests

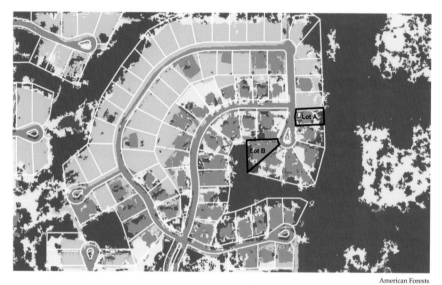

American Forests

Figure 3-11. Sanctuary Conservation Development Lots A and B.

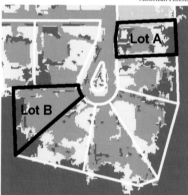

Development scenario	Percent tree canopy of site	Percent open space of site	Percent impervious of site
Lot A	29	43	29
Lot B	23	8.6	69

American Forests

Table 3-9. Sanctuary's Built Lot Land Cover (100 Acres)

scenarios when compared to the pre-development condition.

Because less tree canopy and open space were preserved under the conventional development scenario, this site would require an additional 27,000 cubic feet in stormwater management, valued at $54,000 when compared to the conservation development site.

Water pollution is a direct result of and can be calculated from stormwater runoff. While the water quality of both developed sites diminished, the conventional site design added more contaminants than the conservation development scenario (Table 3-8).

Built lot modeling. While lot size is an important consideration when conserving open space, the amount of stormwater runoff is also greatly affected by the land cover percentages once the lot is built. For example, an urban ecosystem analysis compared Sanctuary's land cover on Lot A and Lot B and their corresponding ecosystem benefits for stormwater runoff and water quality. The lots are identified in Figure 3-11 and the land cover percentages are summarized in Table 3-9.

The analysis findings show that compared to developed Lot A, an additional 1,286 cubic feet of stormwater runoff occurs in developed Lot B, at a cost of $2,573. Reducing the building footprint, sidewalk, and streets (impervious surfaces) and enhancing the tree canopy and other vegetation (green infrastructure) reduce the cost of managing stormwater runoff and protecting water quality. (See Table 3-10 on the following page.)

The Cross Timbers Conservation Development District. When the ecosystem benefits of the Sanctuary Conservation Development are applied to the

Water Pollutants (percentage)	Lot A versus Lot B
Biological Oxygen Demand	40
Cadmium	49
Chromium	58
Chemical Oxygen Demand	61
Copper	33
Lead	18
Nitrogen	24
Phosphorous	46
Suspended Solids	40
Zinc	13

Table 3-10. *Percent Increase in Water Contaminant Loading*

American Forests

larger Cross Timbers Conservation Development District, the ecosystem benefits of conservation development are multiplied many times. The predevelopment site contains 59 percent open space, 33 percent tree canopy, and 4 percent impervious surface (Figure 3-12). The pre-development tree canopy in this district provides 20 million cubic feet in stormwater management, valued at $40 million. The land cover also absorbs 259,000 pounds of air pollutants annually. This service is valued at $648,000 per year.

Original Conditions, 2001+

**Current Conditions, 2006
Conservation Development**

**Schematic Conventional Development
Two-Acre Plots**

Figure 3-12. *Ecosystem Benefits of Conservation Development, Sanctuary Conservation Development*

American Forests

	Storm event* runoff	Number of dwelling units	Runoff (cubic feet) per dwelling unit
Original	537,438	not applicable	not applicable
0.5-acre plots	693,060	89	7,787
2.0-acre polts	611,639	42	14,563

Source: Town of Flower Mound

*Stormwater runoff values are determined using the TR–55 model developed by the Natural Resource Conservation Service (NRCS). The amount of runoff is based on an average two-year, 24-hour storm event of 3.75 inches.

Tables 3-11 and 3-12 summarize the scenario comparison between pre-development and full buildout using both conventional and conservation development scenarios. Both development designs use the same averaged land cover percentages for seven developed lots in Sanctuary. As described above, an average land cover from seven of the built lots is: 40 percent impervious surface, 30 percent open space/grass, and 30 percent tree canopy. These land cover percentages were extrapolated to the entire Cross Timbers District.

Table 3-11. Cross Timbers Conservation District Land Cover and Stormwater Management Costs (2,791 acres)*

Development scenario	Percent tree canopy of site	Percent open space of site	Percent impervious of site	Percent lots** of site	Stormwater management costs (cubic feet) and dollar value
Predevelopment site	33	59	4	0	not applicable
Residential (one-acre lots)	0	0	5	95	14.7/$29,000,000
Residential (half-acre lots) at full buildout	31	12	10	47	4.7/$251,000

American Forests

* The average land cover of seven currently built lots on Sanctuary site is 30 percent per tree canopy, 30 percent open space, and 40 percent impervious. These percentages were used to calculate ecosystem benefits to the site as a whole.

**Percentages may not total 100 due to rounding.

Table 3-12. Cross Timbers Conservation District Percent Increase in Water Contaminants from Pre- to Post-Modeled Development

Water Pollutants	One-half-acre development (percent)	One-acre development (percent)
Biological Oxygen Demand	9	26
Cadmium	11	32
Chromium	13	39
Chemical Oxygen Demand	13	42
Copper	7	21
Lead	4	11
Nitrogen	5	15
Phosphorous	10	30
Suspended Solids	9	26
Zinc	3	8

American Forests

Applying Urban Ecosystem Analyses to planning. Urban Ecosystem Analysis not only quantified the ecological and economic benefits of conservation development, but more importantly provided digital data and software for the town planning staff to use. Several agencies within the town have jurisdiction regarding green infrastructure, including the environmental resources division, the environmental conservation commission, which addresses tree preservation and open space issues, the department of engineering, and the planning division. The environmental conservation commission and the town council view the analysis as a good public education tool. Matthew Woods, director of environmental services, envisions that he and his staff will use the data and tools to fulfill the goals mandated in the town's existing planning mechanisms for new development:

1. Staff can conduct an Urban Ecosystem Analysis as part of the required environmental survey for conservation development projects.

2. Staff will run ecosystem benefit scenarios to quantify the impacts of different development project designs.

3. Staff will use the modeling capabilities of CITYgreen software to enhance conservation development techniques related to preserving or achieving land cover percentages for the town as a whole, as well as within an individual development.

4. Staff will use the data for updating the current and future town master plans.

Urban Ecosystem Analysis provided a baseline measure of 28 percent overall tree canopy. The environmental resources staff sets an overall tree canopy goal at 30 to 40 percent. In addition to this general goal, the environmental conservation commission and town council will use the data and tools to establish their own canopy goals to fulfill the town's stormwater requirements.

The town is required to monitor and meet water quality standards under Phase II of the Clean Water Act. Flower Mound must submit a five-year stormwater management plan to meet or exceed the law's goals. Town staff will use the Urban Ecosystem Analysis data as a baseline to measure their current status and use green infrastructure as a best management practice to meet its Phase II requirements.

The town is located within a region currently in nonattainment for air quality because it is located within the Dallas area airshed. The town has no monitoring stations and is not bound by local regulations for air quality. If it were required, the town could incorporate trees as a best management practice and quantify its benefits.

The initial Urban Ecosystem Analysis project and the environmental resources staff's ongoing use of the tools and data are funded through the general budget (50 percent) and through the town's Tree Preservation Fund (50 percent).

Mecklenburg County now has interactive analytical tools that measure the ecosystem benefits of its land cover and can thereby evaluate the effectiveness of its newly created policies and standards.

REGIONAL APPROACHES

McDowell Creek Watershed, North Carolina

By Cheryl Kollin

Within the lush green landscape of Central North Carolina, Mecklenburg County faces a conundrum because the region is such a desirable place to live. This once rural setting is now one of the fastest-growing areas in the state, its population having increased by 300 percent since 1980. Mountain Island Lake (MIL) Watershed, a 70-square-mile area within the county, provides 80 percent of the drinking water for the 700,000 people who live there. This rapid development has severely threatened the community's water quality. The water entering Mountain Island Lake from McDowell Creek, one of its larger subwatersheds, is already unhealthy for swimming. McDowell Creek Watershed's 30 square miles has thousands of existing homes, and many more are planned. (See Figures 3-13 and 3-14 below.)

This case study shows how the benefits of natural systems, derived from land cover measurements, can be used to address stormwater and water quality needs. From a planning perspective, Mecklenburg County and local communities within the McDowell Creek Watershed demonstrate how they are aggressively tackling their water quality issues in a new and innovative way. The county now has interactive analytical tools that measure the ecosystem benefits of its land cover and can thereby evaluate the effectiveness of its newly created policies and standards. County staff will adjust their strategies as needed to insure long-term water quality for residents. The town of Huntersville, 12 miles north of Charlotte, is an early adopter of Mecklenburg County's new water quality standards. It requires low-impact development design and thus serves as an innovative model to both guide new development and improve water quality in the watershed.

Background. In the 1990s, land development around Charlotte and the need for more electric power provided the catalysts to spur rapid growth in the Mountain Island Lake Watershed. Duke Power, the local utility company, obtained land adjacent to Catawba River by eminent domain. The company

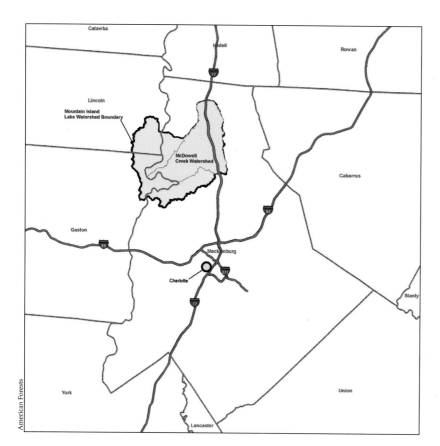

Figure 3-13. *Mountain Island Lake (MIL) Watershed*

Figure 3-14. *McDowell Creek Watershed*

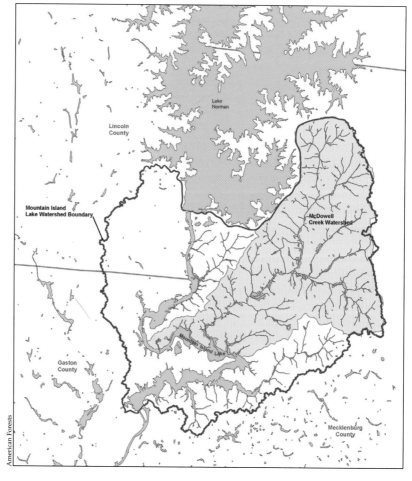

dammed the river to create several lakes needed to generate hydroelectric power. Real estate value around these man-made lakes skyrocketed. Duke formed a real estate company and parceled the land for residential lots. Major highways were constructed, which provided easy access to the lakes region.

As homes sold, the land cover converted from forest and fields to houses, pavement, and lawn. As a result, the enormous influx in stormwater runoff and pollutants was carried into tributaries, McDowell Creek, and other water bodies, all pouring into Mountain Island Lake. Even with water quality controls in place, such as stream buffers and impervious limits, the water quality of Mountain Island Lake was still at risk. The real estate market drove development without regard for the negative consequences its success would create. A land cover assessment and comprehensive plan should have preceded development; the county is now aggressively trying to reverse the damage done. Within a broader regional context, the future of water rights is at stake. As the region continues to grow, decision makers in adjacent counties and even in South Carolina must grapple with shifting water across watersheds.

Urban Ecosystem Analysis. Mecklenburg County stormwater engineers and most of the public officials recognized the urgent need to improve their drinking water supply. Even though the lower third of McDowell Creek, closest to where the water enters Mountain Island Lake, had watershed protections in place, the upper 20 percent had no restrictions on development. This allowed polluted water to enter stream channels. Thus, McDowell Creek still delivered polluted water into Mountain Island Lake.

The Charlotte-Mecklenburg Stormwater Services staff developed the McDowell Creek Watershed Management Plan (2005), which sets water quality goals and presents a detailed plan of action to achieve them. American Forests conducted an Urban Ecosystem Analysis of the McDowell Creek Watershed, providing a method to measure and model the effect that land cover has on slowing stormwater runoff and improving water quality. The initial analysis quantified the extent of the problem from a land cover perspective. The analysis compared land cover between 1984 and 2003. The findings showed a 14 percent increase in flooding potential (as measured by the increase in flow depth) due to a decrease in natural land cover and an increase in urban areas. An additional 17.3 million cubic feet of stormwater valued at $34.7 million would need to be managed as a result of the loss in natural land cover. (See Figure 3-15 below.)

American Forests also prepared a GIS digital map of land cover using 2001 high-resolution imagery. An analysis of this "green data layer" details the stratification of land cover in the McDowell Creek watershed (Table 3-13 below). The findings show that land cover provides valuable ecosystem services by retaining 52.67 million cubic feet of stormwater. These services, valued at $105 million, allow water to infiltrate into the soil that would otherwise run off the land and need to be managed. In addition, when less water runs off the land, fewer pollutants are picked up and carried into tributaries that feed into McDowell Creek. If the land cover were not present to filter pollutants, the additional pollutants could be calculated using stormwater runoff values. Table 3-13 displays the percent increase in contaminant loading that would occur.

The staff uses CITYgreen software to model increases in tree canopy and the resulting water quality improvement to determine the extent of planting needed to achieve its water quality standards. The high-resolution data also reveal breaches in riparian buffers pinpointing where reforestation is needed. The Stormwater Services staff has identified, prioritized, and measured tree-

The Charlotte-Mecklenburg Stormwater Services staff developed the McDowell Creek Watershed Management Plan (2005), which sets water quality goals and presents a detailed plan of action to achieve them.

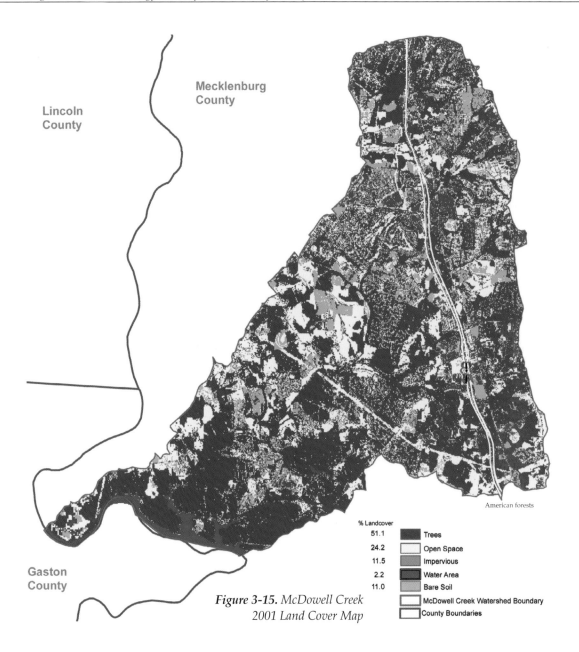

% Landcover	
51.1	Trees
24.2	Open Space
11.5	Impervious
2.2	Water Area
11.0	Bare Soil
	McDowell Creek Watershed Boundary
	County Boundaries

American forests

Figure 3-15. *McDowell Creek 2001 Land Cover Map*

Table 3-13. *Land Cover and Stormwater Benefits in McDowell Creek Watershed (2001)**

Land Cover type	Acres	Percent of land cover
Tree canopy	10,618	51
Open space	5,038	24
Impervious	2,385	12
Bare soil/agricultural	2,292	11
Water	449	2
Total	**20,782**	**100**

American Forests

*This urban ecosystem analysis used one-meter multispectral imagery from 2001 classified into five land cover classes.

save areas for stream bank restoration and stabilization. Staff could also use the analysis to prioritize reforestation areas by creating vegetative zones in proximity to tributaries and measuring the contributions that reforestation in a particular zone will have on water quality. Overall, the data will provide a baseline for future assessments, monitoring how effective the Watershed Management Plan has been and what adjustments need to be made.

Water Pollutants	Percent Increase
Biological Oxygen Demand	80
Cadmium	102
Chromium	134
Chemical Oxygen Demand	144
Copper	62
Lead	30
Nitrogen	41
Phosphorous	95
Suspended Solids	79
Zinc	22

American Forests

Table 3-14. Percent *Increase in Water Contaminant Loading, McDowell Creek Watershed*

Public policy. The public policy goals for the McDowell Creek watershed grew out of the McDowell Creek Watershed Management Plan. On October 15, 1996, the Mecklenburg County Board of County Commissioners took a stand in support of clean, usable surface waters through the adoption of the community's first "Creek Use Policy" calling for all Mecklenburg County surface waters to be "suitable for prolonged human contact and recreational opportunities and supportive of varied species of aquatic life." At that time, only about 15 percent of Mecklenburg County's creeks met this goal. Much work was needed to protect the cleaner creeks, and those creeks with poorer water quality needed to be restored. At the board's direction, a panel of stakeholders was convened in February 1997, including representatives from development and environmental interest groups. This panel worked with city and county staff toward the development of a comprehensive strategy aimed at fulfilling the board's policy statement.

In January 1998, the panel reported back to the board with a three-phased approach for achieving its "Creek Use Policy." The board approved the approach, and the implementation of Phase I began in FY 1998–1999. The approach, Surface Water Improvement & Management (SWIM), prioritized creek basins and tasks using the philosophy of:

- preventing further degradation;
- preserving the best waters;
- improving the good; and
- remediating the worst waters.

The following principles are used to guide SWIM efforts:

- Use of a holistic approach in addressing the community's water quality, quantity, and green space issues
- Basin-level community involvement and support
- Basin-specific analysis using modeling and stream assessment
- Use of proven, scientifically sound watershed management techniques

Through the SWIM Program, McDowell Creek was targeted as a high-priority watershed for restoration due to its location upstream of Charlotte-Mecklenburg's drinking water supply in Mountain Island Lake. As part of the SWIM Program, increased water quality monitoring activities were implemented in the creek and the cove of the lake where the creek drains. In June 2000, Mecklenburg County hired a private consulting firm, Tetra Tech, to develop a water quality model for the watershed using the data American Forests had collected to quantify existing water quality conditions, to identify sources of pollution, and to predict future water quality based on approved land-use plans. The county also asked the consultant to propose a strategy for protecting water quality from further degradation using the model. In December 2002, Tetra Tech completed its baseline assessment report for McDowell Creek, which identified a three-fold increase in pollutants in McDowell Creek and the cove at buildout in the watershed. This was alarming because water quality in the creek and cove is already significantly affected.

This data was presented to the elected officials in the Town of Huntersville. In February 2003, the town adopted the Low Impact Development (LID) Ordinance suggested by Tetra Tech (using the model) to prevent further degradation at buildout. Mecklenburg County agreed to support the town in its efforts to protect McDowell Creek by committing to restore preexisting conditions in the creek in exchange for its adoption of the ordinance. It was this promise that led to the development of the McDowell Creek Watershed Management Plan, which is based on the same modeling that led to the adoption of the LID Ordinance. It was also this promise that led to the grants used to comply with water quality standards.

The NPDES Permit required by the Clean Water Act also prompted the Mecklenburg County Land Use and Environmental Services Agency to develop tougher water quality standards. A companion design manual provides the details and specifications for implementing the standards using LID techniques, including tree canopy cover.

Stormwater runoff from McDowell Creek Watershed enters Mountain Island Lake.

Rusty Rozelle

Connecting land cover, development, and water quality. Prior to the adoption of the 2005 water quality standards, the county had impervious surface restrictions and stream buffer standards in place, but McDowell Creek's water quality was still being impaired, primarily because of new development. In 2003, amendments to the Clean Water Act required Mecklenburg County and all six of its towns to implement a Stormwater Phase II pollution prevention program. This coincided with Huntersville adopting the county's new water quality standards, including its cache of LID design techniques. Developers must now use a site evaluation tool that compares pre- and post-development land cover and measures the impacts these changes have on water quality. As an added incentive for communities like Huntersville to implement mandatory standards, Mecklenburg County has secured $1.5 million in grants including EPA's 319 grant (see Table 3-15 below) to retrofit existing development so that it is in compliance with water quality standards.

Huntersville is particularly concerned with new development in the far eastern and western sides of the community, areas noted for their rural character, steep slopes, and many streams. Prior to the adoption in 2003 of the water quality standards and zoning/subdivision amendments, density was 2.5 units per acre with 15 percent open space and no designated minimum lot size in areas that through the 1980s were rural in character. Mass grading in new subdivisions exacerbated soil erosion. As a result, in early 2003 the town reduced density, established minimum lot sizes, required that significant portions of subdivisions be designated as open space, and established water quality standards.

Improving water quality in a watershed is a long-term process, one that requires commitment from both local and county leaders. Local communities can increase their natural land cover and implement LID provisions on new and retrofit development. The town is a model of local action to protect its watershed. In addition to requiring a pre- and post-development site evaluation, staff could also aggregate and measure the benefits of their water quality improvements by using Urban Ecosystem Analysis in tandem with their site-level tools.

Mecklenburg County will continue to monitor the watershed as a whole and periodically reevaluate its water quality standards. The county could use Urban Ecosystem Analysis to monitor sections of tributaries of greatest concern, modeling land cover scenarios within these smaller subwatersheds to determine optimum tree canopy stocking. Now that the ecosystem services of land cover can be measured, local and county staff can add green infrastructure, along with other nonstructural measures, to their arsenal of planning and management tools. In doing so, they not only plan for future development wisely, but improve the long-term viability of their drinking water.

Improving water quality in a watershed is a long-term process, one that requires commitment from both local and county leaders. Local communities can increase their natural land cover and implement LID provisions on new and retrofit development.

Funding Sources

- Federal (Clean Water Act: Section 319 Program). Section 319 of the Clean Water Act provides grant money for nonpoint-source demonstration projects. USEPA, the granting agency, allocates approximately $4.6 million for Section 319 in North Carolina. From 1992 to 2004, approximately $1,427,000 was allocated by the Section 319 Program to initiate or complete projects in the Catawba River basin.

- State (North Carolina Agriculture Cost Share Program). The North Carolina Agriculture Cost Share Program was established in 1984 to help reduce the sources of agricultural nonpoint-source pollution to the state's waters. The program helps owners by using Best Management Practices (BMPs). These BMPs include vegetative, structural, or management

American Forests

Figures 3-16a and 3-16b.
Mountain Island Lake 2003
and 1984 Land Cover Images

urbanized

forest cover

open space (grassland)

systems that can improve the efficiency of farming operations while reducing the potential for surface and groundwater pollution. This voluntary program reimburses farmers up to 75 percent of the cost of installing an approved BMP. The annual statewide budget for BMP cost sharing is approximately $6.9 million.

• Local (North Carolina's Clean Water Management Trust Fund (CWMTF)). Established by the General Assembly in 1996 (Article 13A; Chapter 113 of the North Carolina General Statutes). At the end of each fiscal year, 6.5 percent of the unreserved credit balance in North Carolina's General Fund (or a minimum of $30 million) goes into the CWMTF. Revenues from the CWMTF are then allocated in the form of grants to local governments, state agencies, and conservation nonprofit organizations to help finance projects that specifically address water pollution problems. In the Catawba River basin, 61 projects were funded between 1997 and 2003, totaling $30,511,123.

Table 3-15 is a list of the grants that Mecklenburg County has received to comply with water quality standards. It includes the sources of the grants and the amount of money that Mecklenburg County has contributed toward the grant match.

Project	Grant	County Match	Total
McDowell BMP	200,000 (Clean Water)	200,000	400,000
McDowell BMP	287,050 (319 Program)	191,366	478,416
McDowell BMP	639,000 (Clean Water)	639,000	1,278,000
McDowell Stream Restoration	95,000 (NCNRCS)	105,000	200,000
Ange Property Project	381,661 (319 Program)	223,406	605,067
North Meck Recycling Center	145,000 (Clean Water)	145,000	290,000
Grand Total	**$1,747,711**	**$1,503,772**	**$3,251,483**

American Forests

Table 3-15. *Funding Sources for Mecklenburg County*

MID-AMERICA REGIONAL COUNCIL (KANSAS CITY)

By Tom Jacobs and Joan Steurer

A broad mix of urban and community forestry programs function in the bi-state Kansas City metro area. Efforts vary considerably in their scope, intensity, impact, and level of political and financial support. A long-standing community culture supports parks and forestry efforts, as currently demonstrated by the 29 member cities in the Arbor Day Foundation Tree City USA program, impressive efforts by two tree-focused nonprofit organizations, and strong collaboration among local and state agencies.

Cover image of MARC's Natural Resource Inventory document, "On the Map."

Emerging regional green infrastructure policies and programs provide an increasingly strong framework to support local forestry programs as well. This case study describes how a broad regional environmental planning agenda supports and facilitates local urban and community forestry efforts. Importantly, substantial opportunities exist for both the planning and forestry professions to increase their level of engagement on environmental issues in urban areas and in urban-rural fringe areas to achieve forestry and community development goals.

Background. The Mid-America Regional Council (MARC) is the regional and metropolitan planning organization for the nine-county, bi-state Kansas City region. As a voluntary association of 129 local governments, MARC provides leadership on a range of regional planning issues such as transportation, environment, and community development.

While MARC has not focused directly on community forestry programs, it has actively leveraged broadly defined green infrastructure protection opportunities to support and advance forestry efforts. Programmatic responsibilities at MARC intersect with urban forestry programs in three major areas: watershed and stormwater management, greenway and open space protection, and air quality conservation. This case study broadly describes the relationship between urban forestry and environmental and urban planning at the regional scale. Opportunities to support forestry programs in each of the three program areas are described in turn.

Regional growth dynamics and environmental planning tools. Growth and development patterns largely frame the context in which regional environmental planning takes place. Current projections estimate that the region will consume approximately 400 square miles of land for development in the coming 25 years as its population grows by 350,000 residents.

Community dialogue about future growth requires explicit deliberation about the relationship of environmental planning issues to urban design,

The "tree price tag" was part of an Arbor Day awareness project in which MARC was involved. The goal was to promote the financial benefits of trees in urban settings in terms of air quality, stormwater management, and other environmental concerns.

Mid-America Regional Council

land use, economic development, transportation, and other factors. Increasingly, MARC strives to facilitate policy and planning initiatives seeking to strengthen such linkages.

A green infrastructure conceptual framework connects environmental protection with public infrastructure development issues in a holistic way. Green infrastructure typically describes a connected network of open spaces, natural areas, parks, greenways, and urban forests.

Various planners, local government staff, and MARC program staff explore areas near the Turkey Creek corridor in Merriam, Kansas, as part of planning new trails and greenways that are part of the regional MetroGreen system.

Mid-America Regional Council

Natural resource assessments routinely show that healthy natural systems are integral to quality of life, just like roads, bridges, and other gray infrastructure. In essence, ecosystem services provided by street trees and community forests (i.e., clean air and water, reduced risk of flooding) cannot be easily or effectively replaced.

Greenways and open space conservation. One key component of the Kansas City region's green infrastructure is MetroGreen, a planned network of 1,144 lineal miles of greenway corridors, many of which follow area streams and rivers. MetroGreen helps conserve and restore streamside forests, offering many oft-cited benefits such as improved water quality, recreation, off-road transportation options, and increased land valuation. These corridors offer opportunities to link communities and high-quality remnant habitats. They also provide a real mechanism to capitalize on ecosystem services at the landscape level.

One innovative tool supportive of conservation planning is a regional natural resources inventory. Completed in 2004, the GIS-based framework provides easily accessible spatial data to help communities appreciate the quality, extent, and distribution of natural assets in their jurisdictions. Data allow proactive consideration of natural resource protection in the course of regional and local decision making related to land use, transportation, greenways, watersheds, and air quality.

The inventory provides regionally consistent land cover data, incorporating the best available wetland, parcel, soils, floodplain, topographic, habitat, and other data with existing land cover data. In highly urbanized Jackson

County, Missouri, additional work was completed to map urban forests. Aerial photographs were then used to refine the GIS-based maps with additional detail, with some modifications done by hand.

Stormwater and watershed management. The Kansas City region has focused substantial effort on using stormwater management tools to protect water quality, reduce the risk of flooding, and create multipurpose community assets like greenway corridors. Not coincidentally, these efforts also advance community forestry programs.

The land development (or redevelopment) process offers many creative opportunities for environmentally sensitive planning and design, whether for new residential or commercial development. Four new tools were jointly developed by area communities, along with the Kansas Chapter of the American Public Works Association, to facilitate this work (see www.marc. org/Environment/Water/local_gov.htm.)

First, new site planning and design guidelines were developed as part of a *Best Management Practices Manual for Protecting Water Quality.* Guidelines now adopted by many communities encourage (and in some instances require) development projects not to increase site runoff above predevelopment levels. These guidelines allow flexible use of a wide range of design practices; chief among them are more integrated site planning, and resource conservation to capture the functional benefits of natural systems.

Various LID strategies, which are closely aligned with urban forestry techniques, are included in this manual. These include planning to proactively conserve native soils and vegetation, restore stream buffers, or plant bioretention facilities and filter strips. Each practice includes detailed discussion of resource inventory needs, planting considerations, and maintenance requirements.

Second, detailed stormwater engineering standards, criteria, and specifications were designed to link engineering strategies with watershed plans. New specifications require consideration of water quality and stream stability and the protection of natural channels for drainage areas that exceed 40 acres (http://kcmetro.apwa.net/kcmetro/specs/APWA5600.pdf).

Similarly, engineering standards were developed for erosion and sediment control (http://kcmetro.apwa.net/kcmetro/specs/APWA5100.pdf). Design criteria, not surprisingly, focus on the need for increased planning, as "the critical process in which land-disturbing activities are formulated and [which] presents the opportune time to minimize impacts." The document includes detailed specifications for filter strips, vegetated stream buffers, tree protection, and permanent seeding with a variety of native plants. Adoption of these standards by communities across the metro area reflects a culture shift supportive of more environmentally friendly development practices.

Last, several communities have adopted stream setback ordinances, restricting development in areas that are prone to flooding or geotechnically unstable, or that include high-quality natural areas. These regulations reduce future liabilities for flood protection while creating valuable community amenities. Conservative estimates on a regional scale show that well more than 50,000 streamside acres are now protected through this mechanism in four unincorporated counties and several municipalities.

Importantly, nearly all of these efforts are conceptualized and implemented using creative partnerships among professional associations, local governments, private development interests, and community and environmental stakeholders. Over time, most of these tools will likely be adopted by the majority of area jurisdictions by ordinance or by administrative rule. Ever-increasing community support for use of these tools derives from their tech-

The Kansas City region has focused substantial effort on using stormwater management tools to protect water quality, reduce the risk of flooding, and create multipurpose community assets like greenway corridors.

nical legitimacy, strong professional education programs, and the strength of underlying collaborative planning processes.

Air quality. Kansas City, Missouri, recently completed a Phase One Climate Protection Plan. Each issue in it has dimensions that can be addressed at scale through comprehensive community forestry and green infrastructure efforts.

Trees provide air quality benefits through both prevention of emissions and metabolic uptake of pollutants. Shading, evapotranspiration (which results in local atmospheric cooling), and wind speed reduction provided by trees reduce energy expenditures, resulting in avoided power plant emissions. Further, trees actively remove ground-level ozone, nitrogen dioxide, sulfur dioxide, and carbon dioxide from the air through metabolic processes. Particulate matter is intercepted by tree surfaces.

Efforts to expand tree inventories and to develop new air quality models will complement regional green infrastructure planning, helping to cut energy use and reduce air pollution. A recent analysis to assess the environmental benefits of city-managed trees in Kansas City, Missouri, demonstrates the substantial air quality benefits of this small subsection of the urban forest. The USDA Forest Service STRATUM model estimates that city-owned street trees reduce carbon dioxide by 127,990 tons annually and other air pollutants by 423 tons annually.

Lessons learned. Common themes in the planning literature reflect the importance of creative partnerships and integrative, collaborative planning. This case study affirms the importance of those issues. Importantly, regional planning efforts are substantially strengthened by a number of state, nonprofit, and corporate efforts.

One notable factor is the relative lack of participation by planners or foresters in the development of the tools described in this case study. Substantially increased involvement by planners in environmental issues, and by foresters in urban issues, would provide invaluable benefits. One might plausibly argue that regional forestry and green infrastructure plans could be designed to comply with the majority of federal air and water quality regulations. A test of this hypothesis at the regional scale will require even greater multi-sector collaboration.

CHAPTER 4

Conclusions and Recommendations

By Cheryl Kollin and James C. Schwab, AICP

Elected officials and municipal planning agencies must balance regional and community growth with environmental quality. While this broad goal is written into many comprehensive plans, implementing it is not easy. Urban forestry is still frequently an afterthought in the process of implementing comprehensive plan goals. Often, there is a fundamental disconnect between the community's vision of environmental quality and the ecosystem functions and services that are the cornerstone for achieving environmental quality and sustainable development.

FRAMING THE ISSUES WITH GREEN INFRASTRUCTURE

Developing robust green infrastructure in cities and counties surrounding an urban core is a good technique for improving the environmental quality and economic viability of the community and the region. Connecting the trees, parks, and other urban green infrastructure at site and neighborhood scales to the surrounding waterways and other regional green infrastructure networks may well become the next great frontier in planning and government services.

Site-specific green infrastructure strategies like Low-Impact Development (LID) are just beginning to supplement traditional, engineered (gray infrastructure) methods of controlling stormwater runoff and improving air and water quality. The need to pay greater attention to how the entire development footprint supports stormwater management and human health is also leading to new initiatives, such as the Leadership in Energy and Environmental Design–Neighborhood Development (LEED-ND), a new certification developed by the U.S. Green Building Council, the Natural Resources Defense Council, and the Congress for New Urbanism. The new LEED-ND, which is patterned after the successful LEED certification for buildings, broadens the architectural scale to evaluate the site-level environmental quality of projects.

Even in communities that have adopted LID or LEED standards, few municipal agencies have the capacity to measure and monitor how well green infrastructure is helping the community meet environmental quality goals. This chapter offers strategies and examples of how to frame planning and development issues in the context of using green infrastructure to meet those goals. The strategies can help planners and local leaders translate goals into policies and implementation methods. Southeast Michigan provides a good example. This nine-county region surrounding Detroit has a host of serious environmental quality issues to tackle in light of the region's demographic and land-use changes. The following statistics from the Southeast Michigan Council of Governments (SEMCOG), the U.S. Environmental Protection Agency (EPA), the *Detroit Free Press*, and American Forests articulate these issues:

- Between 1990 and 2000, the amount of land converted to development in Southeast Michigan grew three times faster than the population (SEMCOG 2003).

- Tree cover and open space in three watersheds—Ecorse, St. Claire, and Rouge—declined significantly between 1991 and 2002. This change resulted in increased stormwater runoff and decreased air and water quality (American Forests 2006).

- In an effort to clean up the most polluted areas in the Great Lakes, EPA has identified the Detroit River, the St. Clair River, and the Rouge River as "Areas of Concern." Their priorities include control of combined sewer overflows (CSOs), control of sanitary sewer overflows (SSOs), and point/nonpoint-source pollution controls (EPA 1998).

- Twenty-five counties near urban areas in Michigan are currently classified as "nonattainment" areas for two air pollutants: ozone and particulates (2.5 microns or less in size). If not addressed, noncompliance with federal clean air regulations could jeopardize federal funding for highways (EPA 2006).

- SEMCOG estimates that it will cost $14 billion to $26 billion over the next 30 years to address the overflow and capacity problems of handling stormwater and sewage (SEMCOG 2003).

- Between 1950 and 1990, the city of Detroit lost half of its tree canopy due to Dutch elm disease, development, and poor maintenance. In the last few years, Emerald ash borer killed 16 million trees statewide, further decreasing the city's tree canopy (*Detroit Free Press* 2006).

• In Detroit, 4,600 acres (66,000 lots) of previously developed land are now vacant as development shifts to suburbs (SEMCOG 2003).

While these statistics highlight serious environmental, economic, regulatory, and planning problems affecting quality of life for Michigan residents and businesses, restoring the region's green infrastructure can tie all of these seemingly disparate issues together. Connecting to and stepping down to the city scale, green infrastructure can also add value to both revitalization and new development. Incorporating urban forestry into redevelopment is a means of enhancing green infrastructure and creating neighborhood vitality. The vision of Detroit's local leaders for a revitalized city offers opportunities to do just that.

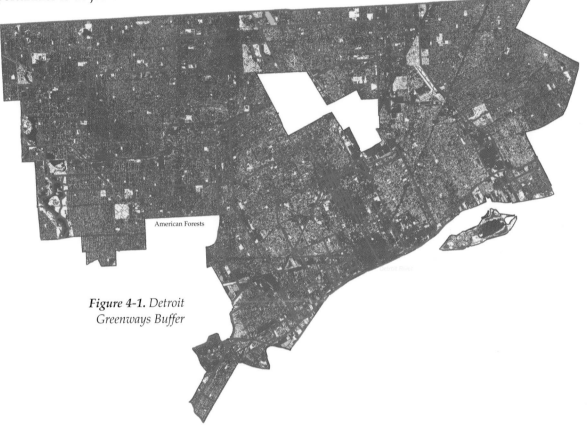

American Forests

Figure 4-1. *Detroit Greenways Buffer*

An example of a land-use revitalization project that could enhance green infrastructure in Detroit is the development of greenways. SEMCOG, the city of Detroit, the Greening of Detroit, and other Southeast Michigan communities have embarked on establishing a regional greenways system that ties several natural systems together. Greenways serve as ideal locations to reestablish and enhance green infrastructure. For example, the Dequindre Cut Greenway (Figure 4-2), an abandoned railroad right-of-way, is slated for phased implementation as a pedestrian and possible light rail corridor. If tree canopy were increased from an existing 31 percent to 40 percent within this 130-acre area, the greenway would reduce the amount of stormwater the city must manage by an additional 92,000 cubic feet at a value of $184,000. If all of Detroit's envisioned greenways were increased from their current 19 percent tree canopy to 25 percent, the green infrastructure of this 3,251-acre area could store an additional 1 million cubic feet of stormwater, valued at $2 million (UEA SE Michigan and Detroit 2006).

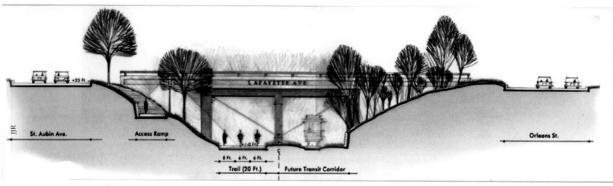

Figure 4-2. The proposed Dequindre Cut Greenway plan for Detroit includes a vegetated buffer, which provides an ideal location for increasing the city's tree canopy. This design was used in the greenway modeling.

The city of Detroit's Riverfront Conservancy is in the process of transforming the riverfront's industrial brownfields into commerce, housing, and recreation. The revitalization has attracted people back to the Detroit River, considered the "heart and soul of Detroit."

Developing a Robust Green Infrastructure by Establishing Tree Canopy Goals

A first step in reincorporating green infrastructure into a community's planning framework is to measure urban forest canopy and set canopy goals. As discussed in Chapter 1, tree canopy is one measure of environmental quality because a sufficient tree canopy can slow stormwater runoff, improve air and water quality, and absorb atmospheric carbon through a process called sequestration. Maintaining a robust tree cover to function as green infrastructure reduces the need and expense of building gray infrastructure to manage air and water resources.

Separate studies conducted by American Forests and the U.S. Department of Agriculture Forest Service estimate that tree canopy cover in urban areas east of the Mississippi has declined by about 30 percent over the last 20 years while the footprint of urban areas has increased by 20 percent. This decline in tree cover is associated with changing land use and the fragmentation of natural systems. It has resulted in significant increases in energy consumption and air and water management costs.

American Forests, the U.S. Conference of Mayors, the Arbor Day Foundation, and many other organizations support climate mitigation strategies that call for planting more trees. American Forests is among the private organizations that recommend every city set a tree canopy goal as an important step in ensuring that this part of its valuable green infrastructure is maintained at minimum thresholds, as the community continues to develop. American Forests offers some general guidelines for canopy goals based on climate conditions and zoning categories (Table 4-1). The

A. *For metropolitan areas east of the Mississippi and in the Pacific Northwest*	
Average tree cover counting all zones	40
Suburban residential zones	50
Urban residential zones	25
Central business districts	15

B. *For metropolitan areas in the Southwest and dry West*	
Average tree cover counting all zones	25
Suburban residential zones	35
Urban residential zones	18
Central business districts	9

American Forests

Table 4-1. American Forests' Tree Canopy Goals.

organization stresses, however, that each community must first inventory its tree canopy cover and then set specific goals based upon its unique combination of climate, geography, land use, and political conditions. Once a specific goal is determined, the local government can pursue that goal using policies, procedures, and budget.

Creating Public Policies that Incorporate Green Infrastructure

While cities and counties generally approve and implement development projects one at a time, having a green infrastructure component for the city or regional comprehensive plan establishes an overall development policy framework. This is especially important because environmental issues like clean water and clean air cross political boundaries. A green infrastructure component links the natural elements of the regional landscape, including streams, forests, and working lands, to the systems of parks, trails, street trees, and other companion elements in cities and communities. Such a plan would provide a strategic framework for tree planting and setting regional tree canopy goals that are appropriate and achievable. Once regional councils (e.g., Councils of Governments (COGs)) establish areawide canopy goals, local governments can use these as a basis to establish their own local canopy goals.

Often, environmental quality targets or goals are cited in local master plans, zoning ordinances, stormwater management plans, natural areas plans, tree and woodland protection ordinances, or other legal documents. Many agencies, however, fail to measure whether their implementation strategies are meeting these stated goals. Once planners begin to measure the ecosystem benefits of green infrastructure, they can better evaluate success and adjust strategies as needed (e.g., see the Baltimore County, Minneapolis, and McDowell Creek Watershed case studies in Chapter 3). In addition to the ability to measure success, project costs can be more easily justified when they can be linked to benefits derived from specific green infrastructure implementation strategies.

The sidebar on this page lists some ways of including the urban forest and its tree canopy into existing public policies, helping establish and manage local and regional green infrastructure.

RECOMMENDATIONS

A primary purpose of assembling a significant series of case studies for this report was to subject our assumptions and principles to what actually seems to work in real communities developing their own urban and community forestry programs. This might be regarded in some ways as a more abstract form of adaptive management: determining not only how best to manage the urban forest in a specific setting by learning over time, but also how best to manage urban forestry programs by looking at the successes and challenges of communities experimenting with new approaches across the country, under a wide variety of circumstances. From those case studies, we distilled the following recommendations.

Create Stable and Adequate Funding

Every program requires adequate, stable funding. In some cases, achieving funding stability may simply be a matter of the local governing body, and by extension the public, remaining committed to allocating sufficient sums from general funds year in and year out. While such support could dwindle in hard times, the potential for urban forestry becoming a target for budget cutting is most likely to depend on perceptions of its benefits to the community. In other words, stable support is generated by a long-term track record of documenting and disseminating those benefits.

PLAN REGIONALLY, IMPLEMENT LOCALLY, TEST THE RESULTS

- In counties that share watersheds, plan collaboratively to ensure water quality downstream. Work through regional council (e.g., COG) to establish an overall tree canopy goal for the region.

- Use regional tree canopy goals as a framework to set compatible local canopy goals.

- Stratify local tree canopy goals by land use. If canopy is lower in one area, then set standards in other areas to reach the overall regional or citywide canopy goal.

- Include metrics for quantifying environmental quality goals in ordinances, plans, and guidelines. Acquire high-resolution aerial or satellite imagery that is classified into land cover categories—creating a green data layer.

- Use the modeling capabilities of green infrastructure software (e.g., CITYgreen) when looking at land-use planning alternatives. Test the impacts of changing tree canopy, impervious surfaces, and other land covers under different development scenarios with environmental quality objectives.

- Assess potential land cover changes and development options. Quantify the environmental benefits of land cover to see if the development option meets stated environmental goals.

- Designate green infrastructure as a public utility (just as gray infrastructure is) in the budget process.

But that is not the only way. Many leaders in urban and community forestry have discovered that stability and innovation, far from being at odds with each other, can be great complements. Innovative approaches to making urban forestry more self-sufficient in funding and less dependent on general revenues have often served to stabilize funding for local programs. Enterprise funding, as with the Landscape Recycling Center in Urbana, Illinois (see that case study in Chapter 3), serves to demonstrate to elected officials that such programs can generate revenue as well as use it. Successful urban forestry program managers in the future may well have an entrepreneurial streak as well as a green thumb.

Identify a Big Enough Vision for the Urban Forest

This report has identified numerous benefits of the urban forest. There is no good reason to think that the urban forest does not have a major role to play in enhancing public welfare. It is important to use some of the tools (e.g., Urban Ecosystem Analysis and similar programs) that American Forests and others have used to help communities document these values in concrete ways, but those numbers must be translated into visions that the public will understand. Do not lose your vision in a forest of technical jargon.

Establishing the role of the urban forest in the public mind will often require some civic and political boldness in laying out a large enough vision so that the community sees urban forestry as an essential component of many of its most cherished public policy goals, such as a cleaner environment, more attractive and livable neighborhoods, and public spaces that help drive economic development. Clearly, these grand visions are lending enormous weight to forestry programs and goals in places like Baltimore County, Minneapolis, and Olympia, Washington, which are linking those visions to the community's policy goals.

Make the Urban Forest an Asset

Positioning the urban forest as an asset in the minds of citizens and elected officials requires more effort than simply assigning management to the city agency responsible for the program. This recommendation is related to but not exactly the same as identifying a vision. It is a matter of changing perceptions. Until the 1990s, most public officials saw urban forestry programs as cost centers that yielded some benefits in terms of aesthetics but which were expendable when the time came to tighten the budget. In many communities, this perception persists. Advocates for the utility of the urban forest have worked hard to reorient that perception so that urban forestry is seen as a sound and even a preferred investment in the community's future, providing valuable insurance against impacts of climate change, stormwater runoff, air pollution, and even the social malaise triggered in treeless public housing environments. Trees are not merely amenities; they are assets that pay regular dividends when well managed. As such, the urban forest should become a magnet for public investment.

Pay Attention to the Details

Beyond every big vision lies the challenge of implementation. Making a program successful means ensuring it is staffed by people with appropriate credentials to know what works and what does not. It means drafting standards, ordinances, and other regulatory tools crafted to achieve precise objectives based on sound research and documented successes. And it means insisting that the program include adequate personnel for plan review, construction monitoring, and enforcement of any requirements regarding trees throughout the development process. Trees require careful planting of the right species in the right places, with careful management, and a willingness to quickly remove those trees that cease to provide the intended benefits, whether due to disease, storm damage, or the need to remedy past mistakes. As in the case of Urbana, a well-managed, well-planned, cost-saving program will become its own best argument for ongoing public support.

Seize the Day (Carpe Diem)

This old Latin slogan applies to many opportunities in the field of planning, but planners and urban foresters need to hitch their wagons to the horses that are winning the race in establishing priorities for public policy. Urban forestry, after all, is versatile. As discussed, it can help solve many problems. In the political world of public decision making, planners and foresters need to be sensitive to which of those problems and resulting public policy priorities can help advance urban forestry goals. This is the central point behind the discussion of public policy drivers. Does the community have an urgent need to improve stormwater management and reduce flooding? Show how urban forestry can play a role. As in Emeryville, California, does the community need to redevelop abandoned sites, including brownfields, in order both to revive the local economy and improve its physical appearance? Again, show how urban forestry can play a role. When opportunity presents itself to show why and how the urban forest can contribute to solving a problem, *seize the day*.

A Green Infrastructure Element
in a Comprehensive Plan

By Donald C. Outen, AICP

In concept, planners understand that the local comprehensive plan spatially covers a jurisdiction's or planning area's built and undeveloped landscapes. While planning has traditionally considered managing elements of the built environment, especially urban land uses and public infrastructure, including transportation and water and sewerage facilities, to accommodate projected demands for population and economic growth, the spaces within and outside the planning area that are not intensively developed have not been "planned." They have instead often been viewed as areas for future planning as growth progresses. Even in jurisdictions where tools such as growth boundaries have been used, the focus has traditionally been on the need to control and to manage urban development, and less so on the values of the areas outside the urban envelope.

Green infrastructure is the term applied to undeveloped lands with high value for their environmental and open space functions. Green infrastructure most commonly refers to forest systems, especially in relationship to the water environment (e.g., wetland and stream systems) and open water bodies (e.g., bays, lakes, and water supply reservoirs). In areas where the forest is not the indigenous vegetative land cover, green infrastructure concepts are still applicable to grasslands or mixed shrub landscapes. This outline of planning for green infrastructure assumes a forest setting because it is the most common.

The premise for green infrastructure planning is that the forest and other vegetative elements of the landscape have important functional values that should be recognized and protected. This appendix offers a primer about green infrastructure planning and is presented as an annotated outline for how communities can compose a comprehensive plan element. Examples of useful, Internet-accessible tools and resources are provided.

GREEN INFRASTRUCTURE ABCs

Understanding the Basis for Green Infrastructure Planning

While all vegetated areas are, in concept, part of an area's green infrastructure, the core of green infrastructure planning involves protecting the forest and vegetated areas with the highest value for providing critical ecosystem functions. These functions include providing wildlife habitat and contributing to clean water and clean air, and they are therefore based in an understanding of ecological process. Fortunately, much work has been done on this subject, and planners have ample sources of information from which to draw regarding the rationale for such planning. Many excellent sources can be identified using Internet search engines. A few examples of excellent sources that cover the scientific rationale and examples of their application suitable for planners include:

- Meyer, Judy L., et al. 2003. *Where Rivers Are Born: The Scientific Imperative for Defending Small Streams and Wetlands*. American Rivers and Sierra Club. (www.sierraclub.org/cleanwater/reports_factsheets/defending_streams.pdf)

- The Biodiversity Partnership (www.biodiversitypartners.org/)

- Duerksen, Christopher, and Cara Snyder. 2005. *Nature-Friendly Communities: Habitat Protection and Land Use Planning*. Island Press. (www.naturefriendlytools.org/book.html)

- Benedict, Mark, and Edward McMahon. 2006. *Green Infrastructure: Linking Landscapes and Communities*. Island Press. (http://conservationfund.org/pubs_product_list/131)

- North East Community Forests. *Green Infrastructure Planning Guide.* (www.greeninfra-structure.eu/images/GREEN_INFRASTRUCTURE_PLANNING_GUIDE.pdf)

Obtaining Data for Delineating Green Infrastructure Elements

The next step after understanding why green infrastructure should be an element of the local comprehensive plan is to gather relevant information and data to delineate what constitutes green infrastructure in a particular planning area. As green infrastructure elements often exist and function on landscape scales, especially in watershed contexts, it is important to be aware of how the green infrastructure in a community might be linked to that in the region. Some states and ecoregion restoration programs have identified wetlands, forests, streams, and sensitive habitats, and have mapped these elements. For example, information about relevant state-level projects in Florida, Oregon, Washington, Maryland, New Jersey, Massachusetts, and other states is available through the Biodiversity partnership (see: http://biodiversitypartners.org/pubs/landuse/07.shtml#flen).

State and regional sources should be investigated and may provide useful data for communities that do not have advanced levels of data or analytical capabilities. Contacting state agencies (natural resources, environment, or planning) and restoration partnership initiatives (e.g., the Chesapeake Bay Program) prevents duplication of effort but also re-inforces an important characteristic of the green infrastructure concept: linkages between elements and places. These structural habitat approaches are useful because data on individual species and guilds are often lacking or are protected by conservation organizations that seek to minimize disturbances. These approaches also address concerns that focusing only on rare or threatened species often ignores the fact that the majority of the landscape not only provides habitat for common species but also functions to provide the bulk of ecosystem services for clean water and clean air at watershed scales.

Green infrastructure planning will be most effective if done at the largest spatial scale possible (smallest land unit) and if done using Geographic Information System (GIS) tools. If the industry standard ArcGIS (www.esri.com/products.html) is not available, free (see http://freegis.org) or alternative GIS software such as Idrisi (www.clarklabs.org/) or even noncomputerized map overlays can be used. An alternative approach is to partner with the next larger unit of government or universities for analysis of spatial data about forest and other land covers. Federal resource agencies are also a good source of data, including:

- U.S. Geological Survey's Integrated Vegetation Mapping Viewer (http://gisdata.usgs.gov/Website/IVM/);

- U.S. Environmental Protection Agency's National Land Cover Data (www.epa.gov/mrlc/nlcd.html); and

- USDA Forest Service's Resources Planning Act (RPA) Assessment (www.fs.fed.us/research/rpa/).

Overall, GIS data that are most useful for green infrastructure analysis, in general order of priority, include: land cover (with forest areas delineated as vector (polygon) features through digitization or as raster (grid cell) features through multi-spectral classification); watershed and subwatershed boundaries; stream center-lines; ownership (public or private or protective conservation easements); zoning; and a cadastral layer (property parcels). A relatively sophisticated landscape-level pattern analysis of forest-based green infrastructure can be performed with these few data layers. This analysis is the next step in green infrastructure planning.

THE PRIORITY GREEN INFRASTRUCTURE NETWORK

Analyzing the Green Infrastructure Resource Network

While all vegetated areas, including urban open spaces and even street trees, are part of a community's green infrastructure, larger areas (e.g., forests with high structural diversity) provide the greatest set of ecological benefits. The objective of analyzing the priority network is to identify those green infrastructure elements with the greatest number of multiple ecosystem benefits. In ecological terms, simple rules of thumb based on research include that "bigger is better." Using GIS, it is possible to identify core green infrastructure areas, often called "hubs," and connecting linear features called "corridors." While the size of these elements is always relative to local settings, regional-scale hubs are often considered to be contiguous areas about 500 acres or larger, and corridors are considered linear features with widths of 200 or more feet, especially if along streams.

At the simplest level, GIS can be used to delineate the size of forest patches and thereby distinguish the ecological "workhorses" of the landscape from isolated, fragmented patches. In the fragmented forest of the eastern U.S., significant patches may be as small as 200 or 300 acres, while many types of forest-dependent wildlife (e.g., forest-interior-dwelling birds) will be associated with forest blocks of 1,000 acres or more. An intermediate-level GIS analysis of forest-based green infrastructure would overlay the local stream system on the land cover and identify forest patches that cover the greatest percentage of the riparian system within a defined watershed. An advanced GIS analysis might include: (1) an entire landscape typology of forest patches that considers, statistically, variation from the mean using the ArcGIS Jenks optimization (see http://blog.aggregatedintelligence.com/2005/08/jenks-optimization-method.html for an explanation) or "natural breaks" classification of output data; or (2) a typology of forest patches according to multiple factors, including patch size as a percentage of watershed forest cover, percentage of stream system covered by the patch, and percentage of patch area with "interior" forest (defined generally as a 300-foot to 500-foot edge, or using a calculated metric, such as perimeter-to-edge ratio or interior-to-edge ratio). These metrics help determine the habitat value of forest patches for many forest-dependent species and can be useful where specific data on wildlife are not available.

Useful data are also available from federal and state natural resource agencies. Forest-interior-dwelling birds are an excellent indicator of high-function habitat, and many states have accessible data on presence of various bird species from breeding bird surveys or "at-lases," part of the U.S. Geological Survey's Gap Analysis Program (see www.gapanalysis.nbii.gov/portal/server.pt; also see the GAP for Community Planning and Maps, Data, and Reports pages). County-level data for a number of forest species, forest health and response to stressors, and general measures of sustainability are available through the U.S. Department of Agriculture Forest Service's Forest Inventory and Analysis (FIA) (http://fia.fs.fed.us/) and Forest Health Monitoring (FHM) programs (http://fhm.fs.fed.us/index.shtm and, for example, reports for 20 northeastern states at: http://fhm.fs.fed.us/pubs/tp/dist_cond/dc.shtm). Surveys are also now including measures of tolerance to air quality stressors such as ozone through measurement of forest lichens.

Valuing and Interpreting Green Infrastructure

Because land as a resource is often described in terms of economic value, it can be helpful to determine the economic value of green infrastructure. Most valuation approaches for green infrastructure seek to estimate the dollar value of the ecosystem services provided by natural resources in terms of human needs, such as stormwater benefits, energy savings, or air quality. A number of useful tools available to planners have been used at multiple spatial scales. For calculating the hydrologic and financial benefits at the development site level of using various "green inventions" (e.g., downspout diversions, green roofs, additional canopy cover, native landscaping, porous pavement, and natural swales), the Center for Neighborhood Technology provides an on-line "Green Values Stormwater Calculator" (http://greenvalues.cnt.org/calculator). For valuing urban tree canopy across a larger area, grant or capital funds can be used to contract for assessments of stormwater, energy, carbon storage, and air quality benefits of urban tree canopies using the American Forests' CITYgreen model (www.amfor.org/productsandpubs/citygreen/) or the USDA Forest Service's Urban Forest Effects (UFORE) model (www.itreetools.org/urban_eco-system/introduction_step1.shtm). Planners can also obtain quick estimates of total forest carbon for an individual county, set of counties in a state, or entire state using the USDA Forest Service's Carbon On-Line Estimator (COLE) (http://ncasi.uml.edu/COLE/), and filters can be applied to segment the analysis by forest ownership group, forest type group, stand size, stand age, and others.

Whether or not planners are able to do a specific economic analysis of the value of the green infrastructure, they can at least appreciate that vegetation nevertheless provides tangible ecosystem services because of inherent ecological processes described above. The green infrastructure element is intended to interpret the value of vegetation with respect to relative importance to the community. Think of green infrastructure as a life support system and ask where retaining and restoring forest cover would be most important. Because forests stabilize watershed hydrology by reducing the "flashiness" of stormwater discharge and ensuring more consistent long-term groundwater discharge, they protect all the values associated with stream systems. And they protect against the dysfunction associated with their absence, including higher rates of erosion and sedimentation, loss of stable and diverse habitat for aquatic resources, loss of leaf litter for the food chain, increase in water temperature, and so on. So green infrastructure often looks to the connection of forest to the water system as a high priority, including "buffers" along streams and surrounding reservoirs.

A GREEN INFRASTRUCTURE ELEMENT IN THE COMPREHENSIVE PLAN

Incorporating the Green Infrastructure Element

Once planners identify and map potential green infrastructure features, those features can be integrated with the other elements of the comprehensive plan, especially the land-use plan. Green infrastructure areas should be overlaid on the land-use map, and areas of conflict with proposed development should be identified. Existing and planned road corridors should also be evaluated, as well as the overall zoning classifications. If green infrastructure areas are understood as critical life support for a community and as areas where ecological functions provide measurable benefits, disturbances of these areas by development are understood as loss of function and value. Wherever possible, the urban land pattern should be revised to avoid development conflicts with priority green infrastructure hubs and corridors. "Keep forest areas forest" is a prime tenant of green infrastructure planning. Some excellent studies at landscape levels (e.g., *The State of Chesapeake Forests*, www.chesapeakebay.net/stateoftheforests.htm) have demonstrated that, in addition to significant levels of historic conversion of forests to nonforest cover, land development through zoning represents a significant potential for future conversion.

Protection of green infrastructure elements through the comprehensive plan is the most cost-effective means to ensure future benefits, and this reduces recurring conflicts later at the site plan stage. As local governments are increasingly being identified as responsible parties for implementing pollution control and ecosystem restoration mandates, such as for ozone nonattainment or stormwater runoff pollution (Phase 1 and Phase 2 under the National Pollutant Discharge Elimination System (NPDES) Municipal Separate Storm Sewer System (MS4) permits, and Total Maximum Daily Load (TMDL) implementation), forests and other green infrastructure features need to be viewed as strategic tools for compliance. The green infrastructure pattern will also reveal areas with potential to expand and connect smaller fragments of forests and wetlands. Closing "gaps" in green infrastructure results in an interconnected network of high-function open spaces that better protect water quality and provide increased interior habitat over the long term. Guides are available for effective strategies for increasing forest cover (see the Center for Watershed Protection's *Urban Watershed Forestry Manual, Part 1: Methods for Increasing Forest Cover in a Watershed*, www.cwp.org/forestry/index.htm#part1).

Protecting Green Infrastructure: Plan Policy

Ideally, not only will the comprehensive plan depict the green infrastructure network graphically, but it will also include policies and recommendations for program enhancements to effectively protect green infrastructure on the ground. The most effective protection is to ensure that critical elements of the green infrastructure network are not zoned for urban development. If such areas are already zoned for development prior to their identification, communities can consider Transfer of Development Rights (TDR) or Purchase of Development Rights (PDR) programs (a wealth of information about planning and zoning tools and their application is available through the American Planning Association's Planning Advisory Service).

Perhaps zoning classifications can be amended to include performance standards to protect the forested and wetland areas. Techniques include limiting the percentage of parcels where natural vegetation can be cleared to 5 percent to 10 percent; requiring setbacks or buffers of 100 feet or more along stream, wetland, and forest edges; or using net density approaches to reduce or eliminate density for those sensitive portions of properties, especially if density zoning (no minimum lot sizes) or clustering can be used to concentrate development in less sensitive portions of parcels. While clustering helps to protect contiguous forests as part of designated conservancy areas, it needs to consider other environmental conditions (e.g., well-to-septic system setbacks and groundwater yield in crystalline formations) such that lot sizes do not become unreasonably small to preclude long-term sustainability of residences on private systems.

Specific protective measures are not often clearly separated between zoning classifications and subdivision regulations. In one county, for example, separate subdivision regulations exist for stream buffers and forest conservation (pursuant to state laws). These regulations apply to all zoning classifications countywide as well as local resource conservation zoning classifications that restrict rural zoning density (net density) for large forest patches and stream buffers, or that restrict the percentage of vegetation that can be cleared for each lot. In more urban areas, green infrastructure protection may be achieved through existing floodplain protection ordinances that restrict building in the active floodplain or through municipal tree protection ordinances.

The comprehensive plan, as well as any zoning classifications and development regulations that protect green infrastructure, should include specific statements regarding the purposes for designating and protecting green infrastructure features and the green infrastructure network. Even though planning documents will contain clear definitions for elements, statements of legislative intent are important for affirming the functional values to the community from green infrastructure. In some areas, such statements make specific reference to national policy (e.g., the Clean Water Act's statement of purpose to protect and restore the chemical, physical, and biological integrity of water). Between plan updates and revisions, the adequacy of protection measures for green infrastructure should be evaluated and improved where possible. Performance standards (e.g., for canopy retention) and evaluation metrics can be useful tools for assuring long-term progress.

By identifying and protecting green infrastructure as an element of the local comprehensive plan, communities can ensure that the biological diversity of areas is reasonably protected and that critical ecosystem services for clean water and clean air, for which they increasingly are responsible parties, are a recognized part of community sustainability.

A Shorthand Guide to Exemplary Urban Forestry Comprehensive Plan Elements and Internet Resources

The overarching theme of this Planning Advisory Service Report has been the incorporation of urban forestry visions and concerns into the planning process, starting with the visioning process that helps identify community goals, to the comprehensive plan, to specific area and functional plans, and finally, to the implementation of such plans through regulations, incentives, and enforcement, including site plan review. The first part of this appendix contains examples of the successful incorporation of urban forestry into community plans, most particularly but not exclusively comprehensive plans, with website links to allow readers to access additional information. The examples include some of our case study communities but also others we examined in the course of compiling the report. Links to each of the plans are also provided.

COMMUNITY PLANS

ANN ARBOR, MICHIGAN
www.a2gov.org/PublicServices/FieldOperations/NaturalAreaPres/nap_main.html

AUSTIN, TEXAS
www.ci.austin.tx.us/parks/forestry.htm

BALTIMORE COUNTY, MARYLAND
www.baltimorecountymd.gov/Agencies/environment/workgroup/index.html

Baltimore County's Master Plan 2010 includes two relevant elements: Natural Environment, and Recreation and Parks. These elements tie into issues like forest restoration, which is discussed extensively in the case study in Chapter 3 of this report, and specific plans directed at forest sustainability. "Managing Forest Resources" is one of the issues highlighted in the Natural Environment element, while the Recreation and Parks element focuses on open space.

BOSTON
www.cityofboston.gov/parks/openspace_doc.asp

CHAPEL HILL, NORTH CAROLINA
www.townofchapelhill.org/index.asp?NID=149

EMERYVILLE, CALIFORNIA
www.ci.emeryville.ca.us/planning/pdf/stormwater_guidelines.pdf

FLAGSTAFF/COCONINO COUNTY, ARIZONA
Community Wildfire Protection Plan:
www.gffp.org/PDF_Pages/CWPP_Report.htm

Comprehensive Plan:
www.coconino.az.gov/comdev.aspx?id=142

The Flagstaff metropolitan area offers examples both in terms of comprehensive planning and visioning and with a hazard-specific plan. The 1996–1997 visioning document, "A Vision for Greater Flagstaff," includes "Healthy Forests" as one of its components and talks about managing the surrounding forest in "ways that are wise and sustainable," including selective logging and appropriate fire management practices.

Five elements of the Coconino County Comprehensive Plan are relevant: The Conservation Framework, Natural Environment, Parks and Recreation, Land Use, and the Implementation Plan. The Natural Environment element directly addresses forest ecosystem health, a central issue in wildfire mitigation. Parks and Recreation includes a section on federal and state lands, an important component of any strategy for managing the wildland/urban interface for wildfire management purposes. Flagstaff is also important because it was early in developing a Community Wildfire Protection Plan, a type of hazard mitigation plan fostered under the federal Healthy Forests Restoration Act of 2003, with support from the USDA Forest Service.

ITHACA, NEW YORK
www.ci.ithaca.ny.us/index.asp

KANSAS CITY (MID-AMERICA REGIONAL COUNCIL)
www.marc.org/Environment/Smart_Growth/index.htm

LOWER MERION, PENNSYLVANIA
www.lowermerion.org/planning/osp_intro.html

A remarkable example of a focused functional plan is the Township of Lower Merion's Open Space and Environmental Resource Protection Plan, issued in spring 2006. Printed in full color with elaborate maps and charts, it is a very thorough piece of work, organized into three sections dealing with Background, Analysis, and Recommendations.

McDOWELL CREEK, NORTH CAROLINA (WATERSHED MANAGEMENT PLAN)
www.charmeck.org/Departments/LUESA/Water+and+Land+Resources/Programs/Water+Quality/McDowell+Creek+Restoration.htm

MINNEAPOLIS
www.ci.minneapolis.mn.us/sustainability/urbantreecanopy.asp

The Minneapolis Plan, adopted in 2000, includes a chapter on Natural Ecology, which outlines 12 environmental goals for the city, one of which encourages the planting and preservation of trees and other vegetation, with the adoption of a tree preservation and replacement ordinance listed as its first implementation step.

OLYMPIA, WASHINGTON
www.olympiawa.gov/cityservices/urbanforest/

Chapter 10 of Olympia's comprehensive plan is Urban Forestry. It details a vision for the city's urban forest, the "Value of an Urban Forestry Program," and a substantial list of goals and policies for achieving the vision. It concludes with a series of ingredients for a forestry program. The level of detail supports the case study observation that, for Olympia, this is a significant local issue central to the city's identity.

PALM BEACH COUNTY, FLORIDA
www.co.palm-beach.fl.us/pzb/Planning/comprehensiveplan/tableofcontent.htm

The county's 1989 Comprehensive Plan includes a significant Conservation Element with five goals. The first four involve protection of: natural resources; native communities and ecosystems; surface water and groundwater quality and quantity; and air quality. The fifth goal concerns a linked open space network with greenways and wildlife corridors.

SALEM, OREGON
www.cityofsalem.net/

SANTA MONICA, CALIFORNIA
www01.smgov.net/osm/Trees/Mgmt_Plan/Complete.pdf

Santa Monica in 1999 adopted a Community Forest Management Plan, which states that it has a relationship that "in many ways supplements both the city's Open Space Element and the Parks and Recreation Master Plan" through specific policies related to the urban forest.

URBANA, ILLINOIS

www.ci.urbana.il.us/Urbana/

As noted in the case study in Chapter 3 of this report, Urbana's 2005 Comprehensive Plan includes Goal 14, focused on increasing the city's inventory of trees and maintaining Urbana's status as a "Tree City." In addition, some related themes are found in Goal 6, "Preserve natural resources."

A Guide to Organizational and Research Websites about Urban and Community Forestry

ALLIANCE FOR COMMUNITY TREES (HTTP://STREETS.ORG/SITE/INDEX.PHP)
The Alliance for Community Trees (ACT) is both the nucleus and catalyst for the fast-growing field of citizen forestry. Along with its 68 community-based member organizations nationwide, ACT's concern is the environment where 80 percent of Americans live and work—cities, towns, and villages. Through information sharing, training, technical assistance, policy and program development, and advocacy, ACT pulls together the pioneering work of citizen foresters across the country to improve the quality of life for all of us.

AMERICAN FORESTS (WWW.AMERICANFORESTS.ORG/)
American Forests is the nation's oldest nonprofit citizens' conservation organization. It is a world leader in planting trees for environmental restoration, a pioneer in the science and practice of urban forestry, and a primary communicator of the benefits of trees and forests.

CENTER FOR URBAN FOREST RESEARCH (WWW.FS.FED.US/PSW/)
One of 13 research work units affiliated with the Pacific Southwest Research Station, a U.S. Department of Agriculture (USDA) Forest Service organization. As part of the center's vision, it works to provide communities with an increased understanding and appreciation of the urban forest, and to encourage them to make an investment in the care and maintenance of community trees to ensure continued health of the urban forest.

CENTER FOR WATERSHED PROTECTION (WWW.CWP.ORG/)
The Center provides local governments, activists, and watershed organizations around the country with the technical tools for protecting some of the nation's most precious natural resources: streams, lakes, and rivers.

GREENINFRASTRUCTURE.NET (HTTP://GREENINFRASTRUCTURE.NET/)
Green infrastructure is our nation's natural life support system—an interconnected network of protected land and water that supports native species, maintains natural ecological processes, sustains air and water resources, and contributes to the health and quality of life for U.S. communities and people. The Conservation Fund and the USDA Forest Service cosponsor the site.

HUMAN DIMENSIONS OF URBAN FORESTRY AND URBAN GREENING (WWW.CFR.WASHINGTON.EDU/RESEARCH.ENVMIND/)
Based in the College of Forest Resources at the University of Washington, this organization promotes research about people's perceptions and behaviors regarding nature in cities.

I-TREE (WWW.ITREETOOLS.ORG/)
i-Tree is a state-of-the-art, peer-reviewed software suite from the USDA Forest Service that provides urban and community forestry analysis and benefits assessment. It currently integrates four urban and community forestry tools: UFORE (Urban Forest Effects Model), STRATUM (Street Tree Resource Analysis Tool for Urban Forest Managers), MCTI (Mobile Community Tree Inventory), and the Storm Damage Assessment Protocol.

INTERNATIONAL SOCIETY OF ARBORICULTURE (WWW.ISA-ARBOR.COM/)

The International Society of Arboriculture (ISA) has served the tree care industry for more than 80 years as a scientific and educational organization.

THE NATIONAL MAP (HTTP://NATIONALMAP.GOV/)

The National Map is a framework for geographic knowledge needed by the nation. It provides public access to high-quality geospatial data and information from multiple partners to help support decision making by resource managers and the public. The National Map is the product of a consortium of federal, state, and local partners who enhance the U.S.'s ability to access, integrate, and apply geospatial data at global, national, and local scales. The U.S. Geological Survey (USGS) is committed to meeting the nation's needs for current base geographic data and maps. Its vision is that, by working with partners, it will ensure that the nation has access to current, accurate, and nationally consistent digital data and topographic maps derived from those data.

NATIONAL URBAN AND COMMUNITY FORESTRY ADVISORY COUNCIL (WWW.TREELINK.ORG/NUCFAC/)

The National Urban and Community Forestry Advisory Council is an organization that supports education, projects, and groups related to urban and community forestry.

SOCIETY OF MUNICIPAL ARBORISTS (WWW.URBAN-FORESTRY.COM/MC/PAGE.DO)

The Society of Municipal Arborists (SMA) is an organization of municipal arborists and urban foresters. The membership also includes consultants, commercial firms, and citizens who actively practice or support some facet of municipal forestry.

TREELINK (WWW.TREELINK.ORG/)

TreeLink is an urban forestry portal. TreeLink's vision is to provide the best technology resources to grow the movement and discipline of urban and community forestry to the widest audience. It plans to expand the canopy of knowledge about urban and community forestry.

U.S. GEOLOGICAL SURVEY, COMPREHENSIVE URBAN ECOSYSTEM STUDIES (HTTP://ROCKYWEB.CR.USGS.GOV/CUES/COcuesHome.HTML)

The Comprehensive Urban Ecosystem Studies unit of the U.S. Geological Survey (USGS) uses USGS data and science expertise to develop decision support tools and other science applications to address critical issues facing the nation's urban areas, including the consequences of urban growth and the conservation and protection of parks, wildlife refuges, and other natural resources.

URBAN FORESTRY SOUTH (WWW.URBANFORESTRYSOUTH.ORG/)

Urban Forestry South is the Internet partnership of the Southern Center for Urban Forestry Research and Information, Southern Regional Extension Forestry, the Southern Group of State Foresters, and the Warnell School of Forest Resources at the University of Georgia. It also hosts the Southern Cooperative Council's work.

Establishing and Preserving
the Urban Forest

By R.J. Laverne

The path to healthy and functional urban forests begins with planting the right trees in the right places and continues with preserving existing natural resources. With proper planning and some help from well-designed tree ordinances, communities can maximize the benefits (while minimizing costs) provided by their urban forest.

TREE PLANTING GUIDELINES

The old Chinese proverb says, "The best time to plant a tree was 20 years ago. The second best time is now." So let's begin. But before we start digging the hole, let's talk a minute about the concept of plant health care. In a nutshell, if you select a plant that is well suited for the site, it will be healthier and more vigorous. Healthy plants usually repel insect pests or diseases more successfully than stressed plants. That means you will spend less money on chemicals, fertilizer, and water, and less time on trying to make the plant look good. Remember, the first (and most important) step in achieving a better landscape at a lower cost is proper plant selection and placement.

What should you consider? First, know what "plant hardiness zone" you are in. Plant hardiness zones are defined by the lowest temperature during an average winter. For example, Chicago (Zone 5) can expect to see temperatures as low as –10 to –20 degrees (Fahrenheit), but Atlanta (Zone 8) will normally only dip to 10 to 20 degrees above zero in the winter. Some tree species, such as paper birch (Betula papyrifera), are very hardy, but won't grow well in hot climates. Others, such as gumbo limbo (Bursera simaruba), like it hot, but quickly die when the mercury drops. A map of U.S. Department of Agriculture (USDA) plant hardiness zones can be found at www.usna.usda.gov/Hardzone/ushzmap.html. (It is worth considering that these zones could be altered in the future as a result of climate change.) Also, make sure that the trees you purchase were not originally grown at a nursery significantly south of your location. Individual trees that are acclimated to sprouting leaves early in the spring can be damaged by late frosts when planted too far north.

Next, consider your soils. You don't need a degree in chemistry or soil science to figure this part out, just a small shovel and a plastic bag. Scoop up enough soil from the first eight to 10 inches down, not just surface soil, to fill half a gallon-size storage bag. Call your local county extension office and find out where to send soil samples for testing.

When you send in your soil samples, tell them you just need to know the pH (how acidic or alkaline the soil is) and texture (is it sandy, silty, loam, or clay?). Just as some plants prefer cold or hot temperatures, some species like acidic soils and some like more alkaline. For example, if you plant pin oaks (Quercus palustris) in alkaline soils, they will have small, yellowish leaves and look sickly. Selecting a different oak that prefers alkaline soils, such as burr oak (Quercus macrocarpa), can make all the difference in how the tree performs. Similarly, different species prefer different textures of soil because texture influences how well a site drains water. Jack pines (Pinus banksiana) love sandy dry soil, so consider another species like bald cypress (Taxodium distichum) if your site has heavy soils and is poorly drained.

And finally, select your new trees for the available space. Know how big the tree will be at maturity, and don't plant it any place smaller than the expected mature dimensions. This is particularly important when the planting site is near utility lines.

One last tip: diversify! If your community is already loaded with maples and oaks, try something different. Having a broad range of genera and species of varying ages will not only make your landscape more interesting, it will protect you from losing most of your trees should a genus-specific pest like Emerald ash borer come along. A good rule of thumb is that your tree population should include no more than 20 percent of a single genus (like maple), and no more than 10 percent of a single species (like red maple). This diversity should occur on each street as well as throughout the community. If you follow these easy guidelines, you will discover a fascinating variety of trees that will enhance your community and cost very little to maintain. There are a lot of great references to help you find the right trees. One of the best is *Trees for Urban and Suburban Landscapes* by Edward Gilman (1997).

John Davey, the father of arboriculture, expressed it best 125 years ago when he said, Do it right or not at all! This philosophy applies to many tasks, but none better than planting trees. Planting a tree properly is easy to do, yet improper tree planting may just be the most commonly encountered landscape problem we see in communities. Here are two good reasons to take a little extra time and effort when planting your landscape trees:

1. Planting the tree properly will result in your tree appreciating in value as it adds value to your landscape (a very smart investment).

2. Planting the tree improperly will result in you paying for it twice—once to put it in the ground and again to have it removed when it dies (a poor return on your investment).

Select the tree species to be planted according to the site conditions, including soil texture, pH, surrounding infrastructure, and drainage. Next, get good quality stock from the nursery. Reject trees that have co-dominant stems, poor branch attachments, and those that have small root masses. Once you have selected the perfect specimen for the site, it's time to dig the hole. But WAIT! Before you put the shovel in the ground, you need to know both the utility locations and what size the hole should be. Although this sounds trivial, it is critically important. Measure the width of the root ball and dig the hole three times as wide and bowl-shaped. Depth is a little more difficult, and it takes some investigation. A number of municipalities have taken detailed arboricultural standards for tree pruning, planting, and fertilization from existing American National Standards Institute (ANSI) standards and placed them in the appendix of a street tree ordinance as "Rules and Regulations for Arbor Work." All work on public trees would have to be done in accordance with these standards. The ordinance proper would define who would have the authority to changes these technical standards found within the appendix without public notice or hearing. The same strategy can be used for community tree plans and other technical documents.

The bottom of the root ball should sit on undisturbed soil so that it doesn't sink into the ground as the soil settles after the tree is planted. The root collar of the tree (the flare at the base of the trunk, if present) should be even or slightly above the original grade. If you plant the tree so that the top of the burlap is level with the ground, you have likely planted the tree several inches too deep. To see the root collar, you must open up the burlap and pull away the loose soil. Now measure the distance from the root collar to the bottom of the root ball. This is how deep your hole should be. Simply digging the hole to the proper depth can make the difference between your tree thriving or dying.

Now you're ready to place the tree in the hole. Caution! Do not pull the tree using the trunk as a handle! This can cause severe damage to the cambium (i.e., a layer of living cells, between the bark and hardwood, that each year produces additional wood and bark cells; this layer is responsible for the diameter growth of a tree). If the burlap and the twine have been removed from the top of the ball, the tree could become bare root if handled in this manner. Carefully maneuver the tree by lifting the root ball. When the tree is positioned in the hole, begin to add soil around the root ball. If the burlap ball is in a wire basket, the top two rings should be cut off and removed. Make sure that any rope is removed from the top of the burlap, and that tree wrap or protective tubing is removed from around the stem. If you feel that stakes are needed to secure the tree, be sure to use flexible ties between the tree and stakes. Do not use wire or ropes that constrict the stem.

After the backfill has been added and settled with plenty of water, add two to four inches of mulch evenly over the entire hole, but don't pile mulch around the root collar. Make sure to remove stakes and guy straps within one year. Record the installation date of your tree and inspect it next year before the warranty expires. With these few tips, you'll have more trees

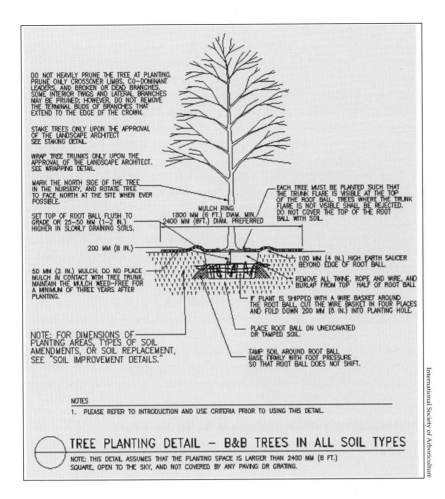

Figure D-1. *Tree planting specifications for balled-and-burlapped trees*

that survive and lower maintenance costs in the future. For more information on planting, visit the International Society of Arboriculture site (www.isa-arbor.com). Figure D-1 shows the proper methods to use when planting a balled-and-burlapped nursery tree.

TREE PRESERVATION: ASSETS VS. LIABILITIES

We will always need to replenish the urban forest with new trees, but preserving the existing trees is essential to maximizing the full range and duration of benefits provided by urban trees. Since large trees provide the most benefits to communities, it's important to protect them throughout their useful life. When trees cannot be preserved due to new development, it is also important for communities to be compensated a fair value for their loss so that new trees can be established in their place.

Before we get into the details of tree preservation, it is useful to understand that, from an urban forest management standpoint, only two kinds of trees exist: those that are assets and those that are liabilities. It is good to preserve the assets, and it is also good to remove the liabilities. Most trees start out as assets (although some can be liabilities right out of the gate). A tree that is an asset can change into a liability, and this change can be very slow (gradual decline from decay) or very rapid (severe structural damage from lightning). All trees are living organisms, and therefore all trees eventually die. So it is easy to see that a healthy, structurally safe tree can be an asset, but when that tree dies or is seriously damaged or decayed, it becomes a liability.

What determines if a tree is an asset or a liability? An asset is a tree that provides benefits greater than the costs of maintaining the tree. A liability is a tree that costs more to maintain than the value of the benefits or that presents unacceptable risks to public safety because of decay or other structural defects. What are some of the benefits provided by urban trees? The list is long and far-reaching, but the benefits can be organized into three groups: environmental, economic, and social (see Chapter 1 of this Planning Advisory Service Report). Some of these benefits are not easy to quantify in monetary terms, and therefore it may be difficult to compare the value of the benefits to the costs of maintenance. What are some of the costs of maintaining a tree? Once again we can look at environmental, economic, and social costs.

It is not always easy to determine if a tree is an asset or a liability; sometimes it depends on a particular person's or agency's perspective. For example, a black cherry tree may be providing beneficial shade to a building, but at the same time its messy fruit is staining the picnic table underneath it. For some people, the benefit of shade may be of greater value than the cost of cleaning up the fruit. For other people, this may not be so. Therefore, conflicts may arise in determining whether a tree is a net asset or a net liability, and also when deciding on whether preserving or removing a tree is the proper course of action. That's OK. Be flexible. Be open. Understand that changing something around the tree without changing the tree may allow the tree to be an asset. Moving the picnic table away from the black cherry tree, for example, solves most of the problem.

The take-home message is this: Tree preservation efforts, including municipal policies and ordinances, are most successful when they protect assets while allowing the removal of liabilities. Keep in mind that the problem causing the liability may be a conflict between the tree and the site that can be resolved without removing the tree. For example, it may be wiser to reroute the sidewalk around the tree than to cut off many roots for the sake of a straight sidewalk. The objective should be to maximize benefits, not just preservation of trees for preservation's sake. Sometimes this means it is best to protect existing trees, using due caution. Sometimes this means it is best to sacrifice existing trees and use the fair compensation or mitigation from their loss to establish new trees elsewhere, preferably with the benefits fully understood. Flexibility and creativity in site design are essential, especially in infill and other crowded development.

FUNDAMENTALS OF TREE PRESERVATION: WHAT WORKS AND WHAT DOESN'T

Organized efforts to preserve trees are usually born from the old proverb, "You don't know what you've got until it's gone," or at least until the trees are nearly gone. Rapid development along urban fringes, frequently referred to as "sprawl," is characterized by changes in land cover and land use. Typically, agricultural fields or undeveloped woodlands are converted to suburban residential or commercial land uses. Many local governments don't recognize the lost value of natural resources, including trees, until most of the woodlands are cleared, and then there is a desperate attempt to preserve the small areas of undisturbed forests that remain.

But it is not just undeveloped woodlands that need our attention. Individual trees in heavily developed areas may also be worthy of protection, particularly if they have historic significance or have attained remarkable age or size. Zoning that encourages infill and higher densities may fail to provide adequate space to preserve larger trees.

Also keep in mind that tree preservation efforts are not solely about preserving specific trees. Tree preservation efforts should be focused more on preserving the benefits that trees provide, recognizing that, even if a specific tree is lost, its benefits may be preserved by the establishment of new trees or the improved maintenance of existing trees. When it comes to balancing tree preservation with economic development, it pays to be flexible. Guard healthy and safe trees, be willing to negotiate options, and recover fair compensation when trees must be removed.

How can local governments effectively preserve valuable natural resources, particularly those that exist on private land? How can a local government be fairly compensated for the loss of trees when those trees are removed from private land? The answer to both questions is through the enactment of a tree preservation ordinance.

Some tips about successful tree preservation methods appear in the following two lists:

Tree Preservation That Works

- Focus tree preservation efforts on trees that are healthy and safe assets and that are likely to live a long time.

- Tree preservation rules should be made official through the adoption of a tree preservation ordinance.

- Tree preservation can be successfully implemented on private lands for many but not all land uses.

- Think of building the specifications for your tree preservation ordinance like a fish net that captures the resources that you wish to preserve while letting those of little value through the net.

- Tree preservation ordinances that apply to private lands must be flexible and reasonable.

- A person, office, or agency responsible for plan review, monitoring, and implementing tree preservation rules must be clearly identified.

- Penalties for failing to meet the provisions of a tree preservation ordinance must be clear, objective, reasonable, and legally defensible.

- Incentives such as fast-tracking permit applications when tree preservation is successfully implemented serve as welcome carrots.

- Remember that tree preservation is not just about keeping the trees you have. It is also about providing for new trees. Therefore, direct tree removal mitigation fines to a dedicated urban forestry fund.

Tree Preservation That Doesn't Work

- Preserving any and all trees for the sake of keeping them is unproductive. Construct your tree preservation guidelines to allow easy removal of liabilities.

- Tree preservation rules that are not given legitimacy through creation of a tree preservation ordinance will usually remain as optional guidelines that are largely ignored.

- Tree preservation laws can be very difficult to pass and enforce on occupied residential properties.

- If you try to preserve everything, you will quickly clog your administrative system with unintended consequences. Focus on those trees that are most important.

- Tree preservation ordinances that severely restrict development can be detrimental to economic growth.

- Tree preservation rules that are not clearly the responsibility of a public official or agency will be ignored.

- Penalties for failing to meet the provisions of a tree protection ordinance that are unreasonable or inconsistently applied are likely to fail legal scrutiny.

- All penalties (sticks) with no incentives (carrots) can lead to more challenges from developers.

- Fines for unlawful tree removal and development mitigation fees that go to the general fund are unlikely to be used for establishing new trees or maintaining existing public trees.

TREE PRESERVATION ORDINANCES

Many municipalities have found a very useful tool in tree preservation ordinances. When properly built and implemented, these local laws protect publicly owned trees and define the circumstances under which developers must preserve trees on private lands.

If properly designed, a tree ordinance can be an effective form of public policy that protects urban forest assets. There are several classes of tree ordinances. The most common type of ordinance is a "street tree" or "public tree" ordinance that applies only to trees growing on property owned by the jurisdiction that issues the ordinance (usually a municipal government). Street tree ordinances generally say that no one is allowed to damage or destroy a tree growing on public property, and then usually defines the penalty for infractions. Street tree ordinances may also list the species of trees that are allowed (or forbidden) to be planted on public property.

The following discussion will focus on another type of tree ordinance—the tree preservation ordinance. Tree preservation ordinances are usually zoning ordinances that apply to trees growing on publicly owned property as well as on some privately owned properties. The purpose of tree preservation ordinances is to prevent unnecessary damage to or destruction of trees during development, and to define some measure of compensation to the community for trees removed or damaged during construction. Most tree preservation ordinances do not apply to the maintenance of trees growing on occupied single-family residential properties. This avoids the usually unwanted consequence of requiring home owners to acquire permits for cutting down trees on their residential property.

But wait! Why should a local government be compensated for lost benefits of trees situated on private property? Doesn't the property owner own the trees? That is true. Some of the values of trees are indeed confined to the tree itself or to the immediate vicinity of the tree. For example, the market value of the wood from timber is a function of the tree itself and is therefore fully owned by the property owner. The direct shade cast by a tree is a highly local benefit.

But understand that many of the benefits provided by trees are not confined to property boundaries or even political boundaries. Take, for example, a tree growing on a slope next to a stream. The roots stabilize the slope and help prevent soil erosion, which has a direct effect on the stream's water quality downstream beyond the property boundaries. Trees that form a visual screen and noise barrier between an industrial site and a residential neighborhood affect the quality of the neighborhood and the property values even though the trees are located on the industrial property. At the largest scale, trees sequester carbon, which from the perspective of climate change has very far-reaching effects. Therefore, it is appropriate for a community to seek to preserve the benefits provided by trees that affect the community.

There are many variations of tree preservation ordinances that have been successfully adopted by municipalities. No two are exactly the same. And yet common threads appear in most of them. First, it is important that existing laws give authority or "enable" a local government to enact zoning and other ordinances that affect land use. State enabling legislation might be found under general laws pertaining to environmental protection, or under existing planning, zoning, or subdivision laws. Several state governments have passed legislation that allows or even requires local governments to implement tree preservation laws.

Another important provision of most successful tree preservation ordinances is a clear description of the purpose of the ordinance. No matter how precisely an ordinance is written, occasions will arise when it is not apparent if or to what extent an ordinance should be applied. A well-written section that articulates the purpose and objectives of the ordinance will allow administrators to understand the "spirit of the law" so that it can be implemented in the manner in which it was intended. From a planning perspective, it is particularly important to tie that purpose statement to the police power that allows local governments to protect the public health, safety, and welfare.

Let's look at an example from the mythical City of Sampleville. Here's a simple introductory statement that frames the objectives of a tree preservation ordinance:

> The City of Sampleville seeks to provide its citizens with a safe and viable community in which to live and work. Natural resources, including trees, play a vital role in public safety, and in the environmental and economic health and welfare of a community.
>
> Recognizing the wide range of environmental, economic, and social benefits provided by trees and natural resources, the City of Sampleville wishes to achieve preservation of natural resources for the health and safety of its citizens and economic growth through thoughtful development.

It is also important to define what is not intended to be affected by the ordinance and to clearly reiterate the objectives:

> It is not an objective of this ordinance to regulate the maintenance, disturbance, or removal of trees on currently developed and occupied residential property, or in commercial tree nurseries. Tree disturbance or removal on all other parcels within the City of Sampleville should consider the loss of benefits that trees provide to the community. Therefore, the purpose of this ordinance is to:
>
> - maximize the environmental, economic, and social benefits provided by trees in the City of Sampleville;
> - during the development process, preserve those trees that have the potential to provide such benefits to the community and to the landowner;

- preserve trees that have historical significance or have obtained outstanding dimensions or age relative to their species;

- establish new trees in areas that are understocked to mitigate the loss of trees during development and maintain a sustainable urban forest canopy within Sampleville;

- assist landowners and developers to achieve both economic and environmental management success through the thoughtful consideration of natural resource integration into flexible and creative development designs;

- provide guidelines and requirements for preparing tree preservation development plans for areas with existing trees, and tree establishment development plans for areas without existing trees; and

- establish a Sampleville Urban Forest Management Account and provide for its funding.

By seeking balance between economic development and environmental preservation, the interests of Sampleville's citizens will best be met.

These concise introductory statements make it clear that a primary purpose of this ordinance is to maximize and to balance the environmental, economic, and social benefits provided by trees in the City of Sampleville.

The next crucial step in designing the tree preservation ordinance is to decide which trees you wish to consider for preservation and which parcels you wish to consider regulating. (Once again, keep in mind it will be difficult to adopt and implement an ordinance that applies to all trees everywhere.) Think of this process as creating a fishing net. The size of the fish trapped by the net is determined by the size of the mesh of the net. Therefore you want to construct your net so that the types of fish you want are captured while the less significant fish pass through the net. For our tree preservation ordinance, we may want the small parcels and less significant trees to slip through the provisions of the ordinance, but we want to efficiently net the larger parcels and highly significant trees.

In some cases, the benefits we wish to preserve may be provided by a single significant tree. In other cases, the benefits may best be provided by groups of trees that by themselves are not necessarily significant, but collectively provide an important function such as slope stabilization. And in areas where there are few trees, environmental and economic health may benefit by the establishment of new trees.

Let's return to Sampleville's Tree Preservation Ordinance to see how they built their fishing net. Since the purpose of this ordinance is to preserve the benefits and functions that existing trees provide and also to provide new benefits of trees to areas without trees, the scope of the ordinance is designed to include three specific goals:

1. Preservation of individual significant trees

2. Preservation of beneficial stands of multiple trees

3. Establishment of trees in nonforested areas

To guide the preservation of individual significant trees, the ordinance identifies specific species of trees worthy of consideration. It also addresses trees that are significant due to age, size, or historical significance, and it provides for the protection of individual trees important for wildlife habitat. In a similar fashion, the ordinance defines the attributes of stands of trees to be preserved. The characteristics to be considered include species composition, total area of the stand, percent of canopy coverage, and the size and density of the trees.

The City of Sampleville wants the small parcels and less significant trees to slip through the provisions of the ordinance, but it wants to efficiently net the larger parcels and highly significant trees. Ideally, it will also want to establish some overall tree canopy coverage goals to ensure the gains it seeks. In order to clarify the process for determining whether a tree or undeveloped parcel is to be included in the scope of the ordinance, a simple "fish net" series of questions can be used:

1. Is the parcel currently a developed and occupied residential lot?

   Yes. The provisions of this ordinance do not apply. No tree preservation plan is needed to remove trees.

No. Go to question 2.

2. Are there individual significant trees on the site? A significant tree meets the following criteria:

   - A significant tree is a species whose species rating is greater than 0.30 (30 percent) as listed in the Sampleville Arboricultural Standards Manual.

   - AND has a trunk diameter (DBH) equal to or greater than the minimum significant diameter as listed for that species in the Sampleville Arboricultural Standards Manual

   - OR is estimated by the Sampleville City Forester to be at least 100 years old

   - OR has known historical significance as determined by the Sample County Historical Society.

   No. Go to question 3.

   Yes. A tree preservation plan must be submitted to the City of Sampleville prior to removal of significant trees. Continue on with question 3 to determine if a preservation plan for stands of trees is also needed.

3. Is the parcel equal to or greater than 1 acre (43,560 square feet) in area?

   No. The parcel is smaller. A tree preservation plan is not needed for stands of trees.

   Yes. Go to question 4.

4. Are there more than 300 trees less than two inches caliper?

   - OR more than 50 trees between 2 inches caliper and 12 inches diameter (DBH)?

   - OR more than 10 trees greater than 12 inches diameter (DBH)?

   Yes. A tree preservation plan must be submitted and approved by the City of Sampleville prior to removal of any trees.

   No. Go to question 5.

5. Is the parcel equal to or greater than 10 acres in area?

   Yes. A tree establishment plan must be submitted and approved by the City of Sampleville.
   No. The parcel is less than 10 acres in size. A tree establishment plan does not need to be submitted.

Once a parcel has been identified as falling within the jurisdiction of the tree preservation ordinance, the property owner or developer is then required to submit a tree preservation plan before a permit will be provided to allow existing trees to be removed or pruned. The depth of detail will vary from community to community, but an inventory and map including information on the health and structure of significant individual trees and stands of trees should be prepared by a qualified forester or arborist. This should be accompanied by details of what trees are to be affected by development with descriptions of the tree preservation actions to be undertaken. Tree preservation plans usually must be approved by the city forester, tree board, or planning commission.

The best tree preservation ordinances recognize it is not necessary to preserve all trees and allow for desired types of development to take place. These ordinances place significant trees in the site design and review process. At the same time, when trees are destroyed during development, a good tree preservation ordinance provides methods for quantifying the value of the lost benefits provided by those trees and creates a mechanism for that value to be returned to the community. For example, an inventory of the trees lost during construction can be used to calculate a monetary value that fairly represents the lost benefits to the community. The developer may be required to pay that amount to the community for use in planting and maintaining trees within the community. The delicate trick is to develop a method that fairly translates the environmental, social, and economic value of trees into a dollar amount. For more information on this topic, visit the U.S. Forest Service i-Tree website at www.itreetools.org/.

The complete step-by-step methods for writing an effective tree preservation ordinance are outside the scope of this chapter, but an excellent discussion of the topic can be found in

Planning Advisory Service Report Number 446, *Tree Conservation Ordinances,* by Christopher Duerksen and Suzanne Richman. Another valuable resource is *Guidelines for Developing and Evaluating Tree Ordinances* (Swiecki and Bernhardt 2001), available through the International Society of Arboriculture website (see www.isa-arbor.com/). Finally, perhaps the most encyclopedic treatment is *U.S. Landscape Ordinances* by Buck Abbey (1998).

Writing, adopting, and effectively implementing a tree preservation ordinance should not be a cookie-cutter exercise. Through a planning process, each community should carefully decide how to balance preservation of natural resources with their other economic and social goals. But the rewards of designing a thoughtful tree preservation ordinance can be great. Consider this list of the helpful tips and dangerous pitfalls frequently encountered in the process.

Tips for Success

- Clearly think through what you want to achieve and why. Then write a clear and concise statement of purpose.

- Seek input from related departments, such as economic development and public works. Understand the objectives of those agencies and dovetail your efforts.

- Start early. Don't wait until your community is 90 percent built out before initiating natural resource preservation efforts.

- Preserving young trees is a good idea. They have the best chance to tolerate adjacent construction activities and have a longer life expectancy than mature trees.

- Keep tree planting, species selection, tree maintenance, and tree preservation specifications in an Arboricultural Standards Manual that can be easily updated. Reference the standards manual in the body of the tree preservation ordinance or in an appendix.

- Enforce your ordinance consistently and impartially.

- Work with property owners and developers closely and cooperatively throughout the preparation of a tree preservation plan. Keep a positive "I'm here to help you" attitude.

Traps to Avoid

- Don't simply copy a generic ordinance template. Study the ordinances that have worked for other communities, but understand your community's specific needs and abilities.

- Seek input but don't be intimidated. Don't accept the attitude or response that it will never work. The most serious threats to implementing a tree preservation ordinance are likely to come from within your local government and not from developers.

- It's best to start early, but it's never too late. Remember that tree preservation isn't just about preserving existing trees—it's also about providing for new trees.

- It's great to preserve those huge old trees, but realize that overmature trees may not be safe and may not live long, even with exceptional care. You may preserve more benefits by preserving several smaller immature trees than by keeping one ancient monarch.

- Don't try to include detailed tree establishment and preservation specs within the body of the tree preservation ordinance. You don't want to rewrite and amend the law every time better tree-care information becomes available.

- It's good to be flexible when enforcing your ordinance, but it's bad to be inconsistent. Doing favors for developers or being intimidated will only lose you respect and credibility.

- Don't wait to enter the tree preservation plan until the final review. Without guidance, either developers will not know how to prepare a good plan, or they will try to cut corners.

A final word on the importance of protecting natural resources in communities: Be tenacious. Once they are destroyed, natural systems, such as streams, wetlands, and forests, are difficult to replace. We increasingly understand the wide-ranging benefits that urban forests provide. We increasingly understand that great communities require great natural resources. Use the environmental protections stated in a community's existing policies, such as those within comprehensive plans and stormwater plans, to tie urban forest benefits to those of air, water, and wildlife habitat protection. Protect the natural resources in your community as if they were in your own backyard because when you consider the air you breathe, the water you drink, and the quality of life you want for your children, your urban forest is truly, in essence, your backyard.

List of References and a
Partially Annotated Bibliography

Abbey, Buck. 1998. *U.S. Landscape Ordinances: An Annotated Reference Handbook.* New York: Wiley.

Ordinances from 41 states. Arranged by state but with an excellent index. Topics include parking lots, buffers and screens, site design standards, tree preservation, and tree protection.

Adler, Catherine S., and Carol A. Krawczyk. 1995. "Tree Preservation." *Environment & Development*, November/December, 6–7.

Agee, James K. 1997. "Management of Greenbelts and Forest Remnants." In *Urban Forest Landscapes: Integrating Multidisciplinary Perspectives,* edited by Gordon A. Bradley. Seattle: University of Washington Press.

Akbari, H., S. Davis, S. Dorsano, J. Huang, and S. Winnett. eds. 1992. *Cooling Our Communities: A Guidebook on Tree Planting and Light-Colored Surfacing.* U.S. Environmental Protection Agency, Office of Policy Analysis, Climate Change Division. Lawrence Berkeley National Laboratory Report No. LBL–31587.

American Forests. 2000. *State of the Urban Forest 2000: Quantifying the Benefits of 100 of the Forests We Live In.* Washington, D.C.

———. 2002. *Urban Ecosystem Analysis of Washington, D.C.* Washington, D.C. www.americanforests.org/resources/urbanforests/analysis.php.

———. 2004. *CITYgreen for ArcGIS Manual.* Washington, D.C.

———. 2005. *Urban Ecosystem Analysis of Jacksonville, Florida.* www.americanforests.org/resources/urbanforests/analysis.php.

———. 2006. *Urban Ecosystem Analysis of S.E. Michigan and the City of Detroit.* www.americanforests.org/resources/urbanforests/analysis.php (listed under Detroit and S.E. Michigan).

———. n.d. *General Tree Canopy Guidelines.* www.americanforests.org/resources/urbanforests/treedeficit.php.

American Society of Landscape Architects (ASLA). 2007. www.asla.org/nonmembers/publicrelations/factshtpr.htm.

Ames, Steven C. 2006. "Community Visioning." In *Planning and Urban Design Standards,* ed. Megan Lewis. New York: Wiley.

ARBOR National Mortgage. 1994. "Realtors Agree Trees Enhance Property Values." News release. April 19.

Arendt, Randall G. 1996. *Conservation Design for Subdivisions.* Washington, D.C.: Island Press.

Arnold, Craig Anthony. 2007. *Fair and Healthy Land Use: Environmental Justice and Planning.* Planning Advisory Service Report No. 549/550. Chicago: American Planning Association.

Arnold, Henry F. 1993. *Trees in Urban Design.* 2nd Ed. New York: Van Nostrand Reinhold.

Bassuk, N.L., and P.L. Trowbridge. 2004. *Trees in the Urban Landscape.* New York: Wiley.

Beattie, Jeff, Cheryl Kollin, and Gary Moll. 2000. "Trees Tackle Clean Water Regs." *American Forests* 106, No. 2 (Summer): 18–19.

A discussion of the use of canopy cover to improve water quality.

Benedict, Mark A., and Edward T. McMahon. 2006. *Green Infrastructure: Linking Landscapes and Communities.* Washington, D.C.: Island Press.

Bowen, Cynthia A. 2004. "Landscape Ordinances: To Define and Protect." *Zoning Practice*, April.

Bradley, Gordon A. ed. 1995. *Urban Forest Landscapes: Integrating Multidisciplinary Perspectives*. Seattle: University of Washington Press.

Divided into four parts. Part 1, "Introduction and Historical Perspective," provides an excellent overview for those new to the topic. Part 2, "The Environmental Setting," includes a chapter on land use controls. Part 3, "Special Purpose Landscapes," looks at specific types of tree environments. Part 4, "Integration: Tradeoffs and Benefits," will probably provide the most insight to planners and foresters.

Burban, Lisa L., and John W. Andresen. 1994. *Storms over the Urban Forest*. 2nd Ed. St. Paul, Minn.: USDA Forest Service, Northeastern Area.

Burgess, Joe. 1999. *Tree Ordinance Development Guidebook*. Stone Mountain, Ga.: Georgia Forestry Commission.

Capiella, Karen, Tom Schueler, and Tiffany Wright. 2005. *Urban Watershed Forestry Manual: Part 1 of a 3-Part Manual Series on Using Trees to Protect and Restore Urban Watersheds*. Newtown Square, Pa.: USDA Forest Service, Northeastern Area State and Private Forestry.

Centers for Disease Control and Prevention. 2006. "Extreme Heat: A Prevention Guide to Promote Your Personal Health and Safety." www.bt.cdc.gov/disasters/extremeheat/heat_guide.asp.

Coder, Kim D. 2004. *Denuding Communities: Tree Canopy Loss Calculations and Public Perceptions*. Warnell School of Forest Resources. Athens: University of Georgia.

A method for calculating past, present, and future tree canopy. Intended to be used during community visioning events.

Council of Tree and Landscape Appraisers. 2000. *Guide for Plant Appraisal*. 9th ed. Champaign, Ill.: International Society of Arboriculture.

Craul, Phillip J. 1999. *Urban Soils: Applications and Practices*. New York: Wiley.

Daniels, Tom, and Katherine Daniels. 2003. *The Environmental Planning Handbook: For Sustainable Communities and Regions*. Chicago: APA Planners Press.

A general treatise on environmental planning for the 21st century. Part III, "Planning for Natural Areas," and Part IV, "Planning for Working Landscapes," contain the most pertinent information for community forestry.

Dannenberg, Andrew L. 2005. Presentation for the Built Environmental Institute of the American Public Health Association (APHA) Conference, Philadelphia, Pa., December 11.

Dickerson, Shawn D., John W. Groninger, and Jean C. Mangun. 2001. "Influences of Community Characteristics on Municipal Tree Ordinances in Illinois, U.S." *Journal of Arboriculture* 27, no. 6 (November): 318–25.

This study explores the relationship between community characteristics and municipal tree ordinances using data from 151 Illinois communities. There are significant correlations between ordinance provisions and a community's characteristics relating to wealth and education.

Dramstad, Wenche E., James D. Olson, and Richard T. T. Forman. 1996. *Landscape Ecology Principles in Landscape Architecture and Land-Use Planning*. Washington, D.C.: Island Press.

Duerksen, Christopher J., and Suzanne Richman. 1993. *Tree Conservation Ordinances*. Planning Advisory Service Report Number 446. Chicago: American Planning Association.

Duerksen, Christopher, and Cara Snyder. 2005. *Nature-Friendly Communities: Habitat Protection and Land Use Planning*. Washington, D.C.: Island Press.

Details successful nature protection programs across the country. Over a dozen case studies are highlighted. Of particular interest are DeKalb County, Georgia's Greenspace Program; Pittsford, New York's Greenprint; and Loudoun County, Virginia's Green Infrastructure plan.

Duryea, Mary L., Eliana Kampf Binelli, and Henry L. Gholz. 2000. "Basic Ecological Principles for Restoration." In *Restoring the Urban Forest Ecosystem*, edited by Mary L. Duryea, Eliana Kampf Binelli, and Lawrence V. Kohrnak. CD–ROM produced by the School of Forest Resources and Conservation, Florida Cooperative Extension Service, Institute of Food and Agricultural Sciences, University of Florida.

Duryea, Mary L., Eliana Kampf Binelli, and Lawrence V. Kohrnak, eds. 2000. *Restoring the Urban Forest Ecosystem*. CD–ROM produced by the School of Forest Resources and Conservation, Florida Cooperative Extension Service, Institute of Food and Agricultural Sciences, University of Florida.

Dwyer, Mark C., and Robert W. Miller. 1999. "Using GIS to Assess Urban Tree Canopy Benefits and Surrounding Greenspace Distributions." *Journal of Arboriculture* 25, no. 2 (March): 102–7.

An analysis of Stevens Point, Wisconsin, using CITYgreen software to assess the environmental and budgetary benefits to urban trees.

Dwyer, John F., David J. Nowak, and Mary Heather Noble. 2003. "Sustaining Urban Forests." *Journal of Arboriculture* 29, no. 1 (January): 49–55.

Ebenreck, Sara. 1989. "The Values of Trees." In *Shading our Cities*, edited by Gary Moll and Sara Ebenreck. Washington, D.C.: Island Press.

Elmendorf, William F., Vincent J. Cotrone, and Joseph T. Mullen. 2003. "Trends in Urban Forestry Practices, Programs, and Sustainability: Contrasting a Pennsylvania, U.S. Study." *Journal of Arboriculture* 29, no. 4. (July): 237–48.

The study examined small town tree commissions in Pennsylvania. It explored attitudes of commission members toward urban forestry and contrasted them with actual accomplishments.

Elmendorf, William F., and A. E. Luloff. 1999. "Using Ecosystem-Based and Traditional Land-Use Planning to Conserve Greenspace." *Journal of Arboriculture* 25, no. 5 (September): 264–73.

_____. 2001. "Using Qualitative Data Collection Methods when Planning for Community Forests." *Journal of Arboriculture* 27, no. 3 (May): 139–51.

Emeryville, California, City of. 2003. "Chapter 10: Urban Forestry Ordinance." Pp. 38–43 of Emeryville Municipal Code Title 7: Public Works. Amended Nov. 20, 2003. www.ci.emeryville.ca.us/code/pdf/title_07.pdf.

_____. 2004. "Title 9: Planning and Zoning." Emeryville Municipal Code. Updated Sept. 7, 2004. www.ci.emeryville.ca.us/code/pdf/title_09.pdf.

_____. 2005a. "Park Avenue District Plan." Aug. 2006. www.ci.emeryville.ca.us/planning/pdf/parkaveplanCouncilAug06.pdf.

_____. 2005b. "Stormwater Guidelines for Green, Dense Development: Stormwater Quality Solutions for the City of Emeryville." Prepared by Community Design + Architecture, Nelson/Nygard Consulting Associates, and Philip Williams Associates. www.ci.emeryville.ca.us/planning/pdf/stormwater_guidelines.pdf [warning: large file (28MB)]

_____. 2006. "Proposed Capital Improvement Program: Fiscal Years 2006–07 through 2010–11." Prepared by Emeryville Finance Department. www.ci.emeryville.ca.us/finance/pdf/2007/cip/cip_2007.pdf.

Envision Utah. 2002. *Urban Planning Tools for Quality Growth.* 1st ed. and 2002 Supplement. Chapter 6: Urban Forestry. Salt Lake City: Envision Utah.

Erickson, Donna. 2006. *MetroGreen: Connecting Open Space in North American Cities.* Washington, D.C.: Island Press.

Fazio, James R. 2003. *Urban and Community Forestry: A Practical Guide to Sustainability.* Lincoln, Neb.: National Arbor Day Foundation.

Flower Mound Master Plan. 2001. Town of Flower Mound, Tex. www.flower-mound.com/cpm/cpm_main.php.

Galvin, Michael F., J. Morgan Grove, and Jarlath O'Neil-Dunne. 2006. *A Report on Baltimore City's Present and Potential Urban Tree Canopy.* Annapolis: Maryland Forest Service. January 19.

Galvin, Michael F., Becky Wilson, and Marian Honeczy. 2000. "Maryland's Forest Conservation Act: a Process for Urban Greenspace Protection during the Development Process." *Journal of Arboriculture* 26, no. 5 (September): 275–80.

Geiger, Jim. 2005. "Air Pollution Control: The Tree Factor." *Urban Forest Research* (January): 1–6.

Georgia Forestry Commission. 2001. *Georgia Model Urban Forest Book.* Stone Mountain, Ga.: Georgia Forestry Commission.

This handbook was created to provide communities and citizens with the information, tools, and references necessary to begin to plan development with the green infrastructure of the urban forest in mind.

Gershuny, Grace, and Joe Smillie. 1999. *The Soul of Soil*. White River Junction, Vt.: Chelsea Green Publishing.

Gilman, Edward F. 1997. *Trees for Urban and Suburban Landscapes*. Albany, N.Y.: Delmar Thomson Learning.

Goetz, S.J., R.K. Wright, A.J. Smith, E. Zineckerb, and E. Schaubb. 2003. "IKONOS Imagery for Resource Management: Tree Cover, Impervious Surfaces, and Riparian Buffer Analyses in the Mid-Atlantic Region." *Remote Sensing of Environment* 88: 195–208.

Great Lakes Areas of Concern. n.d. www.epa.gov/glnpo/aoc/index.html.

The Greening of Detroit. n.d. www.greeningofdetroit.com/index2.htm.

Grado, Stephen C., et al. 2006. "Status, Needs, and Knowledge Levels of Mississippi's Communities Relative to Urban Forestry." *Arboriculture & Urban Forestry* 32, no. 1 (January): 24–31.

A survey of Mississippi communities to determine levels of knowledge and participation in urban and community forestry programs.

Grey, Gene W. 1996. *The Urban Forest: Comprehensive Management*. New York: Wiley.

Grey defines urban forestry as "that which must be done to make trees compatible and functional in the urban environment." This volume is an elaboration on that theme.

Growth Management Committee. 1998. *Title 3 Model Ordinance*. Portland, Ore.: Metro.

Title 3 is the section of Portland's Urban Growth Management Functional Plan that refers to "Water quality, flood management, and fish and wildlife conservation." This particular model ordinance provides for the protection of the region's floodplains, water quality and reduction of flood hazards, and the implementation of erosion control practices.

Hair, Marty. 2006. "Less Cash to Fight Ash Borer This Year: State Waits for Emergency Funds." *Detroit Free Press*, January 27.

Hammitt, William E. 2002. "Urban Forests and Parks as Privacy Refuges." *Journal of Arboriculture* 28, no. 1 (January): 19–26.

Results of a survey of park users in Cleveland, Ohio, indicate that "reflective thought" is a popular use of forests and parks. Visitors spend an average of two-plus hours within these settings.

Harnik, Peter. 2008. "How Much Value Does the City of Philadelphia Receive from Its Parks and Recreation System?" www.tpl.org/content_documents/PhilaParkValueReport.pdf.

Hartel, Dudley. 2004. "Trees as Capital Assets." *City Trees* 40, no. 2: 10–12.

Heisler, Gordon M., Richard H. Grant, and W. Gao. 2002. "Urban Tree Influences on Ultraviolet Irradiance." In *Proceedings of the SPIE* 4482, January 17.

Helms, John A., ed. 1998. *The Dictionary of Forestry*. Bethesda, Md.: Society of American Foresters.

Houston Advanced Research Center. 2004. *Cool Houston: A Plan for Cooling the Region*. The Woodlands, Tex.: Houston Advanced Research Center.

This plan is divided into three sections, the third of which is devoted to trees and the role they can play in improving air quality, quality of life, and other environmental and social benefits.

International Council for Local Environmental Initiatives. 2007. "Cities for Climate Protection." www.iclei.org/index.php?id=800.

Jensen, Ryan R., James R. Boulton, and Bruce T. Harper. 2003. "The Relationship between Urban Leaf Area and Household Energy Usage in Terre Haute, Indiana, U.S." *Journal of Arboriculture* 29, no. 4 (July): 226–30.

This study provides a mixed methodological approach, combining remote sensing technology with standard statistical analysis. It is intended to provide planners, landscape architects, and governmental officials with a method of demonstrating the economic importance of urban forests.

Keating, Janis. 2002. "Trees: The Oldest New Thing in Storm Water Treatment? How Much Do Tree Canopies Really Affect Runoff Volume." *Stormwater* 3, no. 2 (March/April): 56–61.

Kielbaso, J. James, and Vincent Cotrone. 1990. "The State of the Urban Forest." Pp. 11–18, in *Proceedings of the Fourth Urban Forestry Conference*, American Forestry Association: Washington, D.C.

Kohrnak, Lawrence V. 2000. "Restoring the Hydrological Cycle in the Urban Forest Eco-system." In *Restoring the Urban Forest Ecosystem*, edited by Mary L. Duryea, Eliana Kampf Binelli, and Lawrence V. Kohrnak. CD–ROM produced by the School of Forest Resources and Conservation, Florida Cooperative Extension Service, Institute of Food and Agricultural Sciences, University of Florida.

Kollin, Cheryl. 1994. "Frederick's Cool Communites Program," Media briefing at Frederick City Hall, Frederick, Md., August 5.

_____. 1997. "Designing with Nature and Showing the Benefits." *Land Development* (Winter): 30–34.

A discussion of the environmental benefits of conserving trees. The Campus Club Apartment complex in Gainesville, Florida, is used as an example. Focus is given to the CITYgreen GIS program and the stormwater management benefits of tree preservation.

_____. 2004. "Money in the Tree Bank." *American Forests* 110, no. 1 (Spring): 45–47.

Konijnendijk, Cecil C., et al. 2006. "Defining Urban Forestry—A Comparative Perspective of North America and Europe." *Urban Forestry & Urban Greening* 4 : 93–103.

Kuo, F.E., and W.C. Sullivan. 2001. "Environment and Crime in the Inner City: Does Vegetation Reduce Crime?" *Environment and Behavior* 33, no. 3 (May): 343–67.

Land Use Change in Southeast Michigan: Causes and Consequences. 2003. www.semcog.org.

Leatherman, Courtney. 2001. "Digging out of a Tree Deficit." *American Forests* 107, No. 3 (Autumn): 39–43.

Using technology to locate tree canopy—or lack thereof—and to plan for the future.

Lohr, Virginia I., et al. 2004. "How Urban Residents Rate and Rank the Benefits and Problems Associated with Trees in Cities." *Journal of Arboriculture* 30, no. 1 (January): 28–35.

A report of the partial results of a nationwide survey of residents in the 112 most populated metropolitan areas in the continental U.S. This reports focuses on the knowledge and attitudes of urban residents regarding trees in cities; how much urbanites agree that trees are important to their quality of life; whether demographic factors influence responses; and whether people's attitudes toward trees and quality of life influence their attitudes toward other characteristics of urban trees.

Louv, Richard. 2005. *Last Child in the Woods: Saving Our Children from Nature-Deficit Disorder.* Chapel Hill, N.C.: Algonquin Books.

Maco, S. E., and E. G. McPherson. 2002. "Assessing Canopy Cover over Streets and Sidewalks in Street Tree Populations." *Journal of Arboriculture* 28, no. 6 (November): 270–76.

Mahon, Jill R., and Robert W. Miller. 2003. "Identifying High–Value Greenspace Prior to Land Development." *Journal of Arboriculture* 29, no. 1 (January): 25–33.

This paper provides a methodology for locating high-value greenspace. Stevens Point, Wisconsin, was used as a case study. Parcels were identified and the ecologic, recreational, and aesthetic value of each parcel was rated.

Mandelker, Daniel R. 2007. *Planned Unit Developments.* Planning Advisory Service Report No. 545. Chicago: American Planning Association.

Maryland Department of Natural Resources (DNR) Forest Service. 2002. *Forest Stewardship Program: Strategic Plan FY2002–2006.* http://dnrweb.dnr.state.md.us/download/forests/fsp_strategic_plan.pdf.

Matheny, Nelda, and James R. Clark. 1998. *Trees and Development: A Technical Guide to Preservation of Trees During Land Development.* Champaign, Ill.: International Society of Arboriculture.

McDonald, L., et al. 2005. "Green Infrastructure Plan Evaluation Frameworks." *Journal of Conservation Planning* 1, No. 1 (March): 12–43.

The paper provides a more structured definition for green infrastructure plans, "best practices" guidelines, and a framework for evaluating green infrastructure plans for different scales of planning.

McElfish, James M., Jr. 2004. *Nature-Friendly Ordinances: Local Measures to Conserve Biodiversity.* Washington, D.C.: Environmental Law Institute.

The lessons of ecology and conservation biology can enable local decision makers to use their familiar land use tools more effectively in making their development and redevelopment more nature friendly.

McFarland, Kevin. 1994. *Community Forestry and Urban Growth: A Tool Box for Incorporating Urban Forestry Elements into Community Plans*. Olympia, Wash.: Washington State Department of Natural Resources.

Publication provides examples of how communities have incorporated urban forestry principles into critical elements of growth management planning.

McHarg, Ian L. 1969. *Design with Nature*. Garden City, N.Y.: Natural History Press.

McPherson, E. Gregory. 1995. "Net Benefits of Healthy and Productive Urban Forests." In *Urban Forest Landscapes: Integrating Multidisciplinary Perspectives*, edited by Gordon A. Bradley. Seattle: University of Washington Press.

_____. 2004a. "Parking Lots and Ordinance Compliance." *Western Arborist* (Fall): 30–32.

_____. 2004b. "Will There Be Space for Trees in Our Future?" *Urban Forest Research* (Winter): 1–3.

McPherson, E. Gregory, D. Nowak, and R.A. Rowntree. eds. 1994. *Chicago's Urban Forest Ecosystem: Results of the Chicago Urban Forest Climate Project*. General Technical Report NE–186. Radnor, Pa.: USDA Forest Service Northeastern Forest Experiment Station.

McPherson, E. Gregory, David Nowak, Gordon Heisler, Sue Grimmond, Catherine Souch, Rich Grant, and Rowan Rowntree. 1997. "Quantifying Urban Forest Structure, Function, and Value: The Chicago Urban Forest Climate Project." *Urban Ecosystems* 1:49–61.

McPherson, E. Gregory, James R. Simpson, Paula J. Peper, Scott E. Maco, and Qingfu Xiao. 2005. "Municipal Forest Benefits and Costs in Five U.S. Cities." *Journal of Forestry* 103, no. 8 (December): 411–16.

McPherson, E. Gregory, et al. 2000. *Tree Guidelines for Coastal Southern California Communities*. Sacramento, Calif.: Local Government Commission.

Guidebook analyzes the benefits—economic and environmental—that trees can provide to communities. Case studies focus on Southern California.

Miller, Robert W. 1997. *Urban Forestry: Planning and Managing Urban Greenspaces*. 2nd Ed. Upper Saddle River, N. J.: Prentice Hall.

A textbook introduction to urban forestry. Appendices include a sample tree ordinance, sample tree protection ordinance, and a sample screening ordinance.

Mitchell, Martha S. 2001. "Green Solutions: Planting Trees for Healthy Watersheds." *Erosion Control* 8, no. 5 (July/August): 36–43.

Moll, Gary. 2005. "Repairing Ecosystems at Home." *American Forests* 111, no. 2 (Summer): 41–43.

Moll, Gary, and Cheryl Kollin. 2000. "Picture This." *American Forest* 106, no. 3 (Autumn): 44–48.

A review of the CITYgreen software.

National Urban and Community Forestry Advisory Council. 2004. *A National Research Plan for Urban Forestry, 2005–2015*. Sugarloaf, Calif.: USDA Forest Service.

Ning, Zhu H., and Kamran K. Abdollahi. eds. 2003. *Urban and Community Forestry: Working Together to Facilitate Change*. Baton Rouge, La.: Southern University.

The proceedings of the first National Urban and Community Forestry Education and Outreach Conference for Minority and Underserved Communities.

Nisenson, Lisa. 2006. *Using Smart Growth Techniques as Stormwater Best Management Practices*. Washington, D.C.: Environmental Protection Agency.

Nonpoint-source pollution is a main contributor to water quality problems in developed areas. This report looks at how stormwater management can be tackled at the site planning level through such principles as minimizing impervious surfaces, preserving contiguous open space areas, and making maximum use of existing infrastructure.

Nowak, David J. 2005. *Houston's Regional Forest: Structure, Functions, Values*. Washington, D.C.: U.S. Forest Service; College Station: Texas Forest Service.

Nowak, D.J., et al. 2000. "A Modeling Study of the Impact of Urban Trees on Ozone." *Atmospheric Environment* 34, no. 10: 1601–13.

Nowak, David J., Daniel E. Crane, and Jack C. Stevens. 2006. "Air Pollution Removal by Urban Trees and Shrubs in the United States." *Urban Forestry & Urban Greening* 4: 115–23.

Nowak, David J., and Paul R. O'Connor. 2001. *Syracuse Urban Forest Master Plan: Guid-*

ing the City's Forest Resource into the 21ˢᵗ Century. Newtown Square, Pa.: USDA Forest Service.

Perlman, Dan L., and Jeffrey C. Milder. 2005. *Practical Ecology for Planners, Developers, and Citizens*. Washington, D.C.: Island Press.

Introduces the science of ecology using the language of planners, architects, and landscape architects. Chapters of particular interest include, "Humans Plan," "An Introduction to Ecology and Biodiversity," "The Ecology of Landscapes," "Nature in the Neighborhood," "Ecologically Based Planning and Design Techniques," and "Principles in Practice."

Perry, Robert C. 1995. "Water Conserving Landscapes." In *Urban Forest Landscapes: Integrating Multidisciplinary Perspectives*, edited by Gordon A. Bradley. Seattle: University of Washington Press.

Petit, Jack, Debra L. Bassert, and Cheryl Kollin. 1995. *Building Greener Neighborhoods: Trees as Part of the Plan*. Washington, D.C.: Home Builder Press.

Platt, Rutherford H., Rowan A. Rowntree, and Pamela C. Muick. eds. 1994. *The Ecological City: Preserving and Restoring Urban Biodiversity*. Amherst, Mass.: University of Massachusetts Press.

A collection of essays focusing on public policy and public-private collaboration. Of special interest is section three, "Urbanization and Terrestrial Ecosystems."

Portland, Oregon, City of. 2002. *Green Streets: Innovative Solutions for Stormwater and Stream Crossings*. Portland, Ore.: Metro.

This handbook communicates basic stormwater management concepts, case study examples of how this approach has been successful elsewhere, practical design solutions and methodologies, and a strategy for implementation of "green" streets in the Portland Metro region.

Randolph, John. 2004. *Environmental Land Use Planning and Management*. Washington, D.C.: Island Press.

An introduction to environmental planning. Of particular interest is the chapter "Landscape Ecology, Urban Forestry, and Wetlands."

Ries, Paul. 2005. "Applying Leadership Lessons to Urban Forestry." *City Trees* 41, no. 2: 14–16.

Rowntree, Rowan. 1995. "Toward Ecosystem Management: Shifts in the Core and the Content of Urban Forest Ecology." In *Urban Forest Landscapes: Integrating Multidisciplinary Perspectives*, edited by Gordon A. Bradley. Seattle: University of Washington Press.

Savard, Jean-Pierre L., Philippe Clergeau, and Gwenaelle Mennechez. 2000. "Biodiversity Concepts and Urban Ecosystems." *Landscape and Urban Planning* 48, no. 3–4 (May): 131–42.

Schoeneman, Rita S. 1996. *Trees in the Community: Managing the Urban Forest*. MIS Report 24, No. 5. Washington, D.C.: International City County Management Association.

Schwab, James, and Stuart Meck. 2005. *Planning for Wildfires*. Planning Advisory Service Report No. 529/530. Chicago: American Planning Association.

Sherrard, David. 1996. "Managing Riparian Open Space." *Environment & Development*, January/February, 6–7.

Skiera, James. 2007. Telephone interview. December 4.

Spirn, Anne Whiston. 1984. *The Granite Garden: Urban Nature and Human Design*. New York: Basic Books.

Sprague, Eric, David Burke, Sally Claggett, and Albert Todd. Eds. 2006. *The State of Chesapeake Forests*. Arlington Va.: The Conservation Fund.

Swiecki, T.J., and E.A. Bernhardt. 2001. *Guidelines for Developing and Evaluating Tree Ordinances*. www.isa-arbor.com/publications/ordinance.aspx.

This Is Smart Growth. The Smart Growth Network, www.smartgrowth.org.

Trust for Public Land. n.d. *How Much Value Does a Park System Bring to a City?* www.tpl.org/tier3_cd.cfm?content_item_id=20878&folder_id=3208.

Weitz, Jerry, and Leora Susan Waldner. 2002. *Smart Growth Audits*. Planning Advisory

Service Report No. 512. Chicago: American Planning Association.

Werner, Jan E. Bisco, et al. 2001. *Trees Mean Business: A Study of the Economic Impacts of Trees and Forests in the Commercial Districts of New York City and New Jersey*. New York: Trees New York with Trees New Jersey.

Westphal, L. 2003. "Urban Greening and Social Benefits: A Study of Empowerment Outcomes." *Agriculture and Urban Forestry* 29: 137–47.

Whitehead, Hugh C. 2001. "Transplanting Existing Trees on Development Sites." *Land Development* (Winter): 12–16.

A review of methods to meet tree cover requirements in rezoning or new development. The article focuses on the relocation of trees from the site to conservation areas.

Willeke, Donald. 1993. Presentation at the 4th National Urban Forest Conference, Minneapolis. September.

Williams, Chuck. 2002. "Green Light." *Columbus Ledger-Inquirer*, June 9, B1, 6.

Williams, Madeline. 1998. "Economical Urban Planning or Environmental Injustice?" Pp. 156–60, in *Proceedings of the 8th National Urban Forest Conference*, edited by Cheryl Kollin. Washington, D.C.: American Forests.

Williamson, Karen S. 2003. *Growing with Green Infrastructure*. Doylestown, Pa.: Heritage Conservancy.

Report provides communities with a six-step process for developing and implementing a green infrastructure plan. The steps are: develop an approach; inventory community resources; envision the future; find the hubs and links; create the plan; and build the system.

Wolf, Kathleen L. 1999. "Nature and Commerce: Human Ecology in Business Districts." Paper presented at Building Cities of Green, the Ninth National Urban Forest Conference, Washington, D.C.

_____. 2004a. "Economics and Public Value of Urban Forests." *Urban Agriculture Magazine* 13 (December): 31–33.

_____. 2004b. "Trees and Business District Preferences: A Case Study of Athens, Georgia, U.S." *Journal of Arboriculture* 30, no. 6 (November): 336–46.

The presence of urban trees was associated with higher visual quality ratings and was perceived to be an integral amenity of the central business district. The study utilized an on-site survey of visitors to the Athens CBD. Quantitative and qualitative research outcomes are included.

_____. 2005. "Nature and Commerce: Human Ecology in Business Districts." In *Proceedings of the 2005 National Conference on Urban Ecosystems*, edited by Cheryl Kollin. Washington, D.C.: American Forests.

Making Great Communities Happen

The American Planning Association provides leadership in the development of vital communities by advocating excellence in community planning, promoting education and citizen empowerment, and providing the tools and support necessary to effect positive change.

For price information, please go to APA's PlanningBooks.com or call 312-786-6344.